God,
Dr. Buzzard,
and the
Bolito Man

To:- Haley

Oct. 30-03

Best to you

God,
Dr. Buzzard,
and the
Bolito Man

A Saltwater Geechee

Talks About Life on Sapelo Island

Cornelia Bailey *Good luck!*

with *Christena Bledsoe*

DOUBLEDAY
New York • London • Toronto • Sydney • Auckland

PUBLISHED BY DOUBLEDAY
a division of Random House, Inc.
1540 Broadway, New York, New York 10036

DOUBLEDAY and the portrayal of an anchor with a dolphin
are trademarks of Doubleday, a division of Random House, Inc.

Book design by Lynne Amft
Map designed by David Cain

In the interest of privacy, some names and personal characteristics
of people discussed in this book have been changed.

Library of Congress Cataloging-in-Publication Data
Bailey, Cornelia.
God, Dr. Buzzard, and the Bolito Man: a saltwater Geechee talks about life on
Sapelo Island / Cornelia Bailey with Christena Bledsoe.—1st ed.
p.   cm.
1. Bailey, Cornelia. 2. Afro-American women—Georgia—Sapelo Island—
Biography. 3. Afro-Americans—Georgia—Sapelo Island—Biography.
4. Afro-American families—Georgia—Sapelo Island—Biography. 5. Sapelo
Island (Ga.)—Biography. 6. Afro-Americans—Georgia—Sapelo Island—Social
life and customs. 7. Sapelo Island (Ga.)—Social life and customs. I. Title: God,
Dr. Buzzard, and the Bolito Man. II. Bledsoe, Christena. III. Title.
F292.M15 B35 2000
975.8'737—dc21
[B]   00-022694

ISBN 0-385-49376-2

To all the souls and spirits of Sapelo . . .
The ones who've gone and the ones who are still here.

Acknowledgments

To Papa, who is my main source of reference and who at the age ninety-seven is still sharp. In memory of my son Greg Bailey. He had love for all the stories of my youth. My mother, Hettie, whom I quote all the time. She has a lot to say. Aunt Mary and Grandma Winnie, whose spunk I have inherited. And to my mother-in-law, Mrs. Catherine, for teaching me tolerance.

To those who have gone beyond: Cousin Annie, Beulah, Miss Rosa, Miss Jessie, Miss Lula, Aunt Ruth, the midwife, Katie Underwood, Miss Mattie and Miss Nancy Green, whom I have learned so much from and who are still with us in spirit.

To all who have supported me in this endeavor: My husband, Julius; my children, Teri and Fred, Julius III (Lix) and Trina, Stanley, Maurice and Mary, Janetta, and Tory. To my brothers and sisters, Asberry, Ada, Barbara, Elise, Shug, Winnie and Gibb. All my grandchildren. My friends Mary Joe, Allan McGregor, Iregene and Yvonne Grovner, Jim Barger, Jr. and to John Wise, who always told me "Cornelia, it's time to come out of the backyard."

Thanks to the Sapelo Foundation and the Fund for Southern Communities for giving us the chance and for having faith in us all along. To Richard Cheppy, a talented photographer whose beautiful photographs grace the cover and inside of this book. To my editor, Janet Hill, and her assistant, Roberta Spivak, and to William

Acknowledgments

Clark, a great guy. And to all the other friends whose assistance was invaluable and greatly appreciated.

Most of all to Christena Bledsoe, who helped me put the soul and spirit in their right places in all of this. She is a true saltwater Geechee, part of my spirit. And to Christena's husband, Joe Shifalo, who never complained.

Contents

Contents

Sapelo Island

Choc'lat

Belle Marsh

King Savannah   Raccoon Bluff

Lumber Landing   First African Baptist Church (old)

BLACKBEARD ISLAND

Hanging Bull

ATLANTIC OCEAN

Post Office Landing   First African Baptist Church

Hog Hammock

CABRETTA BEACH

DUPLIN RIVER

Behavior Cemetery   St. Luke's Church

Marsh Landing

Meridian Landing

GEORGIA

Shell Hammock   Big House

DOBOY SOUND   Marine Institute

Sapelo Lighthouse

Sapelo Island

SEA ISLANDS

N

0   Miles   1

Ibo Proverb: All stories are true.
—from *Jarell* by JOHN EDGAR WIDEMAN

God,
Dr. Buzzard,
and the
Bolito Man

Dayclean

MY TALE BEGINS JUST BEFORE THE RISING OF THE
sun, in that brief instant of time when the night clouds are being
cleared away and the first rays of light are streaking across the sky.
Dayclean, we call this, when the day is new and the world is made
fresh again.

If you had been standing on the white sands of this island at dayclean in 1803, or a little later, you might have seen a tall, dark-
skinned man with narrow features, his head covered with a cap
resembling a Turkish fez, unfold his prayer mat, kneel and pray to
the east while the sun rose. This was Bilali, the most famous and
powerful of all the Africans who lived on this island during slavery
days, and the first of my ancestors I can name.

Today, you would see children rising in the dark of winter or the
light of spring so they can board a large, white ferry run by the state
of Georgia that takes them to the mainland where they go to school.
Like myself, they are the descendants of Bilali. Some of us are still
here two hundred years later.

Sapelo Island is south of Savannah, Georgia, and north of Jacksonville, Florida, in the Sea Islands, a chain of islands hugging the coastlines of South Carolina, Georgia and the northern part of Florida on the Eastern Seaboard of the United States.

It's a location that puts us on the edge of the Atlantic Ocean, the ocean that brought my people from Africa to clear the land, build dikes and dig drainage canals so that the island could be flooded and drained as needed to grow rice and cotton and other crops. When my ancestors got just a little bit over the terror of being stripped from their homeland and families and carried across the water in giant ships to who knows what fate, they would have looked around this island and seen similarities to the West African coast.

The climate on Sapelo was hot and humid and buggy, just like it was in West Africa. There were tidal streams and marshes similar to those they knew in Africa. There were seabirds and fish that were similar. There were lima beans, okra, sweet potatoes and other vegetables that were similar, and they could simmer vegetables and seafood together and serve them over rice in ways that they knew.

So, they would have taken a deep breath and said, "Okay, this reminds me of home. Maybe we can go on," and found the strength to make a new beginning.

Dayclean! You see, you can think of the Africans as being victims, and in a sense they were, but they were also great survivors. If they survived the Middle Passage, and a lot of people didn't, then they survived everything that was thrown at them. They were determined people.

They were expected to conform to the ways of the European slaveholders and they did just enough of that to get by, but they didn't want to lose all of their African selves. They hung onto their customs and beliefs as much as they could and in doing so they kept a good bit of their pride. Then they passed their traditions down so successfully that many of the Geechee ways I learned as a child can be traced directly back to Africa.

Even "dayclean" came from Africa. In Africa, you can still hear people speak of it today. Our word for dayclean is a little different from theirs, that's all, because like almost everything my ancestors brought with them to this new shore, our version changed some over time.

The Sea Islands are famed for their beauty, for the superior rice and cotton once grown on them, and for being the home of the Geechee and the Gullah peoples.

Rice was grown in Africa long before it was in the Sea Islands. When the planters in the Sea Islands discovered in about 1700 that rice could be grown on these islands, they didn't really know how to grow it at first. They just knew there were fortunes to be made if they could get people with the right skills and know-how to grow it for them, and their desire to find such workers touched off a whole new wave of slave trading in Africa.

The slave traders looked to the traditional rice-growing areas of West Africa to fill the demand, especially to the Sierra Leone region, stretching from Senegal down to Sierra Leone and Liberia. Tens of thousands of West Africans were seized and sent to the slave markets of Charleston and Savannah and were sold to planters on the Sea Islands.

The planters bought so many people from tribes in Sierra Leone and surrounding countries that they soon outnumbered everyone else in the Sea Islands and they stamped these islands with their culture. But first, they had to learn a common tongue and common ways.

What they learned to speak is called Creole, and that's a lot like throwing everything into a huge pot, blending it together and simmering it into a delicious soup served over rice. It was based on the English language, yes and it included bits and pieces from the French and Portuguese and all the other Europeans that the Africans had come in contact with, but the onions, the okra and the black pepper in it—the seasonings that gave it an exciting taste— came from African words, speech patterns and grammar.

The customs and ways of their tribes were thrown into that pot too, and once the pot got stirred, everyone in these islands of African descent became known either as Geechee or Gullah.

As to the labels "Geechee" and "Gullah," there's a line of thinking that they came from two neighboring tribes in West Africa—the Kissi, pronounced "Geezee," who lived where the modern-day countries of Sierra Leone, Liberia and Guinea converge; and the Gola, a tribe on the Sierra Leone–Liberia border. A lot of members from both of these tribes were brought to these islands, and while it has never been proven—the people who study such things will be arguing about it for years to come—it could very well be that what we were called stemmed from the two tribal names.

It used to be said that black people on the Georgia Sea Islands were Geechee and those on the South Carolina islands were Gullah, but there were always people in areas like Charleston who called themselves Geechee. I think it just depended on the area you were from and what you preferred to be called.

People on each of the islands once had a few different traits to their speech, and if you were knowledgeable, you could listen and say, "Aah, he's from St. John's. She's from Ossabaw." But after generations of marrying each other and moving back and forth between islands, we Geechee and Gullah people sound pretty much alike. Our eating habits are alike, our folklore is just alike, and we pray just alike. We have become almost one and the same people.

There are about five hundred thousand of us in the United States and at least that many more who have kept traces of Geechee and Gullah speech, and these days we usually all get lumped together under the heading Gullah.

The term "Gullah" somehow got very popular during the 1970s and all of a sudden, over here on Sapelo, we heard people describing us as Gullah. We looked at each other and said, "We're not Gullah. We're Geechee."

There's not a thing wrong with "Gullah" if that's what you identify with, but a lot of us, including me, have always thought of ourselves as Geechee and we want to be known by our traditional name. Matter of fact, we're Saltwater Geechee.

Here on the Georgia islands, Saltwater Geechee was what we called ourselves, and black people who lived about thirty miles inland, around freshwater, were Freshwater Geechee. It was a bantering thing, a teasing thing we called ourselves just for fun.

We liked saltwater fish. They liked freshwater fish. We thought our speech was a bit more musical than theirs, because we talked a little faster, with fewer rest stops between our words, so that everything we said ran together. We'd listen to them and say, "Can't they talk any faster than that? People don't have all day." Then we'd shake our heads and say," Ah, those Freshwater Geechee, what do they know?"

You gotta have some fun. It's as much a part of our life over here as pain and beauty and loss. Geechee culture is rich with humor. Our story can't be told without it.

Sapelo is a small island you can reach only by boat. These days the island is almost totally owned by the state of Georgia. If you were coming to Sapelo island, as thirty thousand visitors a year do for a brief three-hour public tour offered by the state, you would come on a state of Georgia ferry. The thirty-minute ride gives you just enough time to smell saltwater, feel a breeze on your face, hear seabirds crying overhead, and maybe see a porpoise or two.

You would see the Sapelo Lighthouse first and then you land at Marsh Landing Dock on the South End of the island and enter a world bathed in a quiet hush. There's no hustle and bustle, condominiums or traffic lights here, more dirt roads than paved ones, and plenty of natural beauty. There are gorgeous beaches, winding tidal creeks, "hammocks" of raised ground that are higher than the surrounding swampland and densely wooded areas that are former fields. We have palmettos, pines, bays, holly trees, cypress, and giant live oaks with gray, Spanish moss and resurrection ferns on the branches that wither when it's cold and dry and spring back green and full when the air is warm and moist.

On the South End of the island the area most visitors see is the old tabby sugar house, an old cotton barn, the Big House, now owned by the state, and buildings now used to house the marine scientists with the University of Georgia Marine Institute.

The last Geechee community, Hog Hammock, lies three miles inland from the Big House. It's a tiny community of 434 acres, wandering paths, big trees, wooden houses, and trailers. About seventy permanent residents, all African American, including myself and my family, plus additional folks who return for vacations or weekends.

But what you see now is not how it was when I was growing up. Back in my youth in the 1940s and 1950s, we had five Geechee communities on Sapelo and more than 450 people. Today, we have one community left and fewer than seventy people; and I fear for the survival of my people on this island.

We have very little land of our own left. Our young leave to go to the mainland and our old die. This pattern is repeated throughout the Sea Islands, except that on most islands, Geechee and Gullah people have been squeezed out as developers have rushed in. On Sapelo, the situation is different, but the results have been the same. Our one remaining community basically is plopped down in the middle of a giant state-owned nature preserve.

When I was growing up, we Geechee and Gullah people were thought to be a peculiar people with funny ways. Today, as our presence on these islands shrinks and our customs fade, folklorists, linguists and anthropologists are taking a second look at us, like "Hold it now—maybe they retained something special." Something that black people in New York, Chicago or San Francisco weren't able to. *Because* we stayed right here in the Sea Islands, where we were more isolated and we were in the majority until the past few decades, we were able to keep alive more of our connections to Africa.

At age fifty-five, I am of the last generation to grow up with all of the old Geechee ways. Our customs and traditions started fading in the mid-1950s when the outside world began crashing in. But I can tell you of our lives before that; how in my early childhood we watched the animals for good- and bad-luck signs, we believed in the healing properties of the earth and all forms of the supernatural, and we believed in God, Dr. Buzzard and the Bolito Man.

A few years ago I was sitting in church and the minister said, as he always does at the close of the service, "And as for me and my family, we shall praise the Lord," and I opened my mouth and added, "and Dr. Buzzard and the Bolito Man."

Everybody around me cracked up. They knew just what I meant, because, while people my age and older grew up praying to God, we also believed in Dr. Buzzard, the root doctor, whom people other places call the voodoo man, and a lot of us played Bolito, the numbers racket. We saw no conflict in that at all because we figured we needed a little extra luck.

My ancestors didn't have a written language. They passed down everything through stories and the stories made you laugh, yes, but they also made you think. That is what I want to do for you too.

When I tell you about the strength of our elders, our views on everything from birth to death and the hereafter, and how I came to fear for my people, I am telling you about who we were and are as a people. I want to hold up our customs and traditions for you to see one at a time, as if each is a bright piece of fabric that I will stitch into a warm Geechee quilt you can look at and say, "Those Geechee people really *did* have a different way of living and believing over there."

I am a storyteller and my tale is of a people so private our story has never been told before. I tell it now for my people, in hopes it will create a new beginning on this island, a shining dayclean, and for people everywhere: you can survive if you believe in yourself and your culture.

This is how I remember it.

Lean back and listen.

◆

Chapter One

A Special Gift

LET ME TELL YOU HOW IT WAS. A SCREECH OWL hooting at your door was a *sure sign* of death. A black cat wasn't bad luck, it was *good* luck. And you never threw water out your door after dark. You might be throwing it on your loved ones, the spirits of your loved ones who came to visit at night. If you just had to throw that water out, you'd stop first and say, "Excuse me, loved ones. Draw aside," and that gave them time to move out of the way.

Back in the 1940s when I was growing up, it was part of everyday life [over here on Sapelo Island] to believe in magic and signs and spirits. My family absolutely believed. That's right. The spirits were always in our lives. *Always.* People talked to the spirits and accused them of playing tricks and being full of mischief. Like when Mama would lose her glasses and she knew, just *knew*, she left them on the table.

She'd say, "Okay, Uncle Shed, I know you're in the house. I know you took my glasses. I know you' playin' a joke on me. Now put my glasses back. You put my glasses right back where you got them from." Uncle Shed was Shadrach Hall, Mama's uncle on her mother's side, who was born in slavery times and lived to be more than one hundred years old. Mama would call on the spirit of Uncle Shed to put her glasses back and then she'd go and do her work and come back, and those glasses would be on the table right where she left them. All of a sudden, they'd reappear.

Some of us saw spirits too, me included, not all the time but sometimes. Of course, there's a reason why I saw them. The old people said I was singled out.

We were living at Belle Marsh, on the west side of Sapelo, on the North End, when I got singled out. There were five small black communities over here then, Belle Marsh, Raccoon Bluff, Lumber Landing, Shell Hammock and Hog Hammock.

Hog Hammock was already the biggest community and Belle Marsh was the smallest, but we all lived on land that had been in our families since shortly after the Civil War. When freedom came, our ancestors knew the only way to stand on their own two feet and feed their families was to have their own land. So as soon as they could, they bought land on the island they had worked the soil of during slavery days.

Belle Marsh was my family's *own* little world. Other than Papa's Uncle Nero, it was just Mama and Papa, my brother Gibb, my sisters Barbara and Ada, Ada's baby son Michael and my brother Asberry and me in the area known as Belle Marsh. That was it.

Anyway, one day when I was three years old, I got sick. *Real* sick. Up to that time, I was a regular little healthy child. Mama and Papa had gone shopping in Brunswick that day. They'd gotten up early that morning and walked down to Marsh Landing at the southern tip of the island to catch the company boat. That was nine miles right there. Then they rode six and one-half miles over the water to Meridian Dock on "the other side," which is what we all call the

A S p e c i a l   G i f t

Georgia mainland. From there, it's another twenty-one miles south
to Brunswick but luckily Mama and Papa got a ride. What I'm getting at though is that they were *far away*.

It was spring, a beautiful Saturday in May, late May, matter of
fact, and back at Belle Marsh, my brother Asberry and I were playing in the sun. There was a pear tree near the house and there were
tiny green pears on the pear tree that were looking good. Mama had
told us not to eat them because they weren't ripe yet. But a kid's
gonna do what a kid's gonna do, especially if your parents aren't
around to catch you, so naturally we ate them. Asberry picked them.
He was two years older than me, which made him five, so he could
reach up and grab them and he gave me some. We had ourselves a
good time eating those pears.

By the time Mama and Papa got back to the Marsh Landing
Dock and walked home to Belle Marsh, it was almost dark. I wasn't
feeling well by then and I got worse quick. That night, I had a fever,
a very high fever, and no matter what Mama and Papa did, nothing
brought the fever down.

We didn't have a doctor on the island, we never had and we still
don't, so people took care of things themselves. They had to most
times, absolutely had to, and Mama and Papa had to this time. They
couldn't have gotten me to a hospital on the mainland because the
company boat didn't run on Saturday night and it was the only way
on and off the island.

Mama and Papa tried every remedy they could and *nothing*
worked. There's a plant here we call the fever bush because you
make a tea out of it to lower your temperature, but that bush isn't
ready to pick until late summer, so they had to try something else.

Mama bathed me in tepid water and that didn't work so Papa
went out and got some leaves from the beauty berry bush, another

11

plant that grows over here. In the fall of the year, the beauty berry bush has clusters of the most gorgeous bright purple berries and that's why it's called the beauty berry bush, but it's the leaves that you use and they're out in the spring. Mama crushed the leaves, mixed them with vinegar and slathered it all over my body to make the fever go down. But that didn't work either.

Mama and Papa sat up all night with me. Nobody in the house went to bed that night. Nobody slept. They were all too scared for me to sleep. Mama was watching and praying the entire night because she knew my fate was in God's hands.

A little before daybreak, I died.

Papa had been tired and worried from staying up all night and he had left the house just minutes before I died, saying, "I'm goin' down to Minus' and get me a drink." His friend, Mr. Minus Banks, lived at Lumber Landing, which is about a three-mile walk from our house. Shortly after he got there, my brother Gibb came running up to tell Papa that I'd died.

Mr. Minus drove a big red company truck that belonged to Mr. Richard Reynolds, the head of what was Reynolds Tobacco then, and is now called RJR Tobacco, and Mr. Reynolds owned most of the island. He wasn't on Sapelo all the time because he had houses in North Carolina and Florida too, but when he was, he lived in a huge house everyone called The Big House on the South End. That house sits on the ground where the old plantation house was before the Civil War.

Anyway, Mr. Minus was a trusted employee of Mr. Reynolds, which is why he had the company truck. At that time, he was one of the few men on the island who had a car of any kind. So while Gibb ran on to Raccoon Bluff to spread the news, Mr. Minus drove Papa back to Belle Marsh, flying fast as he could.

A Special Gift

Papa was having an absolute fit because I was his daughter, his *baby* daughter. Mama and Papa had lost two other children before I was born, Hicks, named after Papa, and Edwin, named after Mama's brother. They were born in 1933 and '35 and they died when they were still "arm babies," small enough to carry in your arms. A fever took them, just like me.

When Gibb got to Raccoon Bluff, he found someone to ring the church bell. We rang the bell for everything back then, 'cause we didn't have telephones, so the church bell was used for many different things. It was a big bell, on a rope you pulled by hand, and there was a certain ring for death, another for disaster and another to signal the beginning of church service. You *knew* each one. When you heard the bell, you knew exactly what each ring meant.

The toll for disaster was loud and sharp, like "Hurry, hurry, hurry!" It had an urgent tone, like come quick, somebody's house is burning. The one for church was *"Bing, bing, bing!"* It was a faster pull of the rope, a brighter sound.

The death bell went *"Bongggg, bongggg, bongggg,"* so slow it went right through every bone in your body. It didn't matter if you were sleeping your heart away in the thin of night, all of a sudden, the bell would go *"bongggg,"* and you'd sit straight up in your bed, thinking, "Oh, no, I heard the bell!" It'd take a few seconds before the rope would come down again, and then you'd hear a second *bongggg.* Then you'd jump into your clothes and fly out the door because you knew you'd heard it right the first time. Someone on the island had died.

Mama's people lived over at Raccoon Bluff, and some of Papa's did too, so people started coming after they heard the bell. By the time they reached Belle Marsh, they were probably fanning themselves with cardboard fans, fans made from old boxes, and wiping their faces with handkerchiefs or clean rags. It was Sunday by then, and since they saved handkerchiefs for Sundays and special occasions outside the home, they might have been using handkerchiefs. Mama and Papa were probably using clean rags because they used those at home.

May on Sapelo can be hot, real hot, so they were gonna bury me that same afternoon. They had to. My family didn't have money for a fancy funeral and they sure weren't gonna wait on the buzzards to come around, because in the summertime that can happen quick.

As soon as Papa had gotten home, he had measured me for a casket. Then he went to the house of the island carpenter, Mr. Freddy Wilson, and they went down to the shop where Mr. Freddy worked and built my casket out of pine. They built the rough outer box and the smooth one that goes inside, and they brought it back to the house.

Mama lined my casket with clean sheets and got it ready. She put something under the sheets to rest my head on and make me look more natural, like I was sleeping. They always did that. You gotta rest your head on a pillow to be comfortable, even in death.

Here on the island the old people had a saying "God sent an angel to get his angel." So Mama set about making me look like an angel. I had long hair, real thick hair, and Mama plaited it in two plaits and she dressed me in my Sunday dress, the only one that wasn't handmade. I still remember that dress. It was a little frilly pink dress with ruffles and lace. Then Mama laid me out on the double bed in the living room that she and Papa slept in, a brown-colored iron bed.

I was dead and Mama was crying.

Mama and Papa and Ada and Barbara couldn't believe I was dead and they checked again for a heartbeat. They couldn't find a pulse and they even did the mirror test—they held a mirror over my mouth to see if it fogged up—but there wasn't any sign that I was breathing. No sign of breath. I was *dead*.

Uncle Nero was there with Papa, and he had been drinking. He was a churchgoing man, but that day he figured he might as well have a couple of shots. Shots of whiskey were big in those days and after he'd had about a pint, Uncle Nero kept saying, "Bury the chile, whatcha y'all waitin' for? Bury the chile."

So, it was time for the cemetery.

Then, Aunt Mary—Mama's sister—came on the scene from Raccoon Bluff. She'd come over in a horse and wagon with her daughter, Cousin Dorothy. Aunt Mary examined me again, and at first, she agreed I was dead. But for some reason or another, a little voice inside her head argued with her. It kept saying, "I don't believe this child is dead."

She told Dorothy, "Pull up some garlic, pull up some garlic," and sent her over to Uncle Nero's house. He had a little garlic patch in his yard and Cousin Dorothy pulled up some garlic and brought it back. Aunt Mary washed the garlic and crushed it up, and packed it in my nose, my mouth and God only knows where else, and I came around.

If it hadn't been for Aunt Mary, I would've been put in that casket and taken to Behavior Cemetery over by Hog Hammock and that would've been the end of me.

But I recovered, I got well, and even today I can remember little snatches from that time, like a dream that I drifted in and out of. I have no memory of being on Mama and Papa's bed, but I remember my casket, because we kept it, and I kinda remember people being around. It had to be a big occasion for people to be around since we were the only family living at Belle Marsh. And I have a fragment of a memory, a day or two later, of people still coming to see me, almost like they'd come to see the baby Jesus. I had become a *special* child.

Mama wouldn't let me eat any more fruit that summer and from then on the old people looked at me like I was different. I had died and come back to life, and that didn't happen every day. Nobody knew of that ever happening on Sapelo, not Papa, not Mama, not Aunt Mary, not Grandma, not Grandpa or anybody. But word spread quickly. Everybody in Raccoon Bluff knew, everybody at Hog Hammock knew—and most of them didn't even know me. Pretty soon, everybody on the island had heard the news.

Sometimes when I'd be out with Mama and Papa somewhere, all eyes would turn to me and people would say, "Oh yeah, you' the one, Hick's and Hettie's youngest baby, the one that died and came back to life. God bless you, baby." I was kinda shy back then, so I just stayed close to Papa, glued up to his leg. I'd glue up close to Mama too, like, "Yeah, that happened, but why don't you leave me alone?"

Some people said I'd died and some said I had been in a trance. Mama believed I died. Grandma said I was in a trance. And while Aunt Mary hadn't seen any sign of life in me, she believed I was in a trance, and somehow she knew the only thing that could bring me out of that trance was garlic.

So had I really died? Was I in a trance?

How could so many people check out a child and say she's dead, if I wasn't? Why did my being dead turn out to be different than people who were pronounced dead and *really* were dead?

Grandpa and Uncle Joe, who was Aunt Mary's husband, and some of the other elders said I would have special powers. They said I would be able to see and hear and *do* things that the ordinary person wouldn't be able to do. It was like a prophecy that I had to fulfill because that's the gift that God blessed me with when I came back to life.

A Special Gift

Growing up over here, the basic thing every child had to do was to satisfy the elders. If the elders said a blessing had been put on you, you *had* to fulfill it. It was a disgrace to prove the old people wrong. So you had to believe in what they said *enough* to make the blessing come forth. You tried your best to prove them right.

But that can be a heavy burden on a child, a *heavy burden*. I didn't really know what the elders expected of me, and I just wanted to be a normal little kid. I didn't want to be able to see the future or predict whether someone was gonna have a baby boy or girl. The only signs I wanted to read were the signs Papa could read from nature, like when the tide is right for fishing.

Papa would swear that I saw things that I didn't. He thought I could see a spirit anytime. If he saw me just sitting down looking at nothing, he would think I was seeing spirits or something he couldn't see.

It was easier for Papa to believe I wasn't seeing spirits if I sat with a book in my hand, so I kept a book in my hand a lot.

One day, we were walking down the road and Papa asked me what I saw. It was just after sunset at the time the old people called dusk-dark and which even today is a time of day some people in Africa consider sacred. Night was coming and day was going and anything could happen at that moment because you're between two worlds. And sometimes as the darkness enters the sky, the rising of the moon catches up with the setting of the sun, and the shadows are so plentiful you see them *all over*. That's how it was that night.

The moon was shining as bright as it could be and it was casting shadows on the trees and shrubs. Those shadows were everywhere and they were moving and flowing and dancing in the moonlight. I kept staring in the woods.

"Whatcha looking at? Whatcha looking at, girl?"

"Nuttun'."

"Aw, I know you see sump'n, chile. You just won't tell me what you see."

"No, sir, Papa, I don't see nuttun'."

"Yeah, you do. I know ya see sump'n. I know ya see sump'n."

Just as we passed by this huge oak tree with moss hanging off it—*whisk!* This warm air started hitting my body like there was something else present—like the spirits were walking, like they were walking on that particular road, right then and there—like they were keeping the road busy, walking with me.

How do you tell Papa that at age five? Shoosh! The safest thing was to leave it alone or just say yes and get it over with.

A *warm* heat went all over my body, everywhere, except my head. The rest of my body was warm and my head got this chilly feeling and tightened up. Even my jaw kinda got a tight feeling, I was tight from the head up and I felt like my hair was standing on end. Every hair was in place, but it *felt* like it was standing on end.

So I said, "Yes, sir, Papa, I see sump'n." And Papa was happy. He didn't ask anything more. He was *sure* I had the power.

Chapter   Two

◆

Paradise to Us

I DIDN'T KNOW WHAT WAS HAPPENING IN THE REST
of the world in the late 1940s or how the post–World War II economy
was booming because it sure wasn't over here, but on our little island
off the coast of Georgia, I was in paradise.

At Belle Marsh, I had everything a little girl could want—her
family, one ox and a hog, orange and other fruit and nut trees, lots of
room to explore and the most beautiful marsh you'd ever want to
see. Even the word "Belle" means beautiful, so the Frenchmen who
owned Sapelo from 1789 through 1802 and named the marsh must
have thought almost as highly of Belle Marsh as I did.

The marsh was directly behind our house, about three hundred
feet away. The high tides on Sapelo are so big that on an especially
big tide like a spring tide, when you looked outside, the whole
marsh would be white with water. Absolutely *white* with water.

But on low tide all you could see from the house was a field of
tall, green, Spartina marsh grass until you got up close. Then there
was nothing but marsh and mud, mud and marsh grass. You
would see tiny clams growing in the mud, the outline of a creek in

the middle of the marsh and everything that's hidden when the tide was in.

We had all kinds of seabirds. We had beautiful white egrets and ibis that draped themselves in the trees, so many seagulls they could block out the light when they flew over you, and tall blue herons stalking the marsh that we called po'jo's— "po'" because they were so skinny they looked poor, and "jo," like they were an everyday working Joe.

Small brown marsh hens clattered away in the marsh too. They nested down in that grass where you could almost never see them, but you could sure hear them calling the tide in and out. God, they made a racket sometimes. They were *loud*.

There was usually a gentle breeze blowing so we had a saltwater smell all the time. On high tide, you'd smell the salt more and on low tide, you'd get a whiff of the sea and everything in it. Either way, the smell meant home to us. "Just smell that marsh," Mama would say proudly. "It smell' so marshy."

So we had a gorgeous view of the water. Matter of fact, we had three water views. In addition to the marsh, we had the Duplin River, which starts off big down at Marsh Landing, but is pretty small by the time it gets to Belle Marsh; just about two hundred feet wide. You could see it from the house looking west. Then there was Belle Marsh Creek, to the south of us, about an eighth of a mile away. You passed it off the road that came near the front of our house.

Whether you were walking, driving a mule-led wagon or riding in a truck, you'd take that road. It was the only road into Belle Marsh, a little dirt road winding past fields and water and big oak trees with long, gray Spanish moss hanging off them, like the tail of a horse.

We lived in a small house that Papa's father, Gibb Walker, built in the early 1900s when he married my grandmother, Ada Jones. The Joneses owned Belle Marsh, all sixty acres or more of it, and had since 1885. In those days, the man always tried to build his bride a house and since there was plenty of land available here, Grandfather Gibb moved to Belle Marsh from Raccoon Bluff to build a house for Grandma Ada.

The house sat up on huge timbers, about four feet off the ground. Nobody's house ever sat on the ground over here. The old people had the sense to know that if there was a real high tide, they'd rather the water go under the house than in it, so, even though the water got close to us sometimes, our house never got flooded.

Like most houses on the island, our house was a simple house. It was made of pine, one board thick, in a style called overlapping single board, and it had four windows—wooden windows, like we were living on the frontier and we were. We were on the edge of the ocean, the Atlantic Ocean. Wood was a lot cheaper than glass and your wooden windows helped you batten down the hatches if a storm was coming.

We had a front stoop on the outside of the house and there were two rooms inside, separated by a hallway. If you went in the front door and turned right, you were in the bedroom where we kids slept, and if you turned left, you were in the combination living room and bedroom where Mama and Papa slept in their iron double bed. The fireplace was in that room, on the outside wall, and there were tables and chairs, but no sofa, and kerosene lamps for light, because nobody on Sapelo who was black had electricity back then.

My little casket was in there too. The one Papa and Mr. Freddy built me. Mama kept it covered with a cloth and used it to store blankets in. We reused everything, we were frugal, and that was a good box. And maybe Mama wasn't going to take any chances. She could still need that casket.

Our kitchen was about twenty feet away from the house, in a separate building. You did your cooking over a wood stove, and the old people said that your kitchen was the biggest fire hazard you had, so in case it caught on fire, you kept it separate to save the rest of your house from burning down.

We had a separate outside toilet too, what most people would call an "outhouse" but we called a "toilet," because we still used a few words from the French era on Sapelo and that was one of them. It was a wooden building, about thirty-six inches square, with a door you could latch for privacy, a built-up wooden platform with a hole cut in it for you to sit on, and a lime and ash pit down below. It was set off about 250 feet from the house and that way you didn't get a whiff of it all the time.

So that was the house we were living in, Mama, Papa, Asberry and me, my teenage sister Barbara, my nephew Michael, who was my sister Ada's son, and occasionally Ada, though usually she was on the mainland picking crabs at a crab factory. That made six of us in the house, sometimes seven, and there would have been a real crowd if my brother Gibb and my sister Winnie had been there. Gibb was twenty-one, married and living in Brunswick by now. Winnie was nineteen and living over at Raccoon Bluff, helping out Mama's parents, Grandma Winnie and Grandpa John Bryant.

Mama was in her thirties. She was a medium person, about five foot seven and slender and she wore gathered skirts and blouses she called "waists." I thought she was pretty but when she was young, Grandma used to say, "Hettie ain't gonna get no husband. Look at her, her forehead's too wide." To Grandma, that meant she was a little unattractive. But Mama's forehead wasn't all that wide and she turned out to be the only one of the children Grandma and Grandpa had together who gave Grandpa any grandchildren. So Mama would laugh whenever she was reminded of that and say, "Yeah, and I ended up with a husband and all these kids."

Mama got her forehead from Grandpa, who was half Native American, but she got Grandma's coloring, which was kinda light. Her hair was almost down to her shoulders and kinda soft. She'd wear it in a pageboy for church but for everyday, she'd split her hair down the middle, make two braids, or plaits, and wrap them around her head, and tuck the ends up underneath. Then, if she was going to the fields to tend our crops, she'd tie an old head rag around her head to cover her hair.

Papa was in his forties. He was darker than Mama and I thought he was good-looking. He had stronger cheekbones than Mama, which was kinda funny since she was part Indian and he wasn't, and he was about the tallest man on the island over here. He was six foot two. The average for men over here was about five foot ten, so Papa's friends called him Big One.

For everyday, Papa wore bib overalls, a shirt and work boots, practical clothes that saw a lot of wear. Like all the men over here, he worked for Richard Reynolds, doing whatever needed to be done, from driving a tractor to working on boats and herding cattle, and he didn't let the fact that he had a leg injury and walked with a limp slow him down one bit.

He had been nineteen and working at the island lumber mill when a log slammed into his leg, right near the ankle bone, and made an ugly wound. His leg healed, but then it opened back up and it had kept on healing and opening back up ever since then. The rest of him was in perfect shape, but that leg had a raw, red, oozing spot, no matter what he used on it.

He would make an agent to bathe his leg with and he dressed it everyday. Mama would make his bandages by cutting old cloth or a sheet into long strips and sewing them together to make them longer, just like women did during the Civil War, then Papa would wrap his leg all the way up to the knee and back down, and continue wrapping it over and over until the leg was good and covered.

There was no doubt about how the accident happened, but that was more than thirty years ago, so why didn't that wound heal? When Mama got mad at him, she'd say, "Yeah, one of them women you' been messing with before you married me, did something to you. They put something on you and that's why it don't heal."

Mama believed in root, in mojo, in what people other places call hoodoo or voodoo. She believed that someone could put root on you and could cause you bodily harm, and jealous women were known to use root.

Papa would look to root too, everybody here believed in root, but he was one who would look to natural causes first. But Mama sure didn't. She was quick to blame everything on root.

"Well, I tell you what," Papa would say, "you believe what you want to believe," and he'd walk off. He wasn't gonna argue with her beliefs. Her beliefs were her beliefs.

My sister Ada was seventeen and she looked like a younger version of Mama and she'd wear her hair in two or three plaits if she was at home and in a pageboy if she was dressing for work. Barbara was the pretty one of the family, now. She was fifteen, slender and tall and she wore her hair short, with bangs, in a modern style.

Asberry was skinny and a little taller than me. I didn't have to like, look up, look up at Asberry, but I couldn't look at him eyeball to eyeball. His hair was short, Papa cut it, and all the boys here had a haircut like that then. My nephew Michael, who Mama called

"Murkel," was a year and a half old and he was walking and talking. He had a slim build and long limbs, so we knew he was going to be tall, and he was nice and well behaved. He was a kid that never complained.

As for me, I was four years old. I wasn't skinny nor fat, and my complexion was a little darker than all of the other kids except for Gibb. Gibb and I were a little richer brown. Mama would plait my hair in three plaits, with one coming down over the right side of my face and two coming over my ear. I looked fine, but when I opened my mouth, I stuttered sometimes and because of that, I didn't talk too much. Other than that, there was nothing too out of the ordinary about me.

I have to tell you right off the bat that I had a pretty normal childhood. I didn't go around performing miracles or anything like that. Mama and Papa may have believed that God had blessed me by bringing me back, but they weren't in any rush to see me do great things. They knew God's ways were God's ways. They can take a *long* time to unfold. Mama and Papa's job was to raise me until I was grown, so I could find out what my purpose was later on, assuming I had one. That was fine with me because I was busy playing.

I made grass babydolls out of marsh grass like my grandmother and great-grandmother had done before me, Asberry and I used vines for jump ropes, heavy sticks and pine cones for playing ball, and Papa made us a balloon out of a hog bladder once. But my favorite thing was playing at the edge of our very own marsh.

There were hundreds of fiddler crabs, tiny crabs with one big claw, scurrying over the sand, and Asberry and I would try to catch them. You'd cup your hand over one and close it up quick so it wouldn't pinch you, then you'd turn it loose and watch it run to its hole. They moved so fast, it was like *zap*. They're gone!

One day Mama said, "Okay, y'all can walk down to the creek there and get crabs. Take a rake and a bucket," and I went racing off with Asberry to catch blue crabs. It was the first time I'd gone to the creek without Mama being with me and that was a lot of trusting on her part, because we were surrounded by water, yes, but the old people always were worried about their children drowning. They'd tell kids, "Stay out of the water. Stay out of that water. Don't go in that water."

They *used* the water, now. To them, the purpose of the water was for getting you from one place to another and for getting your fish and seafood to feed your family. They just had a fear of actually getting in it and that fear had been passed down for generations. It was like they distrusted the water because that water had carried our ancestors here from their home in Africa.

Asberry and I got a bucketful of crabs and took them home to Mama and she boiled them, picked them, and made what we call a soup out of them, but is basically like a stew, and served it for dinner over rice. I had helped provide for the family and I was proud of it. Mama was pleased too, and it wasn't long before she decided I was old enough to go fishing with her.

Mama harvested some clams from the marsh, broke them open and cut out the tough part of the clams, the muscle, and put them in a can for bait. We went down to where Papa's rowboat was tied up, just below the house, on the Duplin River.

So we were out there in the rowboat. The water was deep and I couldn't swim, Barbara couldn't swim, Ada was home and she couldn't swim, and Mama couldn't swim. Papa could but Mama couldn't. The ladies over here couldn't swim a lick but they'd go fishing in the water all the time and think nothing of it. But they were careful and they never had any problems.

We were using a drop line—no pole, just a line with a hook—and I was on the back seat of the boat. Mama had tied my line to the boat so I wouldn't lose it and it was warm and sunny and I went to sleep. The next thing I knew, Mama was going, "Wake up. Wake up. Time to go home. We're rowing in."

I started pulling my line up and all of a sudden, the line started jerking and something started fighting and I started yelling, "I got a fish, I got a fish, I got *a fish*!" Barbara helped me get it in and it was a big croaker, a fish that's every bit as sweet tasting as a trout.

It was my first time fishing and I'd caught a fish. Mama fried it for me for dinner and put it on my plate and it was delicious.

After that you couldn't keep me away from the water. I wanted to be there no matter what, so one day when Asberry said, "Sis, let's see if we can get that box down in the water and make a boat out of it," I said okay.

Mama had gone over to Raccoon Bluff to see Grandma. Barbara was supposed to be watching us, but she wasn't paying any attention. It was a gorgeous day, the sun was shining and she was busy day-dreaming or taking a nap. If Mama had been there, we never would have gotten from the house to the marsh with that casket without her missing us, because she would call at regular intervals. "Asberry? Cornelius? Murkel?" She'd call a couple of times and then she'd go looking, because when it got quiet and Mama didn't see you, she knew you were up to something.

Asberry and I took the lid off the casket and put it aside and emptied the quilts and blankets out and that made it lighter, but we still had to get that box all the way down to the marsh. Asberry pulled the box and I pushed and it wasn't easy, but we got it there. We took Michael with us because he liked playing with us.

We got the box into shallow water and it started leaking right away. We pushed it on out anyhow, because we were determined to play with it, and we put Michael in it and we had fun. We just couldn't float it.

Now, it happened that Papa got off early from work that particular day and he was going to go gannet hunting on the high tide. A gannet was a game bird that was good to eat. Whenever the old people would see one they'd say, "Feasting time tonight, there's a gannet overhead." Gannets are large birds, with wingspans up to seventy inches, found up and down the Eastern Seaboard.

If you didn't have a real big family, you shared the meat of a gannet. You had to, really. Since you didn't have electricity, you didn't have a refrigerator. We didn't have an ice box either. We couldn't afford it, and the only way to get ice anyway was to bring it from the mainland by boat. So when Papa killed a gannet, he always sent some of it over to Grandma and Grandpa or someone else.

Well that day, Papa saw a flock going overhead and he got his shotgun and his sack and came down to the marsh and looked off a distance, to where he was expecting the gannet to feed.

We were sitting down in the middle of the marsh, playing with the box. Asberry and I were behind the grasses, so Papa couldn't see us, but he could see Michael. Michael stood out in his little white shirt, and his skin was black, of course, and the gannet is white and black. It's white on its chest and body, with black wing tips and black tail feathers.

All Papa saw was the white and black he was looking for, this thing moving in the grass in the marsh, which could be a gannet. He looked down the barrel of his gun, and *just before* he pulled the trigger, he saw it was Michael.

Boy, did he call us in.

"What the hell y'all doin' out here? Do your Mama know y'all out here? Get your ass out of that water and I mean now." While he was talking, Papa was getting him a switch off of one of the trees.

Papa *never* spanked. If any spanking was to be done, Mama did the spanking. But this day Papa could very well have shot his grandson. He was scared out of his wits. So, he broke the rule of not spanking. He grabbed Asberry's arm and he tore his butt up with that switch. The whole time he was doing it, he was preaching to him.

"You' the oldest one and you know better than that. You got no business takin' that box from out of that house and takin' it down to that water. You could have had your little nephew killed."

I got scared and figured I was gonna be next and I ran to the house and hid under the bed. I knew I was at fault too. Papa never did come looking for me, but I stayed under that bed until Mama got home and came and got me. My braids got caught on the spring then and I needed help. Mama got me out and she said, "That's what you get for running under this bed hiding."

Papa got the box out of the water, and once it was cleaned and dried out, Mama put her quilts back in it and put it back in the living room where it had rested before we tried to make a boat out of it. After that, I left that casket *alone*. If Michael had died that day, he would have been buried in that casket. It would have been his.

But Mama kept that box. She wasn't gonna get rid of that box. She still might need it for its real purpose sometime. It was her just-in-case insurance. She was keeping it *just in case*.

The Spirit of Grandma Ada

EVERYTHING WE KIDS KNEW WE LEARNED FROM OUR parents. That's how the old ways got passed down, including our beliefs about the spirits.

As early as I can remember, I knew better than to throw the water out the door after dark and by the time I was four, I knew the spirits could play harmless little tricks on you. But there was one other thing I needed to know if I wanted to live a long life. Mama said that I must *never* answer an unseen voice.

I learned this after I thought I heard somebody call my name one time and I answered without really thinking about it. Mama was out the door in a flash. "Who you talkin' to?"

"I thought I heard somebody call me."

"Who they sound like?"

"I don't know, Mama, I just thought I heard someone call my name."

She promptly got me in the house and she fussed at me. "Didn't I tell you not to do that? Don't you do that again. You were lucky that time."

Mama hadn't heard the voice of any living person. She believed it could very well have been the spirit of someone or a family member who was dead calling me to join it in the afterlife so she set me down and told me about the spirits.

We didn't believe just in the body and the soul. We believed in the body, the soul *and* the spirit, just like the people in Africa had believed. The way it worked was that when a person died, the body went to the grave and the soul rested in peace, and the spirit remained on earth. So the spirit was *always* here. It stayed until it was reconnected with the body on Judgment Day.

If you were wise, you didn't underestimate the spirits. They were just as real as any flesh-and-blood person so they were quite powerful, and there was such a thin veil between this world and the next that they could make themselves known. And, even though you wanted to believe that all of them were good, a spirit could be good or bad, depending on the nature of person they had been.

Some spirits would do their best to give you helpful signs. Papa would see all his relatives in a dream and he'd go, "Well, they're coming for someone, maybe even me." Because the spirits of his loved ones were coming back and telling him someone in the family was going to die soon, so it wouldn't be as much of a shock when it happened. But there were spirits you had to guard against. They were the ones that would try to trick you into an early death so you would join them in the spirit world.

If you heard a voice calling you off in the woods and you didn't see anyone but answered, "I'm comin'," that's when you could get yourself in trouble. You'd go out to where you thought you heard that voice and it'd call you from a little further off, so you'd go on to where you thought it was and it would call from a little further off again, and all of a sudden, you'd be hopelessly lost in the woods.

You'd be going around in circles and all the oak trees and the red bays and the pine trees would look alike. Even that deer you just saw would look just like the deer you saw before, and you'd be so befuddled you wouldn't know what was happening to you at all.

Mama said that when people got lost following the spirits, they were usually talking out of their head when they were found. You would get them home and take care of them and if they were lucky, they would recover. Some people would come down with a high fever though and after that, they were never completely in their right mind. They'd walk around mumbling to themselves, they'd catch one thing after another, and they'd get sicker and sicker, and finally they would die and join the spirit that called them.

Mama knew about the spirits calling people. She'd seen it almost happen to Gibb, her firstborn child and my oldest brother, when he was just a baby. He was not quite one year old at the time.

Papa brought Mama over to Belle Marsh when they got married in 1929 and Papa's mama, Grandma Ada, was still living then. Papa's father, Grandpa Gibb, was gone. He was of the wandering kind. He had a little gypsy in his soul and he went down to Florida, to Jacksonville, to visit his half-sister's family and never came back. "He left the old lady, he left his wife, and didn't ever look back," Mama said.

Grandma Ada was expecting him back but when he didn't come, she got sick. She wasn't old, she was only in her early forties, but she got weaker and weaker. She might have been heartbroken, because she loved that husband of hers.

She latched onto Papa because Papa was her only living child, and Papa took real good care of his mama. He was her *hand and foot*. He did everything for her and bought her everything he could to try to make up for her husband being gone.

But that just made Mama a little bit jealous. I know that because when she'd get mad at Papa, she'd say, "Yeah, when your mama was alive, you treat your mama better than me. You buy her butter and fancy bread from the store. I don't remember you buying me no butter. You buy me ol' lard."

But naturally, Mama did take care of his mama. Grandma Ada would just lie in the bed and Mama bathed and fed her like she was a child and took care of her round the clock. She did her best by Grandma Ada but Mama said Grandma Ada was hell, and I don't think Grandma Ada liked Mama too much either.

But Grandma Ada was *crazy* about little Gibb. He was her first grandchild and he was named after her husband. She carried on about him day and night and Gibb liked her too.

Grandma Ada kept getting worse and worse and not long after Mama came over to Belle Marsh, Grandma Ada died. But her spirit stayed nearby because she loved her grandchild too much to leave him.

Mama was in the bed one night right after Papa's mama died and she had Gibb beside her, because back then parents mostly kept the little kids in bed with them, and all of a sudden Mama woke up. She raised up like somebody was calling and she looked around to check on Gibb and Gibb wasn't there.

Gibb was floating through the air.

Mama was never so scared in her life.

There was her baby dressed in his nightclothes, floating through the air, going toward the door. Mama *knew* that was the spirit of Papa's mama coming back to get her grandson.

Gibb's hands were outstretched like he was going into the waiting arms of his grandmother, the spirit of his grandmother. Gibb was too young to understand the meaning of death. When he heard her voice, he would have thought, "Oh, she's back. I'm going to Grandma."

Mama jumped out of bed and grabbed hold of her son just before he got to the door, and she told the spirit of Grandma Ada in no uncertain terms, "Leave my son alone. Don't be *bothering my chile.* You ain't taking my chile with you."

Mama would have tied Gibb down if she'd needed to, but it wasn't necessary. The spirt of Grandma Ada backed off and she didn't come back.

Really, her spirit was probably just lonely and what better company could she find than the grandson she loved? But even if she did want him in the afterlife with her, she didn't want to see Gibb hurt on earth. Her job was to protect and guide him—that's what spirits are supposed to do anyway—and she showed that she knew this when he was two years old. Gibb was a walking and talking little boy then.

It was laundry day and Mama always started her washing early. She would be out in the yard by eight o'clock or earlier, with her fire going and an iron pot on that fire. She would scrub and boil the clothes to get out any dirt and then she'd rinse them in a tub filled with cold water. So Mama was washing and hanging out clothes, and she turned around and Gibb was gone.

"Where's my baby? Where's my baby at?"

She went running around that yard yelling, "Gibb, Gibb," and he didn't answer. He always answered Mama. Then she remembered the well.

We got our water from an outside well. It was just a hole in the ground, level to the ground, with a flat cover on it. It was open that day because Mama needed water.

Mama ran to the well and looked down and there was Gibb.

"My God, my baby's in the well!"

Gibb was inside the well, sitting on a little narrow piece of board that went across it. The well was about six to eight feet deep and that board wasn't deep down, but it was down there. If Gibb had slipped just a little, he would have fallen in that water and drowned. But Gibb was not wet or anything, he was just sitting on that thing in the well.

Mama knew the spirit of Grandma Ada had caught him just in time and set him up nice on that piece of board and her spirit was staying nearby to make sure he didn't drown. "There ain't no other way a child that little could fall in the well and not hit the water," she told me. "I knowed it was nobody but his grandma protecting him from going all the way down."

Mama was scared but Gibb never said a word. Not a word. Most little kids would be crying up a storm because all they could see was a black hole below them, down to that water, but not Gibb. He was just sitting there, tongue-tied.

Mama lay down on her stomach and reached down into that well and she grabbed Gibb off that board. Even if he'd fallen all the way down, Mama would have found some way of getting down into that well and getting him. Papa was off at work and it was up to her. She didn't hesitate at all, she just reached down and pulled him out and brought Gibb back to safety.

A little after that, Mama and Papa got themselves a hand pump so you could pump the water straight into a bucket and Papa filled the well up with sand. It must have taken Papa a lot of sand to fill the well but he did. Nobody ever fell down that hole again.

Mama felt a bit more kindly toward the spirit of Grandma Ada after that because she had saved Gibb. Grandma Ada probably kept watching Gibb though. She'd proved she was good at that. But Gibb never was in serious danger again while he was a kid, so that was the last time the spirit of Grandma Ada made her presence known.

◆
_____

Chapter Four

A Make-Do or Do-Without Family

AT PLANTING TIME ON SAPELO, WE RELIED ON SIGNS
from nature that the soil was ready to receive new seed and our beliefs
about our bonds to the earth.

We were a make-do or do-without family, and the spring I was
four I learned how much *everything* we had counted toward our survival. If our flour had weevils in it, Mama sifted it and used it anyway. Our sugar was kept in a container set in a pan of water with a
greased rim so that the sugar ants couldn't get to it. And you know
that if our staples were that precious, our crops were more so. We
depended on those crops. What we grew was what we ate, along
with the fish we got from the sea and Papa's hunting, and the few
staples we bought. So Mama and Papa were careful to do everything
just right with our crop.

If there was a pregnant woman around at planting time, she
dropped the seed. A pregnant woman was the best planter there was
because she was carrying new life in her. Your seed would get up
faster, your crops would grow faster and they would bear better, all
because of her, and if she dropped the seed for watermelon, they

would grow like crazy. Your field would practically explode; you would have watermelon everywhere. Ada was in the field dropping the seed this particular spring and if I had been a little older, it might have made me wonder if she was in the family way. But I was too young to know about things like that. Besides, I was in the fields too.

If you didn't have a pregnant woman around, you'd get a young child to drop the seed, the younger the better, because little hands were full of life. The seed would grow just as fast as a growing child. Sometimes a family would even borrow a young child if they didn't have one.

I was dropping the seed before I was two years old, before I could even talk. I was just big enough to walk that row. Mama had me in real bib overalls, a long shirt, and I was barefoot. The weather was warm and it was barefoot time.

Mama had patience with me galore. She would hold my hand in hers, give me three or four seeds, whatever was supposed to go in the hole, and show me just where to put them. She'd say, "Put it right there. That's fine. Go to the next one. Okay, now drop one right here." I got the hang of it and I would drop the seed and she would push and stamp it in the dirt. I was out there thinking I was as big as my mama and daddy. They let me plant the fields and it was neat.

Old hands were the worst to have around at planting time. We believed that old hands should never drop seed because your crop will always take longer to grow. They didn't have much planting life left in them; they were going back to the earth, not coming from it. The old people would say, "Yeah, girl, I'm going backwards every day," and that meant they were closer to death than you.

We had other rules for planting too. We never planted when the tide was out, we planted when the tide was coming in, because if the tide was low or going out, we believed it would stunt the growth of your plants. We always tried to plant on the new moon, just as it was beginning to grow and swell. If we didn't plant on the new moon, Papa would say, "We'll plant on the fullest of the moon," because that was the second-best time.

Our early crops went in the ground in February and March and then come Good Friday, Mama would say, "Okay, it's Good Friday, so I'm planting my lima beans." That day was blessed by God, so your beans would do better if you planted them then.

For certain crops, you had to be sure that danger of a late frost was over before you planted. Mama said nothing can fool the pecan trees so we watched the pecan trees and when they were putting out their blossoms, we knew it was safe to plant okra or anything else.

Papa would get everything ready. He would burn the fields off so he could get a plow through and spread lime over the soil to make it better. He made his own lime by burning oyster shells from a pile we kept near the house, and if he wanted to spread ashes too, he'd get them from a pile of ashes we saved from our wood stove and chimney. Then he would hitch our ox, Bully, to the plow and plow the fields.

Bully was a black ox with sorrowful-looking eyes and big horns that curved way up. During slavery, Thomas Spalding, the biggest plantation owner over here, had about ninety oxen that were used for hauling sugar cane to the sugar mill and other plantation uses. His grandson said that the "more privileged Negroes" were allowed to own horses and cattle too, so Bilali, the most famous of the Africans on Sapelo, probably had a team of oxen too that he used to plow his own garden.

After slavery, when people were farming strictly for themselves, an ox would have been a prized possession because it is the strongest of all the work animals. They were available too, because an ox is nothing but a bull that was picked out when it was young and castrated and then it grew big and you made it into a work cow.

President Calvin Coolidge went hunting in an ox-drawn cart when he came here in 1928. By the end of the forties, most people in the United States used tractors and other people mainly used mules. So oxen were almost relics by the time I came along. There were only five left on the island, including Bully.

Papa inherited Bully from his father, and God, was Bully huge! He weighed about three-quarters of a ton, fifteen hundred pounds. He was probably one of the biggest work cows ever. Most people's oxen came up to their shoulders but Bully was over most people's heads. He was almost level with Papa, and Papa was quite tall so they were like two giants going through the fields. They made a handsome pair.

Most mornings Bully would be tethered out across from the house, lying down resting. When I'd walk up to him and rub his face, he would turn to me with his big ol' cow eyes so soft and gentle like he was saying, "Hello, what have you got for me?" and I would give him water. I was never afraid of him; he was just sweet-tempered and nice. Most oxen were. They were slow-moving and lumbering, but steady, not stubborn like a mule, a true beast of burden.

Papa would hitch Bully to a cart to carry wood for our fireplace and wood stove, or to a wagon to bring back the staples from Hog Hammock that he and Mama bought, and Bully could even take my whole family to church over at Raccoon Bluff in the wagon. You would see a whole line of mules, oxen and a few horses hitched up in front of the church that people had used to get there from all over the island.

We didn't use Bully too much for a Sunday ride unless someone was ailing but still wanted to go to church. That wagon saved your feet, yes, but if you were young and healthy you would rather walk than ride in a *sloooow* wagon with a *sloooow* cow. You walked if you were going for speed. But at plowing time I would watch Papa and Bully work, and to me, Bully, with his black body glistening in the sun, was the star of the show.

Some of the food we planted was brought over by the early slave-holders after they realized we couldn't adapt to their diet. We always planted collard greens, rice, onions, sweet potatoes, white potatoes, corn, peanuts, okra, squash, pumpkin, red peas and lima beans. At harvesttime, *everything* had a purpose. You didn't toss anything away. Mama even grew our rice until the early 1940s when it became cheaper to buy it. By the 1950s, she could get a hundred-pound bag of rice for eight dollars which could last a whole year depending on the size of your family.

We had delicious corn back then. Delicious green corn. By green I mean fresh, not the color green. You'd eat the corn off the cob and then since it's soft still, you'd give the cob to your pig or your cow and it would eat the whole thing.

The cornstalks were left in the field to dry. Then the leaves on the stalks were bundled and saved for fodder during the winter for your cow, if you had one. You used the cornstalks for making potato banks, or houses, so that you could have sweet potatoes most of the winter and some seed potatoes to plant the next spring. You had three plantings of sweet potatoes and then the vines became fodder too. Absolutely nothing went to waste.

We planted lots of corn because we used corn for everything from feeding ourselves to feeding our animals. We would grind it into grits and cornmeal using a small stone mill that may have belonged to Papa's great-grandfather Charles, who had been freed from slavery. The mill had two flat, heavy stones, a hole for pouring the corn in and a handle that took a lot of muscle to turn. Your first grinding would get you grits and the second one got you a fine grade of cornmeal.

There was one other use for your corn too. *Moonshine*. That's right.

Everybody over here made their own moonshine then. You used some for medicine: for a hot toddy if you were chilled, with a little honey in it for a cold, with water for gastritis, and for an awful concoction of whiskey over parched hog hooves for kidney problems. You would drink your moonshine too, naturally, and most people, including Mama, kept some to sell. The little bit of money she made from it was an important part of our livelihood. It was her spending money.

People would stop by different houses to buy a drink of moonshine, depending on who they wanted to see, whose whiskey they liked—everyone's was blended a little differently—and who had some right then. You never made too much whiskey at one time. But there was one house in Hog Hammock where you could count on getting whiskey, and that was Mama Lizzie's.

Mama Lizzie was known for selling whiskey by the shot, pint or quart. She was also known for being a root worker, and I don't mean good root either. That didn't seem to bother the menfolks; actually, it probably just intrigued them. They loved to sit there and drink and talk, but they tried their best not to fall to sleep when they stopped at Mama Lizzie's. You could be relieved of your money at Mama Lizzie's. If she didn't get you, her family would. Papa found this out firsthand.

Times were tough and Papa didn't have no other choice, so one day he sold Bully to the Reynolds people. They didn't give him what Bully was worth, they just gave him five dollars, and Papa handed Bully over with Bully looking at him like, "Where are you going and who are these new men?"

Papa was feeling quite low and by the time he got to Hog Hammock he needed a drink, so he stopped off at Mama Lizzie's house for some moonshine. He had a drink or two and then fell asleep.

When he woke up, his pocket was empty. The money he got for his only cow was gone. Papa walked the distance back to Belle Marsh, angry and ashamed and knowing he wasn't going home to be consoled for losing that money.

Mama was looking for Papa to see how much money he got to feed the family, and when she found out he didn't have anything to show for the fact he sold his cow, she hit the roof. She raised some Cain. She couldn't believe Papa messed around and got his pocket picked. We *needed* that money. We were worse off than before.

Papa lost the money and the cow to boot. "He hung his head and cried like a baby," Mama said. He bawled his heart out and then as he said about things, with the words rolling out fast, it was *"kitty-byth'do'r."* Kitty-by-the-door. Like a cat streaking out a cracked door. Like "I'm finished with it. It's done. Leave it alone." He wasn't going to let himself be defeated by regret.

Grandpa let Papa use his ox, Spring, to plow the fields and the crops bore well. How could they not with Ada and me dropping the seed? But it was a hard go for Papa. Spring was a little red ox, a *mean* little thing. Papa kept yelling to us kids, "Stay away from Spring, stay away from that cow," because Spring would chase you and knock you down.

After that we didn't have an ox of our own for plowing, hauling wood or staples, or a Sunday ride if we needed one. The only thing we had left was Mike and Charlie—our right foot and our left foot. I don't know for sure where those names came from but they probably came from two Irishmen. There used to be some hardworking Irish fishermen in this area on Blackbeard Island, just across from Raccoon Bluff. Most white people along the coast looked down on them, but the Irish and the black people got along well because the Irish had spunk.

The old people on Sapelo knew all about getting by with what they had. They would look straight at you and say, "If you know like me, you'll take Mike and Charlie and get on down that road," and that's what we did. We made do with Mike and Charlie and we kept on going down the road.

◆

Chapter Five

Grandma Winnie

FROM AS EARLY AS I CAN REMEMBER, WE WALKED TO the Bluff, Raccoon Bluff, to see Grandma. We were always walking, walking, walking. We *walked*.

Asberry and I kicked pine cones and chased them while we walked, so we were always up ahead or back behind Mama. She would turn around and go, "C'mon kids, c'mon up," and we'd run and catch up with Mama and Michael and Barbara and then we'd go ahead of them. Then she'd say, "Kids, there's some sparkle berries and there's some blackberries," and what we couldn't reach, she'd reach for us. So we didn't just take a long, dry, boring walk. We had fun.

We walked over to see Grandma even more after one spring day when it was raining and some guys with the timber company had stopped by to buy a drink of Mama's moonshine. Grandma was down to Belle Marsh that day and my sister Winnie was with her. Winnie lived with Grandma and would come over to see Mama, and Winnie's son Capus was just a baby, so naturally Winnie had him with her, and they were all in the kitchen.

Grandma was about seventy and she was a little woman and light skinned. She was five foot one or two at best, and slender. Her hair was gray and she wore it plaited. Grandma was blind in one eye, and you know how a lot of people are blind but they still have their eyes open? Not Grandma. I never saw an eyeball or anything. Her left eye was sealed shut. It was totally closed, like it was forever sleeping.

She was born sighted but something went wrong when she was a young girl, about eleven or twelve years old. The old people said that Grandma got hold of a handkerchief that was meant for somebody else and that the handkerchief had something on it—it had root on it. When Grandma wiped her face with that handkerchief, her left eye burned like crazy and she went blind. Her family believed it was an accident that she got hold of that handkerchief, because people over here never put root deliberately on children, you never wanted to hurt the young, but they definitely believed it was root.

I asked Mama one time, "Mama, what happened to Grandma's eye?" and when Mama told me that it was caused by root, my reaction was, "That must have been some *strong* root."

My sister Winnie was nineteen at this time and she and Mama were the same size and the same height. She had Mama's coloring but she was a dead ringer for Papa. She swung her arms like him. Both Papa's and Winnie's arms didn't just hang down, it was like there was a curve to them when they swung them, and she held her shoulders like him. Papa's shoulders kinda came forward a little and Winnie's did too.

After Grandma had a few drinks of moonshine with the fellows, she told Winnie, "Bring that child and come on. Let's go home."

"Winnie ain't going nowhere with that baby," Mama said. "That baby is too young and it's raining out there and she ain't going anywhere. She'll catch a death of cold." When Mama said a dead of cold, she meant consumption.

Grandma could get mean when she drank and she just ignored Mama and said, "Winnie, you just wanta stay down here because them men folks are down here." Grandma did have reason to be worried, really, because Winnie was kinda sweet on one of the men that was there drinking. She just had Capus and she didn't have a husband and Grandma didn't want any more babies under her roof.

Mama turned to Grandma and said, "Mama, there's no need for you to go. Let's wait and see if the rain stops some."

"No, John's waiting on me and I'm going home," Grandma said. She was speaking of Grandpa, my Grandpa John Bryant. "Winnie can stay if she wants."

"Miss Winnie," one of the guys said, because Winnie was Grandma's name too, "we'll carry you home in a little bit."

"I'm going now."

There was no reasoning with Grandma when she'd had a few. She was going home to John, to her matey. So Mama gave her some fish to carry home, some smoked mullet, and she put it in a five-pound grits bag, a blue-and-white Jim Dandy grits bag. We saved everything, and we would always empty the grits out of the bag and save it to use again.

So Grandma got her fish and took off. She left.

The rain did let up enough for Winnie to go home later, so Winnie walked home to Raccoon Bluff. And when Winnie got home, she asked Grandpa where was Mama. (She said Mama, not Grandma, because when Mama and Grandma were together, she called one Belle Marsh Mama and the other Bluff Mama.) But when Winnie got back home, she asked where was Mama, because the other Mama wasn't there.

So Winnie just said, "Where's Mama?"

Grandpa said, "I thought she was with you."

"No, Bluff Mama left well ahead of me so she should be home."

Where was Grandma?

Grandpa and Winnie and Capus walked back up King Savannah toward Belle Marsh looking for Grandma, because Grandma would have been coming through King Savannah. She had walked that road all her life. There was no way she could get lost. A savannah's an open prairie-type area where you see nothing but grass and sometimes stubby trees, and King Savannah was the biggest one around. Grandma always walked through King Savannah.

They looked to see if they could find any tracks in the road, because although it rained all day, they might have found a track or two of hers. But they looked up and down that road and didn't find any trace of Grandma.

There was one road that swings off before you actually get to King Savannah, and it goes to what's called Fanny Garry Gap. That was the only road they hadn't looked for Grandma on, so they went and took that road. They found the bag of fish first, that blue-and-white bag, a little up the road. About a half a mile or so up that road, she had dropped the bag of fish.

They were scared now, really scared, and then they found Grandma. They found her sitting in the road, in that wet road, in all that rain. Grandma was just sitting there, not knowing where she was. She had been there for hours in that soaking rain. Winnie said Grandma was confused and talking out of her head. "Racoon Bluff Mama didn't even know us. She didn't know who we were when we walked up on her."

They got Grandma up, and Grandpa got on one side of her and Winnie got on the other, and they helped her back home. Grandpa was walking with his walking cane and Winnie was walking with a baby on her hip, and they supported her in between them for almost three miles. And they got Grandma home and bathed her off and put dry clothes on her and gave her a hot toddy to drink, and then she came around. She wasn't confused anymore, but she never took that road again.

Grandma's arthritis set in after that. She couldn't ever walk as good again and she spent a lot of time sitting in a chair. Mama said if Grandma wasn't so hard headed, if she had waited till the rain let up, she wouldn't be suffering like this. Then she said that nobody could ever tell Grandma what to do, not even Grandma's mother.

Grandma's mama was Harriet, that was my great-grandmother Harriet, and she was a Hall. Everybody called her Ma'am, and that was a term of respect. Mama remembered her a little from when she was a little girl and she had a photograph of Ma'am hanging in the living room. It was a brown-and-white old-fashioned photograph and in it Ma'am is young and pretty. She has on a white blouse with ruffled sleeves and a high neck with lace around the top, and her hair is thick and wavy and she has it pulled back, because that's what was popular at the time. She is light skinned in that photograph, and that's the way Mama said she was. Ma'am was so light skinned she almost looked white.

Ma'am was born in 1854 and she was a young girl when freedom came. She married Samuel Grovner when she grew up, the son of Cotto and John Grovner. John Grovner was a forward-looking man. He registered to vote two years after the Civil War and along with two other black men, William Hillery and Bilali Bell, in 1871 managed somehow to scrape up enough money for a five-hundred-dollar down payment to buy land at Raccoon Bluff.

After the Civil War, a lot of people on Sapelo didn't want anything to do with the old communities they had lived in during slavery and they started abandoning them pretty quick. Within ten years, most of the old slave communities had totally disappeared.

Uncle Nero Jones and his parents, for instance, moved to Belle Marsh from the slave settlement behind the mansion house on the South End and that community closed. The settlements at New Barn Creek and Behavior, also on the South End, closed. On the west side of the island, people moved away from Bourbon Field, and Hanging Bull dwindled and died. Hanging Bull took a little while to close because the First African Baptist Church was built there after the war. There also were old people at Hanging Bull that no one would have wanted to uproot, so Hanging Bull wouldn't have closed until after they died. My great-great-great-grandmother Hester, was among the old people there. She was in her nineties when the Civil War ended.

Getting back to John Grovner, he had moved to the Raccoon Bluff area even before land was available to buy there and as soon as it was, he and the other two men formed a land company, Hillery and Company, and bought between 700 and 800 acres of land. They kept about 105 acres of land for themselves and divided the rest into tracts of 33 to 35 acres each. They then sold the tracts to seventeen other freed families who had lived on Sapelo before the war, and that was how the community of Raccoon Bluff was founded. People from Hanging Bull, Bourbon Field and other places on the island poured into the Bluff so they could get a fresh start in a new community of their own making.

Each year for three years, on or around New Year's Day, the men of Hillery and Company rowed to the mainland, went to the Bank of Darien and made another payment of five hundred dollars, which worked out to be twenty-five dollars a family. That was a lot of money then. If some families didn't have all of their share, others pitched in extra, because everyone was determined to get that land, and in 1874, the land at Raccoon Bluff belonged lock, stock and barrel to black people.

So, Samuel, being the son of John Grovner, and Harriet, being a granddaughter of Bilali, were upstanding people in the community. They had eight children, four that lived and four that died, and their children didn't have too many children, just one or two kids each, and all the others, except Grandma, didn't have outside children. Every child belonged to a proper husband-and-wife team until Grandma came of age.

Ma'am was very religious, very strict, and she tried to keep a lid on my grandma Winnie when she got to where she liked to have some fun. Ma'am would shut the door to the bedroom Winnie was in and lock her in her room every night. But Grandma would wait till everything got quiet and her parents had gone to sleep. Then she'd open the wooden window in her bedroom and crawl through, and she was free to meet a young man and have a drink or two. Then Grandma would crawl back through the window in her room and go to bed. In the morning, Ma'am would open the door, see Winnie in her bed and think she'd been in the bed all night.

So Grandma kept sneaking out the window and she got pregnant, and she had Maggie, and then she kept going. She had Edwin, she had Ferdinand, she had Della, and she had Mary, and still no husband.

In those days, you did not have a child out of wedlock, it absolutely was not right. If a young lady was expecting a baby and she wasn't married, the elders of the church, the deacons, would call on the young man that was responsible. Six deacons would be staring in the face of that young man and asking him what his intentions are. "Aaaah, marry her," he'd answer, and they got married before that baby came. There weren't many babies born out of wedlock in Grandma's time.

When Grandma's first child was born, the deacons called Grandma to church conference to find out who the father was, but Grandma wouldn't go. She broke all the rules by refusing to go. They tried again when her second child was born and Grandma still wouldn't come. The deacons kept on calling her to conference after each child was born, and Grandma wouldn't go.

Finally, my Aunt Mary was born in January of 1905. That was Grandma's fifth child and Grandma was getting tired of the deacons pestering her. So when they called her to conference, "to question," they called it, she went. She got dressed up and she went and the church was crowded. Just about everybody in the Bluff came to hear Grandma confess who the father of all her children were.

"Sister Winnie, this is enough," the deacons said. "You have to tell us who's the father of your children."

Grandma looked at the deacons up front, all men. She looked at the deaconesses, which were the wives of the deacons, and at her friends' families in the pews. The women were all sitting on the edge of their seats saying, "Lord, I hope she don't call my man's name."

She looked straight at the deacons and she said, "Now, if I tell you all which one of you up there is the father of my children, or which one of you up there could have been the father of my children, there wouldn't be nobody in this church but me now, would there?"

All heads bowed, like when God said Let he who is without sin cast the first stone. One of them up there condemning her was the father of one of her children, and the others had propositioned her or wanted to, so they were all guilty. Hymns were hummed and church was let out and they didn't bother Grandma no more. So she put it to them like, how dare you, and she stopped that dog from sucking eggs.

She knew who her children belonged to. One was a Walker and one was a Green and another was a Jackson and so forth. Each one belonged to someone different, every one of them. She didn't have two by the same man. She could very well have named one and had the church made him do the right thing, but she didn't.

Each man would just use her. She got pregnant and had a baby, and then they left her alone and went with someone else. They married someone who was "whole," that's what they called it then, and Grandma had that blind eye. Grandma wasn't gonna have anything to do with them then. Naming one of them and being forced into marrying him would have killed her spunk. She lived with her mama and papa and everybody pitched in and helped raise her kids and she waited for one that liked her.

Then Grandpa came to Sapelo and he was a mystery man. He was half black and half Indian and he had long, black wavy hair. He wore it down his back, and the women all said he was one handsome man, he was a fine-looking man. Not many men moved to Sapelo and stayed. The last one that had was Mr. Charles Banks, and that was nineteen years before Grandpa did. So, it was like, "Aaaah, a new one."

There were rumors about why Grandpa came here, but nothing was ever proven. He never stole, he was never a man to do that, he didn't fit the character of such a thing, but he might have gotten in a fight and somebody got killed and he took off and run, and he ended up down here. He came to Sapelo on a turpentine boat, never to send a letter home, as if he didn't want his family or the law to know where he was. He never spoke about where he came from, he never did, except to tell us of his birth, that he was part Indian and part black. And that was all over him, there was no question about that. The waviness in his hair came from the black part of him and that jet black color of it came from the Indian part. He was tall, kinda high cheekboned, and he was dark complexioned and his skin had almost a reddish hue to it.

So he never said, and Grandma didn't divulge that secret, so nobody knew for sure. Even Mama didn't know where he came from. I asked her and she just said, "Well, to tell the truth, I never asked." Mama just accepted her papa. Now her sister, Aunt Harriet, said he was from around Macon, Georgia, and that his name was Brunson or Brinson. But he was John Bryant when he got here, and so he was John Bryant from then on. Everybody called him Bryan'. They didn't say Bryant, they said Bryan'.

There was a lady he was going with before he started going with Grandma, so Grandma wasn't his first choice when he got off that turpentine boat. And who knows what Grandpa was thinking, because it took him awhile before he got around to marrying Grandma. About six months. She almost didn't get Grandpa, matter of fact, because there were a couple of other ladies that were running after him, trying to catch him. Grandma didn't look that appealing and everybody was going, why was somebody so handsome getting ahold of someone that look like Grandma? So they all tried their best to get ahold of John Bryan'.

Grandma was no young chippy, she was about thirty-one then, and Grandpa was twenty-nine. But Grandma must have had something, because she snagged that younger man. I think he liked her because Grandma was such an independent cuss and Grandpa was too. Grandma agreed with most things that Grandpa did and he didn't argue too much about the things that Grandma did. So it seems like they forged this bond.

They got married August the tenth, 1910, and Mama was born in October. So they made it to the altar in time, just in time. Some of Grandma's children were grown by then. My Aunt Maggie was married and she came to Grandma's wedding, so it must have been an unusual wedding. But that was the end of that running-around episode in Grandma's life.

After Mama was born, Grandma and Grandpa had two more children, both girls, Harriet and Lucinda, and Grandpa helped raise two of her earlier children, Aunt Mary and Aunt Della. Grandma stayed home then, except if she was out with her drinking buddies, because Grandma liked her tea, that's for sure, or if she was going to church or coming to Belle Marsh to see Mama. At least that's the way everything was until the day when Grandma said the spirits "swing" her head and confused her and lost her on that road.

Grandma never came back to Belle Marsh. She didn't trust the spirits, she didn't want the spirits bothering her anymore.

Grandma said some spirit just took her down that road and lost her and left her wet and so confused she didn't know anything. She blamed it on the spirits, not the moonshine, and it could have been a spirit, an evil spirit. The spirit of some vengeful woman getting back at Grandma, like, "I'll fix her for messin' with my man." It could have happened just the way Grandma said. *She* believed it did.

"It was the spirits, gal," Grandma said. "It had nuttin' to do with that moonshine. It was the spirits."

◆

Chapter Six

At the Bluff

ALL THE OLD PEOPLE WERE SOMETHING AND GRAND-
ma and Grandpa really were. I never knew anyone like them. They
each had their own power and neither of them gave up their power to
the other.

The Bluff was Grandma's seat of power. After Grandma and
Grandpa married, he shared it with her, she didn't share it with him.
They had a good marriage, I think, but they weren't like one husband-and-wife team over here, Ben Brown and Katie Brown, who
was a famous midwife on Sapelo. Ben Brown died first and he had a
little headstone in the cemetery that said Ben Brown, Husband of
Katie Brown, and that's all it said. "Well, we know who the boss
of that family was," people would say. But no one could say that of
Grandma and Grandpa. There wasn't a boss in their household, just
a struggle of wills.

Grandpa John Bryant was a good fisherman, a good trapper and
the best alligator skinner there was. He and Papa and Uncle Joe,
who was Aunt Mary's husband, and Cousin Luke Walker would go
gator hunting at night with their pine torches blazing—their flam-

beaux, we called them—and a single-shot rifle, shovels to dig a gator out its hole if they needed to, and a long pole with a big hook on the end of it to grab a gator with.

There were a lot of gators in freshwater ponds and creeks, and the men would have studied the gator's habits ahead of time, so they knew just where a gator hole was. They'd shine their flambeaux on the water and if there was a gator swimming there, his eyes would be glowing red like two cigarette butts in the dark. The further apart those red eyes were, the bigger the gator was, and they wanted the big ones because they were going to sell the hides. They'd aim their rifle right between the eyes and shoot, and when they could get to him—that gator was gonna be snapping at them, he was one angry gator—they'd hook him in his mouth and strong-arm him in—all six to twelve feet of tail-lashing gator.

They'd get the gator home and they'd skin it and split the meat among them, cure the hide and wrap it in brown paper, tie it with string, and send it off to Jake's Furriers in Savannah. A week or so later a check for something like thirty dollars a hide would come in the mail and they'd share it equally. Grandpa trapped otter and mink too and sold their hides and most of the time he didn't work for anybody else. He worked for himself.

He was an educated man too. Grandpa went to school through the third grade and that was a good bit for a black man back then. He was no professor, but he could read, write, decipher and order things through the mail and that put him in the educated class. A lot of the men at the Bluff could read and write simple letters and sign their names, so they didn't have to do X's. But none of them could read the way Grandpa did.

Everybody had their Bible, the Sears catalog and maybe Montgomery Ward too, but we never saw regular books at other people's

houses. Grandpa had a whole collection of books. He read everything he could put his hands on and he knew a lot of things that
most of the other men didn't and people held him in esteem—especially after the first airplane flew over Sapelo.

It must have happened before 1929, because Charles Lindbergh,
the famous aviator, flew to Sapelo that year to see Howard Coffin,
the wealthy Detroit auto engineer who owned most of the island
from 1912 until 1934. The only wage-paying jobs on the island were
under Coffin and he had up to two hundred people planting crops,
tending his dairy, taking his guests hunting, rebuilding and taking
care of the Big House. It had burned down during the Civil War
and no one had the money to have it rebuilt until Coffin came.
Grandpa would work for Coffin every now and then to get some
cash money and on this particular occasion, Grandpa and some of
the men were out working in the fields for Coffin.

The men were out there doing their thing when this loud noise
came overhead. They looked up in the sky and all of a sudden they
saw this funny-looking thing in the air with things on it that were
turning around.

They all went to church and the preacher preached about damna-
tion and brimstone and things falling from the sky on Judgment
Day, so, naturally the first thing they thought about was Judgment
Day, and they ran off in all different directions into the woods. The
only one left in the field was Grandpa, or Ol' man Bryan', as they
called him. He was just a-hoeing and not paying a bit of attention.

That thing went streaking across the sky and after they couldn't
see or hear it anymore, everybody came sneaking back out of the
woods. They got back in the field where Grandpa was and they said.
"Well, Bryan'. How come you wasn't afraid? How come you didn't
run?"

Grandpa said, "Nothin' to be afraid of. Just a man-made thing called a airplane. That's all it was." He'd read about it somewhere.

So, he was a little superior in some ways and Grandma knew it and she was proud of it. After Grandma and Grandpa married, Grandma would get dressed to the nines and the two of them would go to church. She'd make her own clothes and she'd make matching hats, and Grandma was one of the best-dressed women in church.

There were two services back then. Church service was *long*, baby. Grandma and Grandpa went to the Sunday School part and that meant they left home at ten. By the time the first part of service was over, it'd be something like two o'clock. Then they'd come back home and eat. You'd have about an hour or so before you'd go back to the next service and it would usually last to four o'clock or so.

Grandma and Grandpa would come in after the Sunday morning services and Mama and her sisters better have the chicken fried, the greens cooked and the rice ready because Grandma would say, "Well, we're bringing home the preacher after church."

They'd start cooking before Grandma and Grandpa left for church and sometimes they had to thrash the rice too, because you left the rice in the husk until you needed it and that helped keep it fresh. Everybody still had a rice field then and after they harvested it, they'd stack the sheaves up, tie them in bundles and keep them in the corn house.

Mama would put the rice in a big wooden mortar made from a hollowed-out cypress log, she'd pick up a wooden pestle that was between two and three feet long and drop it on the rice, being careful not to drop it too hard because that would break the grain. Then she'd winnow the rice: she'd put it in a large, shallow basket called a rice fanner, and shake it gently so the wind would catch the chaff and blow it off. People used to pray that the wind would come up, because that made winnowing it easier, and a long time ago they would sing a song that went, "Blow, wind, blow."

Mama hated it when the preacher came, because a Baptist preacher would eat you out of house and home and not even think about the kids. Mama and her sisters would get the chicken foot and the gizzard, the liver and the neck and backbone, and the preacher and Grandma and Grandpa would sit around and eat and then they'd go back to that second service.

Grandma wasn't going back with the same clothes on, now. She'd wash off and put on a clean set of clothes and they'd go. Grandpa would have his suit on, his creases all sharp, and Mama said they made a handsome couple walking down the road. Grandma loved showing off her clothes and her man. She wanted everybody to see she had a man. She didn't have to mess with their men no more. She had a husband of her own now.

But while Grandma's running-around days were over, Grandpa was a rogue. He was the mysterious new kid on the block and either the women chased him or he chased them.

All the women liked Grandpa and when he was out visiting and his hair was hanging down with all those waves, they would go completely bonkers about Grandpa. Mama's sister, my Aunt Harriet, said that after they got married, Grandma almost lost him to another woman, Miss Ida. Miss Ida was married, solemnly married, but she almost took Grandpa from Grandma.

There was a story too about Grandpa having a girlfriend in the Bluff and suspecting another guy of going to see her. Grandpa was going to Hog Hammock and when he got down to Miller's Pump, which is just as you're coming into the Bluff, he met Mr. Richard Bens heading for the Bluff. Grandpa stopped Richard Bens in the middle of the road and said, "Where you goin'? I heard you been tryin' to tear my kingdom down." Richard Bens always called Grandpa "King," a lot of the men did because Grandpa was powerful in his own way, so Mr. Richard said, "King, o' King. It's not *me* tryin' to tear your kingdom down. It's somebody else."

So, Grandpa had a kingdom and Grandma wouldn't have liked it one bit. I don't know if she yelled at him or what, but she put up with it somehow, and he put up with the fact that she liked her drinks.

He wouldn't touch a drop of whiskey himself, not even at Christmas, but on weekends, Grandma and her friend, Miss Frances Grovner, would go to different houses in the Bluff and get a drink. Grandma always had a little spending change in her apron pocket to buy a drink and Grandpa didn't like drinking but he gave it to her. She'd kill him if he didn't, she'd nag him to death. They had their own balancing act. They saw eye to eye on most things but where they didn't, they both did what they wanted to do.

We always called it "the Bluff," we never said Raccoon Bluff. Everything centered around the Bluff to us. I didn't know much about the community of Hog Hammock then, and the Bluff was the biggest thing I had ever seen. That's where your relatives were, that's where the school was and that's where the church was. There were nearly seventy people there. It was a jumping, hopping place.

The community was located on the east side of Sapelo, at the far edge of the island, and there's a high bluff there that the community was named after. It drops off suddenly, down to Blackbeard Creek, and that's a saltwater creek that's big enough that you could think it was a river. Everybody had their own landing at the creek and all the men kept a boat tied up there.

Back during Reconstruction, the community of Raccoon Bluff was a major port for black people on the North End. They rowed their crops straight to the mainland and got a higher price for them than if they went through a middleman, and they didn't have to dock on the South End and be reminded of slavery days.

By the early 1900s, they had formed an organization to cooperatively market their crops and built the Farmer's Alliance Hall, which also doubled as a social hall for the community, so people at the Bluff had their own social hall, their own school, their own church, their own general store, their own midwife and even a constable and a mailman—someone who picked up the mail down at the post office on the South End and delivered it to your door for a dime.

So, the Bluff was a totally separate community. You could live there and not have to go to the South End at all, except on occasions when you went to a funeral down there.

Even in my time, there were some highly independent people at the Bluff. A lot of the people worked for themselves and some of the men rowed their boats across the creek and worked for the federal government on Blackbeard Island.

Blackbeard Island is a big island that's so close to the bluff that it almost looks like it's part of Sapelo. It supposedly was a hiding spot for the famous British pirate Blackbeard, who terrorized the South Atlantic in the early 1700s, and that's how it got its name. It's been a federal wildlife refuge ever since 1914, but before that, there was a hospital there for sailors who got yellow fever.

Yellow fever was a huge problem up and down the entire Atlantic coast in the late 1800s. It killed hundreds of people along the Georgia coast. Epidemics would strike when the weather got warm and ships from the West Indies and Latin America came into port with sick sailors on board. There was a lot of ship traffic along this area of the coast, so the government started a quarantine station and hospital on Blackbeard, in 1880. A lot of people from the Bluff worked there. Grandma worked there as a cook and a nurse when she was young.

Ships would pull in and the sick would be rushed to the hospital. The other sailors would be quarantined and watched to see if they were gonna catch yellow fever too, and sulphur gas would be pumped into the ships' holds to try to kill the disease.

The hospital lasted until the hurricane of 1898, which was a really bad storm. High winds tore the hospital apart and sent the lumber from it floating over toward the Bluff. The people at the Bluff asked permission to get the lumber and then they rowed out and gathered it up and they built themselves a new church. And that's how the church came to be located at the Bluff.

It was quite providential because people at the Bluff needed a new church. The original First African Baptist Church at Hanging Bull was too small and no one lived there anymore and people were still having to walk over there to go to church. And suddenly, there was lumber to build a bigger church at the Bluff.

The old people would have said, "Well, good things come from bad," and it worked that way. Jobs were lost because the hospital wasn't needed as much anymore and it was never rebuilt, but there was a new church in the Bluff that everyone was proud of.

All of that happened before my time though. I didn't know how Blackbeard Island got its name or much about the yellow fever hospital. Mostly, I knew that there was a little, sandy beach at the creek at low tide that I loved to play at. It was one of the things I would do at the Bluff.

Miss Mary Hall and her husband, Mr. Eddie Hall, had a little store that I loved to go to also, and Asberry and I would sometimes get a Nehi soda or coconut candy that was pure sugar with some coconut and peanuts in it. Miss Mary would cook it and pour it out on wax paper, and you'd get a round piece of candy that was three inches across and up to three-quarters of an inch thick, and sometimes it would be tinted pink. You could nibble on that thing for days, or if you were like some kids, you could eat it all at once.

We never left the Bluff hungry. Allen Green, Uncle Allen to me, had a store too and on Sundays he'd have homemade ice cream, sodas and peanuts that were roasted in the oven. Grandpa would give us a snack every time we went through his yard too and Aunt Mary and other people would have a snack for us when we stopped by their houses also.

I was going to school now, so I was at the Bluff a lot. Mama had signed me up a year early because everybody said I was ready to go, and I'd walk over from Belle Marsh with Asberry every weekday morning.

When we'd get close enough to the Bluff in the mornings, we could smell Grandpa's coffee. We'd always know when he was brewing coffee; there was no such thing as weak coffee when Grandpa made it.

We had tea at home mostly. We never had coffee. Mama would parch grits in a skillet, she'd brown them slowly and make a hot drink from them for Papa. It had its own taste, but it was dark brown like coffee and we called it coffee. Grandpa did that too when Mama was young but now that he was older and didn't have kids to raise anymore, he could afford real coffee.

He would wash out his pot on Monday, put grounds in that pot and boil it on the stove and he had this delicious fresh coffee. You could smell it like two miles down the road on Monday if the wind was right. On Tuesday, Grandpa's going. "There's nothing wrong with this coffee. Why get rid of good coffee?" So he'd sprinkle a teaspoon or so of new coffee on top of those old grounds and distribute them carefully. He kept on adding him a spoonful of coffee on top of those grounds every day for a week. He was the only one I knew who used his coffee grounds for a full week. Then he'd dump them all out, clean his pot out, and start over.

We didn't always stop at Grandma and Grandpa's in the mornings, but we always stopped there in the afternoons after school. Grandpa had about an acre fenced in and he had corn and peanuts and sweet potato and white potatoes in there, and a little okra patch on the lower end. We'd enter through the side gate most times, go through the field and walk on a narrow dirt footpath up to the front door.

The yard was sand, it was white sand, the color of beach sand. Grandpa would hoe any grass out of it and then he'd rake it. Everyone had rakes by the time I came along, and before that they used to sweep their yard with a straw broom. You kept your yard *clean*.

There weren't any trees up close to the house. Trees have a habit of falling down, so they were planted a distance away. But there was a pink rosebush in the front and some palmettos, and a piney willow tree a little ways off that had tiny yellow fruit on it that you could actually eat.

The house was a two-room house with wooden shingles on the roof and a separate kitchen, about like the one we had at Belle Marsh. It sat up on oak posts about three feet off the ground and it faced to the east, toward the creek. The front door of just about every house faced the bluff to catch the breeze. A few people further into the community had their front door facing inland, because that's where the road was. But the houses mostly faced the bluff and from Grandpa's house, you could see a wide open area that you knew was the bluff.

We'd go inside and Grandma and Grandpa would be in the living room.

Grandma would be sitting down sewing and smoking her pipe, like a lot of Geechee women did, with her handkerchief ready at all times to clean that eye of hers. It was always leaking water, like she was crying under that lid. She was more aged-looking than Grandpa, especially after her arthritis set in. Whenever you'd see Grandma, you knew she had her nubie with her. She was the only one on Sapelo who had a nubie and she never went anywhere without it. Not anywhere. The nubie was a very old bit of magic that she probably learned from her mother, Harriet, or her grandmother Sally and for some reason she'd kept it up and nobody else had. She kept it in the pocket of her apron and sometimes I'd see her pull out that nubie and ask it something secret.

I never knew how it got its name, but the nubie is an object on a piece of string that you use to divine answers to your questions. Grandma's object was a small glass dresser knob, crystal-clear pure glass, and the string was about twelve inches long.

She believed that the power of your soul rests in the palm of your hands and the soles of your feet, so she would rub her hands together first to stir up her powers. Then she'd take the nubie, hold it in the center of her hand with the glass knob hanging down, and ask her question. She didn't ever say a word, she would just concentrate hard, and all of a sudden, the nubie would start moving. If it went around in a circle, the answer to her question was "yes." If it swung back and forth like a pendulum, the answer was "no."

She'd get her answer, put her nubie up, and hum a short, little up-and-down singsong thing to herself and I couldn't tell from that whether she was contented or not with the answer she got. Whatever she asked, it was between her and the nubie. I'd stare and wonder what did she ask? It was mysterious.

Grandpa would be sitting in a straight-back chair with his legs crossed and a book in his hand, no matter what. He was about sixty-eight and his hair was still mostly black. There was very little gray in it, but the top was bald and he kept it shorter, to the ear, at his age. He was a medium-size person, he was trim, he didn't have excess fat and he walked stiffly, like somebody with a bad artificial leg. He had his walking cane and that helped, but he would just swing that left leg out from the hip.

He believed in magic too and he wore an amulet around his waist all his life. It was a little, white cotton bag, about one and a half inches square, sewn onto a piece of string. He always wore it, he never took it off, he never washed it. No one else on Sapelo had that tradition, so it may have been passed down in his family, and he gave out amulets to some of the other men on Sapelo, including Papa, to bring them good luck, good health and strength.

After Grandpa died, I opened the little bag and pulled the paper out and it said, "With God, all things are possible." I later found out that Muslim clerics in Africa used to hand out little sealed pouches with religious sayings in them. The men carried the sealed pouches on their bodies and believed them to ward off evil. So, the amulets Grandpa handed out were like a modern version of that, but I didn't know any of that as a kid.

By this time, Grandpa wasn't doing much trapping anymore and he was an entrepreneur, an entrepreneur from the heart. Everything he could find, even an ad on a matchbook cover that said "Send for me," Grandpa was going to try it out.

He sold suits for men. He had a catalog and swatches and they got to choose from navy blue and black and gray suits, solid or pin-striped. The men would come to the house and he'd measure them along the back, and around the waist, and measure the inseam to see how long the pants should be. He'd order shoes for men too and gardenia perfume and honeysuckle and rose perfume for the women and they were the neatest-smelling things, all essence of natural things. The women would smell so good when they'd wear it.

He'd put his knapsack on his back, his olive drab knapsack, and he would go from house to house and sell his wares and take orders, and in about a month Grandpa would get the products back in the mail and he would deliver them to your door.

As soon as we came in the door, Grandpa would put his book down, mark that page and ask us how school was. Asberry and I would answer, but, really, we were more interested in looking around the room to see what Grandpa had. There were two tables and some regular chairs in that room and an iron bed that Grandma and Grandpa slept in, and Grandpa had stuff all over that room. We could hardly see the floor under Grandma and Grandpa's bed, because Grandpa had boxes there.

The stuff that he knew children wasn't gonna bother with, like small metal washbasins and liniment and hardware and glasses, were stacked in the other room. But the stuff that he had like instant pudding and powdered Kool-Aid and perfume, he kept that stuff under the bed in the living room, and that was enticing. We didn't want to get caught sneaking under that bed and helping ourselves though. Grandpa wasn't to be taken lightly. He'd set you straight in no time at all.

Mama said when she was growing up Grandpa would set traps for mice and rats, we called them all rats, and he'd set one in the main house and one in the kitchen and one in the corn house. She and her sisters had to check them every morning and that was their job. They had to empty those rat traps and tote them out. They'd put them in a basket, a shallow basket like a rice fanner, and they'd tote those rats out in that basket on their head. Mama said she couldn't stand those long tails. She hated those tails. They were still limber. So when she walked, those tails would be waving in her face.

Grandpa kept a big leather strap and if he got home and Mama and her sisters hadn't done their chores, he'd get that strap out. It was just a regular strap but he had trimmed it down and cut a little split in the end, about three or four inches in, so you felt that spanking more. In those days, when they spanked somebody, they spanked somebody, and Grandpa kept that strap just for spanking.

After one or two spankings, Mama didn't want any more. "But my sister Harriet was a devil," Mama said. "She didn't care whether she got that spanking. She'd rather have one than deny herself a trip down the road with her friends." Mama would hate for her to get a spanking, so lots of times Mama would do Harriet's work for her to keep her out of hot water. She said, "Yep, I saved her behind from gettin' many a beatin' by doing her work." Aunt Harriet lived it up, she had her share of fun, even if it meant trouble, and I kinda think Asberry took after her.

Asberry and I loved playing under Grandma and Grandpa's house. One day Asberry got some wood shavings from the packages Grandpa had that were sent from Blair, that's a company he ordered from that's still around, and he stole a match from Grandpa.

You'd have to steal matches because Grandpa didn't give you matches to waste. He would give you one match and he would tear a little piece off the corner of the box that had the friction part on the side of the box, and say, "Here, catch that fire." You'd have to hold the match and that piece of box in your hand and strike it, hoping that match would stay lit. The first time he told me to light the fire in the stove in the kitchen, I used a match and it didn't catch. I had to go back and get another one. Matter of fact, I had to get a couple matches and he let me have it. He said, "You better be sure that do." I knew Grandpa was running out of patience.

So Asberry stole a match and he lit a fire under the house. My sister Winnie was in the kitchen frying a yard chicken and she saw the smoke. She yelled for Grandpa and he grabbed his hoe and got the stuff out from under the house and stamped on it and put it out before it really got blazing. He got it in time, no thanks to Asberry. Then he asked Asberry, "Who did this?" Asberry goes, "Cornelia did."

I was over by the well playing on a fifty-five-gallon drum and I had nothing to do with it, absolutely nothing to do with it. But I couldn't get my words out fast enough, I stuttered, so Grandpa went and he got his leather strap and he gave me a couple of nice licks with it. He hurt my feelings and my backside before I could tell him I didn't do it, and when I did, he went and gave Asberry a real good spanking.

Then he went in the kitchen where Winnie was frying chicken, and he called me and gave me the chicken gizzard. He knew I liked the gizzard of the chicken, and that was sorta like making up for the spanking. But I wouldn't have anything to do with that chicken gizzard. When he turned his back, I gave it to Michael. I was going, "Don't give me a spanking for something I didn't do. You can keep your gizzard." But I didn't say it so he could hear. You didn't back-talk the old people. They better not hear you mumbling, or they'd go, "Hey, what did you say? Mess around, I'll make you eat them words." Then, shoot, you better be quick on your feet or you'd get a backhand in a jiffy. Back talk was worse than anything you could do. That's right.

Grandma still had good days, her arthritis wasn't too bad yet. I know that because when Asberry and I were walking home from the Bluff one day, there was a bull in the road at King Savannah. It snorted and pawed and carried on and wouldn't let us pass. So we went back to the Bluff and Grandma said, "Chirren, whatcha y'all doing back here?" We said, "We back, Grandma, because this big, white bull in the road wouldn't let us by."

So she said, "Okay, chirren, come on." She got the pitchfork and we followed her and she walked to King Savannah, and that bull was still there standing in that road minding his territory.

Grandma walked up to him waving her hands and stomping her feet and saying, "Shoo. Shoo, shoo. Git. Git! Carry your butt o'er there. *Git, Git.*" And the bull, once she got close to him with that pitchfork and he saw us, he swung around. When he swung around, Grandma rushed him and let him have it, *whang*! She stuck that pitchfork in his back part where it hurts. That's right.

That bull took off running across King Savannah. Grandma said, "Now chirren, y'all can go on home," and we took off and were gone. We ran. I looked back and Grandma was taking her sweet time going back home. She knew she'd stuck him where it hurt.

When Grandma's arthritis did start getting worse, Grandpa mostly stayed home then and he took care of Grandma and he fed her and he ordered her clothes. He did everything he could for her, but he was still his own person and she was too. Just because they were old, the fire hadn't gone out of either of them.

One day Asberry and I were playing outside and there was a little narrow catwalk, no more than twenty-four inches wide, that went from the back of the house to the kitchen. It was about two or three feet off the ground, the same height as the house, and you could go from the main house to the kitchen without having to step down, like we did at Belle Marsh.

Grandma was coming out of that kitchen and Grandpa was coming out of the house, and they met in the middle of the catwalk. Grandma was little, but she pulled herself up for all her worth and said, "John, you move because I ain't backing up." Grandpa says, "You move, Winnie, so I can go in the kitchen." And Grandma says, "I ain't gonna move." And Grandpa says, "Well, I ain't gonna move."

Neither one of them would back up and Asberry and I were watching and going, "Which one's gonna win? Which one's gonna give in and back up?"

Grandpa upped his cane and *bap*! He knocked Grandma on the side of her head with the business end of the cane and she fell off that catwalk. He wasn't gonna argue very long. He found a quick means to end it. Grandma hit the ground and she was mad but she got up and dusted the sand off herself and walked around the house and went in the front door and she didn't say a word. She wasn't gonna give him that satisfaction. That was a tough old bird.

Asberry and I were standing there with our mouths hanging open. We weren't expecting that. We were expecting one of them to give in and back up. We didn't expect one of them to get the upper hand altogether. Grandpa hit Grandma? He would take that stick sometimes and whack one of us, but only gently. But we didn't dare laugh. *No sirree*. We would have been in hot water then and Grandma would have been madder than Grandpa. She was a spitfire. If she'd had the cane, matter of fact, she'd probably have used it on him.

They were hard-headed, strong-minded people and never one to give an inch, not either of them. They had a life and they lived it. They *lived* their lives.

◆

Chapter Seven

The Babydoll

A SHOOTING STAR WAS A SIGN OF BIRTH OVER HERE and the old people would see one in the sky and go, "Aah, there's gonna be a new addition in someone's family soon." But if there was a shooting star foretelling a birth in our family the winter I was four and a half, nobody told me about it. That's for sure. I didn't even know that my sister Ada was expecting a baby.

I didn't know it back in the spring when Ada helped plant the crops, and it was December now and time for her to give birth, and I still didn't know it. I was totally ignorant of the fact. Mama wasn't gonna tell me anything about Ada being in the family way. The old people didn't tell you things until they thought you were old enough to know them and I was just a kid. The only baby I knew anything about was the babydoll my brother Gibb was gonna get me for Christmas.

The Sears Christmas catalog was out with all its toys by Thanksgiving, when Gibb was home. I was staring at the babydolls in that catalog and Gibb went, "Aah, Sis, I'm gonna get you a babydoll, a doll that cries and opens its eyes and can walk. I'll get it for you for Christmas." So *that* was the baby I was looking for.

Ada had gone to see the midwife, to see Miss Katie, because it was the midwife who birthed babies over here. All of Mama's babies were delivered by a midwife. All of Grandma's babies were delivered by a midwife. All of Great-Grandma Harriet's were. There was a whole line of babies birthed by midwives, going all the way back to the days of slavery on Sapelo.

There were always women on a plantation who became midwives and it was an honored position. A highly honored position. The midwives were black, yes, and they delivered the babies of all the women who were black, but they delivered the babies of the white slaveholders too. At least they did over here. Sapelo was miles from the mainland, remember, and when it was time for a baby to be born, you needed the midwife right then. So the midwives were it. They had the skill to birth babies and the mother wit.

Now, Miss Katie was born a Hall and she married an Underwood so she was Miss Katie Underwood and she was a first cousin to Grandma. She was a short woman with a reddish brown complexion, a kinda broad nose and thin lips that let you see right off that she was in charge. She was the only midwife left on the island. Each community on Sapelo had its own midwives once, but there was less need for them now—there weren't as many people—and the other midwives had slowly died off or retired.

Miss Katie would go from one end of Sapelo to the other birthing babies. She was up in age herself, close to seventy, but her mind was *sharp*. She didn't have no problem delivering your baby, and, really, there weren't that many complications usually. If the carrying period was fine and normal and if the woman was healthy, you were pretty well set. The only problem birth I know of was with one baby believed to be stillborn.

The baby was not breathing at all. The mother begged Miss

Katie, "Miss Katie, *please* make him breathe." Miss Katie tried every trick up her sleeve and when those didn't work, she reached back in her memory and sent someone to get a basin of water. *Cold* water. Miss Katie held the baby in the basin of water. Face down. She just held that baby there. All of a sudden, you could see these tiny, little bubbles in the water and the baby started to struggle. Miss Katie pulled his head out and he let out a wail. A *big* wail. It was the happiest sound that mother had ever heard in her life.

So Ada went to see Miss Katie and Miss Katie asked all kinds of questions to find out how Ada and her baby were doing. Ada knew a lot of what she had to say because she'd already had one child, Michael, but you always talked to the midwife anyway. Miss Katie reminded Ada of all the technical things, like what to eat and how to make a simple quilt of newspapers sewn between clean cloth to have as padding on your bed during and after the birth. Then she reminded Ada of our traditional ways, like not to do too much hanging laundry out in the last few days, because if you're reaching overhead, the umbilical cord can actually get wrapped around the baby's neck.

Ada was ready for her baby to come and early in the night of December thirteenth, she started having labor pains. Papa walked seven miles down to Hog Hammock in the dark of the night, with only the moon and the stars for light, to get Miss Katie.

Asberry and Michael and I were sleeping in the same bedroom as my sisters Ada and Barbara were, so while Papa was gone, Mama came in and took the three of us kids out to the living room and put us on a pallet on the floor in front of the fireplace. I was sleeping so soundly, I didn't wake up when Miss Katie came in.

Miss Katie came in ready for business, with her hair tied up in a white cloth and her long white apron on. She made sure that Ada was propped up right, mopped Ada's forehead and sent Barbara out to start some water boiling on the stove to sterilize her scissors and the string she needed to tie the umbilical cord with. And while I wasn't in that room, I know pretty much what went on, because I learned those ways when I got older.

Mama was holding Ada's hand and telling jokes about what had happened when she gave birth, and Miss Katie sat by the bed and talked to Ada the whole time. They kept the room lively with their conversation so Ada wouldn't have much time to think about the pain. Miss Katie was busy telling Ada, "Okay, baby. *Pray baby*. Don't worry, that baby is gonna get here. It's not comin' till God want it to, so just have a little patience. I know the pain hurt, but just hold on in there, now. When it's supposed to come, it's gonna come, and nothing's gonna stop it from coming."

She gave Ada a soothing cup of pennyroyal tea, which is an herb we used for women's problems that grows over here. That was all you got for childbirth pain most times, though Miss Katie did keep a bottle of whiskey in her black bag for times when the pain got real bad.

She didn't have to give Ada a shot of moonshine though. Ada was young and healthy, she was seventeen, and she'd already had one baby, Michael. And in the middle of the night, I heard a baby cry, a girl Ada named Elise.

I woke up in front of a big fire going in the living room fireplace, thinking, "What am I doing here? This isn't my bedroom." Then I heard another cry and I sat straight up.

Time to a little kid doesn't mean much and I knew it was getting close to Christmas.

"Mama, Mama, is that my babydoll?" I yelled.

"Yep, that's your babydoll," Mama said. She thought I was just kidding around, but that was absolutely the wrong thing to say.

"I want my babydoll, Mama, I want my babydoll."

"You'll get your babydoll later," she said, and with that, I started crying because she wouldn't let me have my babydoll.

"*Sshhh, Sshhh!* That's not your babydoll. Santa's not coming now."

I had an absolute fit. She was gonna have to give me proof that wasn't my babydoll if she wanted me to stop crying.

So, as soon as Miss Katie got the baby cleaned up, Mama came out of the bedroom with this bundled-up wiggling baby in her arms and she gave it to me to hold. It was a fat little red-brown baby. I'd never seen a baby before, but I knew instantly it was a *real*, live baby. It wasn't some toy babydoll from the Sears book. After Mama let me hold the baby, I was satisfied and I went back to sleep. I was still going to get my toy babydoll later, and I had a new baby to play with to boot.

Now, if Elise had been Ada's first child, Miss Katie would have read the knots in the afterbirth, as the midwife always did after the first child was born. By that, I mean she would have counted the knots when the first child came and predicted how many more kids you would have. Miss Katie would read those knots, and lots of time she'd say, "Oh Lord, plenty of knots in this one. You' gonna have plenty chirren." Or she might go, "That's the only one you're gonna have, baby. You ain't gonna have no more," and then that one was all the woman usually had.

Miss Katie probably told Ada to love that baby good, because there must not have been too many knots in the afterbirth when Michael was born, and Elise was the last child she had. Then Miss Katie went and got Papa and said, "I got a job for you now, Hicks," and they went outside to bury the afterbirth.

That was the man's job and if there wasn't a man present, Miss Katie would bury it herself. The other women weren't allowed to help. I don't know why that was. Maybe it was just because the man was thought to be stronger and could dig a better hole, but that was our way.

Papa dug a deep hole and he buried the afterbirth. He put a big, heavy block of wood on top of the hole so that no animal could get to it, because you protected that afterbirth, you treated it with respect. This was the first part of you that went back to the earth. The rest of you would follow later, when you died, but the afterbirth went first, and that connected you to the earth then and to Sapelo. Wherever else you might go, Sapelo would be your true home.

The next morning Mama fixed this delicious breakfast of grits and butter and milk and fried ham, because you always pampered the new mother. She was given the best of what you could afford to help her produce milk and to get her strength back.

The ham was fried hard so that all the fat was out of it, because the women here nursed their babies, and whatever they ate would be passed down in the milk. So if you were a new mother, you were forbidden to eat anything that might give your baby an upset stomach. And when the time came for Elise to get her first solid food, Mama would stew fish, and take the stock off of it and pour it over grits to make it soupy-like. That was always the first meal over here because it was easy on the system.

Just as with childbirth, we had all these strict do's and don'ts for the early part of a child's life. Some of these were practical and some were traditional. The new baby would wear binders to strengthen its back. You always covered the baby's head so it wouldn't get sick. Even if it was summer, you'd take a blanket and put part of that blanket loosely over the baby's face if you were going outside. And before you took that baby anywhere, you would call the baby by its name.

You didn't say "baby." You said its name. That way you were calling the *whole baby*—the spirit of the baby along with the actual baby. If you were to take the baby somewhere but the spirit was left behind, that baby was gonna be fretful. So you always called the baby's name.

You'd tell the baby and its spirit whose house it was going to or where it was going, and you'd do the same thing when you'd get ready to go home. When you got back to your house then, the spirit was with the baby.

When Elise was seven days old, Mama took Elise outside to introduce her to the world. Ada was still in bed then. The new mother couldn't go anywhere until the midwife came and told her she could get up, so Mama was the one to take Elise out.

"C'mon, Elise, let's go. One week old now, time for you to go outside."

Mama bundled Elise up and took her outside in the morning, when the world was new. She held her kinda at arms' length and turned around slowly in a circle, telling Elise about everything in sight, like Elise could understand everything she said even at that tender age. Everything Mama described was something that God had made.

"Elise, baby, it's kinda nippy out here today, but the sun's nice and blue. Can you feel the sun on your face, Elise? Everything smell' so fresh. The world is clean. That's the marsh and the river back there. See it? See that bird? That seagull? It can just take wing and fly. Take wing and fly over the ocean."

It was a ceremony that went back to the beginning of our time on this island and to Africa before that. The reasoning for it was lost to us but the ritual had been passed down through the generations. You did it because it felt right.

Mama held Elise out in front of her, introducing her to God's world. It was like a vibration going from the ancestors to that child, a vibration from Grandma Ada and Great-Grandma Harriet and Uncle Shed and all the old ones who come before us. All the wisdom the elders would bestow on Elise began right then and there. And their wisdom would go right into her very being and be a part of her for the rest of her life.

◆

Chapter Eight

Around the Fire

WE WERE ON THE WEST SIDE OF THE ISLAND AT Belle Marsh and we never saw the sun come up. There wasn't a clear area near us, so we'd see rays of light coming through the trees first, and then the sun would top the trees and be up in the sky, all fresh-looking and light golden. It'd be about seven o'clock when we saw the sun climbing into the sky in the springtime and about an hour later in the fall and winter.

So we didn't see the sun come up but we could always see it go down. Every evening the sun would slide down over the marsh, making the sky all red and orange and lavender and pink, but really, we didn't pay that sunset no mind. We never stood there and just watched that magic act of it disappearing. Asberry and I were too busy playing. We'd know the sun was going down by the shadows cast and by the way the light looked on the trees. In summertime, the light would be a hard gold, but by fall and winter, that light on the trees had a different hue, like it was tired. It'd look like it was trying hard to give you a golden glow, but it was weaker, and it just couldn't give you the same thing.

We'd keep on playing until Mama called us.

"Okay, y'all, come in. The sun going down now. Time to come in."

Mama would feed us first and then Papa came in and she'd feed him.

One afternoon Papa walked home from the South End where he worked at. It was wintertime, and when he got home he found there was nothing to eat—there was no "soup," that's what we called it. We had some rice and grits but there was nothing to put on the rice and grits, no soup. Mama cooked what she had for us kids but there wasn't nothing much to fill a hungry man up with and nothing for Papa to put in his lunch pail the next day to go to work with.

So Papa went outside to get his cast net, the net he used for fishing. You know what a cast net is? It's a long net you throw. It's narrow at the top and opens out into a wide skirt with lead weights on it. When you throw it just right, it glides out over the water, opens up in a big, wide circle and sinks down over any fish that happen to be in that spot. You draw it up then, it's got what we call a tucking system, and when you draw up the line, the net draws up like a bag, and that holds the fish in.

But Papa's net was all in shambles, it had holes in it, big holes. Fish was a large part of what we ate and Papa used that net a lot, but he must not have used it lately.

You can use that net a long time but sooner or later, your net is gonna get tore up from getting hung up on oyster shells. You learn where the oyster shell beds are and you try to miss them, but it can be tricky. Sometimes the tide will go one way and pull your net onto those oyster shells, and a lot of times, the more you pull on it, the worse it tears up. Those shells can tear it completely to smithereens.

"Dang, this net ain't gonna catch no fish. There's too many holes in it."

Now, Papa was one of the best cast-net makers on this island. He learned how from his father and his grandfather and from Uncle Nero. Uncle Nero paid a lot of attention to him, teaching him how to make those nets. But Papa didn't have any new thread, cotton thread, to make a net with this night and he didn't have any money to buy thread with. Times were tough.

So Papa set down in front of that fire and started to unravel that net with the holes in it. He cut off the foot line first, the hem, and then he started unraveling that net, pulling out the cotton thread, that heavy cotton twine, so he could reuse it. He was gonna redo his net so he could catch some fish for breakfast and lunch tomorrow, come hell or high water.

Mama and Papa pulled up chairs in front of the fire, they were regular straight-back chairs, in the same position every night. Papa was on the right side of the fire and Mama on the left, and Asberry and me and Michael were in the middle, on a quilt on the floor. Barbara was a little further off, by a table.

The fireplace was built out of old bricks, pale red, and we had an old-fashioned, small fireplace. The opening was small, because the fireplace was only about three feet wide and not too tall, but it was big enough to make a good hot fire in it. We had a "bacca chunk" in the back of the chimney, what we call a bacca chunk, a large log that would burn all day and cast heat out. There would be other wood on top of it and in front of it, but the bacca chunk's what kept the fire going and kept us warm.

It was cold this night but it wasn't as cold as sometimes, because it would get real cold over here. Sometimes the water in the water bucket in the kitchen would freeze, the water in the ditches outside would freeze and the top layer of the ground would be frozen. The ground made a hollow sound, a light thumping sound, when you'd walk on it.

That freezing cold would just stay a couple of days and then everything would melt away, so it was never a steady cold. But it was a damp cold usually and that made it extra bad. The dampness settles in and once it settles in, it's like it's settling in your bones. You need that fire, that fire feels good and it's the only heat you got. So we set around that fire every night in the fall and wintertime.

Most evenings, Papa'd bring his wooden box traps in to repair them and then Mama make him take them out in the morning, or he'd whittle spokes for the wagon or he'd recast bullets. It was neat to watch Papa recast those bullets.

Papa only had small shot for his gun and small shot's not powerful enough to kill something big like a deer. So Papa set down by the fire, dismantled that small shot and picked up his file and his wire cutter. He would take nails, cut the points off nails, and repack the shells with the nails and make his own buckshot, and they'd be ready for the next time he went hunting.

There wasn't nothing Papa couldn't do, but this night was kinda like a test, a strong test, because it takes days to make a cast net usually. Days and days.

While Papa unraveled that net, Mama decided to tell us a story. We grew up on stories, they were a part of life. Everybody told stories: Mama, Papa, Grandma, Grandpa, Aunty Mary, Uncle Joe, Cousin Annie and all the old people told stories. Sometimes they'd tell true stories, about people we knew, and sometimes they'd tell us about the animals, and we learned those stories by heart.

This night Mama start in on Brer Rabbit and the Sweet Potatoes. She learned this story from her mama and her mama learned it from her mama, my great-grandmother, and she probably learned it from her mama too.

Brer Wolf work hard in his field all day plowin' and preparin' his field for plantin,' while Brer Rabbit play. Brer Wolf start makin' his rows, he bed up his rows, neat rows, task rows, and he gather up his seed tater so he could plant his sweet potatoes.

Brer Rabbit came by.

"Hey, Brer Wolf. Whatcha doin'?"

"Gettin' ready to plant."

"Why you plantin' so much?"

"Well, accordin' to the signs it's gonna be a hard winter."

"Aaah, don't pay that no attention."

Brer Rabbit keep on playin' but he get to thinkin'. "Hmnn, there may be sump'n to what Brer Wolf talkin' 'bout."

He go back.

"Hey, Brer Wolf. Want a hand with this?"

"Nope, I'm doin' okay."

"But Brer Wolf, I can tell ya a better way to do it, a way to make them grow bigger and faster."

"Yeah, Brer Rabbit."

"Listen good. Now, you take the biggest and the best potato' you got. You take those and boil 'em, jis a li'le. Not too much, not too done, you boil them jis a li'le bit. Then you take each one and you put it in a clean rag and you put it in a hill, one at a time, in neat rows. And in two or three days, they'll get up and they'll be the biggest, and the best sweet potatoes you ever had."

"Yup, Brer Rabbit said, thata work. It'll work."

So Brer Wolf went and he got his biggest and best taters and he boiled them jis a little bit and put them in nice clean pieces of rag and he put 'em in hills in neat rows and he planted his whole task with nuttin' but sweet potato' boiled jis a little bit.

Brer Wolf wait two or three days and he went out to the field and he looked but he didn't see anything sprouting up and he decide to check 'em. So he dug up a hill and there was nuttin' there. He dug up another hill and there was nuttin' there, and he kept diggin' and diggin' till he dug up his whole entire field, and there was no sweet potatoes there or clean rags. Yep, you guess it. He realize Brer Rabbit tricked him again. Some folks, or in this case, some wolf, never learn.

That very same night, after Brer Wolf planted all those sweet potatoes and put them in clean rags, Brer Rabbit return to the field with a clean sack, dug up all the potato' and took 'em home and put 'em in his sweet potato house for the winter. So he had something to eat and Brer Wolf didn't. That winter was especially hard and Brer Wolf didn't have any sweet potatoes.

Mama said, "So there's such a thing as over trusting," and that was the lesson of that story.

Most evenings, there were sweet potatoes baking in the ashes in the fireplace. Before he'd start whittling or something, Papa would pick up the fire iron he used to poke the fire, and he'd made a trench in the coals and ashes, lay the sweet potatoes in the trench and cover them back up with ashes and coals, and just leave them there. Then he'd go on with what he's doing.

When those sweet potatoes are ready, all of a sudden you hear *pooofff*! And you look and they're shooting steam up. They're like little geysers with the steam going *pooofff*! And they smell so good. You roast them in ashes and they'll beat any sweet potatoes you can cook in the oven.

But there weren't any sweet potatoes in the fire this night. There weren't any sweet potatoes left for eating at all, because it was so late in the winter and late winter can be one of the leanest times. That's when you depend on the sea more for your dinner. Mama and Papa were saving what sweet potatoes they had for seed taters to start the new crop with.

I was sitting there, wishing we had some nice, delicious sweet potatoes from the fire. It gave me a new feeling for Brer Wolf, what that winter must have been like with no sweet potatoes.

I looked at Papa and he had just finished pulling threads out of his old net. He had that net dismantled and he was ready to start knitting it all over again. He used a little narrow wooden gauge that looked kinda like a Popsicle stick to measure the mesh size. You use a different mesh size for different nets.

There's a three-fourth-inch mesh and that's for what we call a shrimp net, and it's only for catching shrimp. We don't even call it a cast net. Papa hated to make those because that mesh is so small it takes forever.

Then you got a one-inch mesh. That's what we call a poor man's net, because that mesh is small enough to hold most things in it. If you're really hungry, you use that net. Everything comes when you pull your net in, whether you desire it or not.

Mullet nets are the quickest to make because they've got two-inch mesh. They're for catching big mullet and trout. Papa was making a mullet net this night, because that's all he'd have time for, so he filled his needle with thread and set to work. The needle was made of soft pine. It had two prongs sticking up in the back with a piece in between them and that's where you wrap your thread.

Papa started knitting at the top, naturally, and that first row was just a tiny circle, no bigger than your wrist. Then you add the next row and the next row and the next, and the circle gets bigger and bigger as you go, till you end up with a real full bottom. You make your net according to the size you are and Papa is big, so his net was six feet long. The skirt on that net must have been twelve feet across at the bottom.

We watched Papa for a while and then Asberry said, "Mama, tell us another one, yeah, yeah? Please, Mama, tell us another one." "Tell us another one, Mama, tell us another one."

"Okay, chirren, just one more. It's about time to go to bed."

We were animal people, we watched and learned from the animals, and the old people said every animal had a reason for being.

You remember how I told you that a hoot owl was a sure sign of death? The old people did everything to try to keep an owl from making that *who-oo-oo who-oo-oo* noise. "Chile, get me those shoes and turn them upside down in that door so I can stop that noise. That owl out there hooting and making that noise about to carry somebody from here." So those upside-down shoes were supposed to choke them so they can't make that noise.

For good luck, there was that black cat, of course, and we also had Aunt Nancy the spider. We called the spider An' Nancy. An' Nancy was quite wise. You could play with that spider all day long but they would not let you harm An' Nancy. We did not harm it, we did not kill it, we did not do anything to it. That spider bring you good luck.

Some people say An' Nancy was the trickster in stories back in Africa, but somehow in this country the trickster got changed to the rabbit and that's how we got the Brer Rabbit stories. Brer Rabbit was the trickster.

Mama started in telling us about Brer Rabbit and Brer Crane.

Once upon a time, Brer Rabbit thought he was the sharpest thing there was with his brown suit and white shirt and white socks and brown shoes. You know how his coloring is. He thought he was the sharpest thing and all the girls, they liked him. But he wanted to go to this party and he wanted to show off. So he went to his friend Brer Crane's house and asked Brer Crane, "Brer Crane, you want to go with me to a party tonight the girls are havin'?"

"Oh, Brer Rabbit, I can't go. I don't feel too good. My stomach is botherin' me," Brer Crane said.

"Oh, come on."

"No, I can't go because I got the back-door trots and I can't go."

"Oh, come on, I'll fix that."

"You can?"

"Yep, give me piece of corn cob."

So he got a piece of corncob and he corked up ol' Brer Crane and he said, "Come on, you can go with me."

So now when he got Brer Crane outside, he hitched Brer Crane to his little wagon so he could pull up to the girls' house with Crane being like his driver or his horse takin' him to the party.

"Whoa, Brer Crane."

And he jump out the little wagon and all the girls came around him and he's havin' a good time and he's dancin'. Crane's just sittin' lookin' pitiful and he decided well why not join the fun. So he went in and he started joinin' the fun and he was all dressed in his white with his yellow shoes and socks on.

The girls liked his nice white outfit that he was dressed in so they all left Brer Rabbit alone with his dowdy brown-and-white outfit. Left him alone and went to Brer Crane. Brer Crane was just dancin' away with the girls to his heart content.

Brer Rabbit sittin' there lookin' very pitiful with his hand to his jaw and he was getting madder and madder by the minute. So when

Brer Crane swing around past him with one of the girls, he politely pulled the corncob out and that was the end of the party.

He uncorked poor Brer Crane and that was it. The party was out.

That's one of Mama's favorite stories and she was tickled now and she was about to laugh. Mama would get tickled all over when she laughed. She's got a laugh out of this world. She belts that laugh out and she throws her hands up in the air, and watch out. Those hands are coming down on something, and if they come down on your shoulders and you're not steady, you'll fall down.

Asberry got it once. Mama was playing with us, playing hop-scotch, and she started laughing, and her hands went up and came down on Asberry and she knocked him off his feet. Mama knocked grown men off their feet. If she was sitting down, her hands would come down on a dresser or something, but when Mama was standing, she was dangerous. I stayed out of the way.

Asberry and me were laughing now, Mama was laughing and Papa was laughing too. His hands were flying. They were moving so fast you could lose sight of where they were at, because a good story does that. You're laughing and the load gets lighter. Papa didn't have to be thinking, "Dang, I worked hard all day and I gotta get back on the road first thing in the morning and there's no food for my family. This net is all tore up, am I gonna get it redone in time, and what if there ain't any fish out there anyway?" The old people would have been doomed a long time ago if they couldn't tell stories and laugh.

Mama said, "Alright, kids, that's enough for tonight. Time for bed," and Asberry and me went on then and left Mama and Papa sitting by the fire. In our house you could not go to bed till you washed your feet. Even if you missed washing your face and everything else, you better not miss washing your feet. You *must* wash your feet. So we was all washed up and we had our nightclothes on. I had my flannel gown on and Asberry had on white cotton long johns.

So we climbed in the bed and crawled under the quilts and in between the sheets, and those sheets was cold. Mama was going, "Put the cover over your head now and blow, blow, blow." Asberry and I'd blow and blow and that warm air coming from your body is like a heater. All of a sudden, it actually gets warmer and you have to take the cover off your head because it's so warm. You get settled in then, with those heavy quilts on you, and you go to sleep nice and peaceful.

Papa kept working till he finished knitting the whole net. Then he had to sew the foot line back on from the old net. It still had all the lead weights on it, and that saved a lot of time, because Papa used a lot of weights. Those lead weights make your net sink down in the water.

He started in on the tucks then, the cotton strings that make your net draw up like a bag, and trap the fish in. The tucks run from the foot line up to the top and are tied at the top to a swivel. Papa saved the tuck strings from the old net so all he had to do was spread the net out on the floor, open it up and retie those strings back on the foot line.

Then he went fishing. Papa went fishing around three o'clock in the morning.

He had a wooden boat, about fifteen feet long, what we call a bateau, that he had made. Everybody here made their own bateau. A man had to do everything, and they sure could say that of Papa. "Yeah, he's a regular jack-of-all-trades, alright." So he went down to Moses Hammock, got his bateau and went out fishing by himself in the cold.

There was a fishing hole not too far behind the house and that's where Papa went. He stood up in the boat and threw his net. If you don't throw your net right, it won't open up and catch anything, but Papa's a good thrower. He can throw a net anytime.

You keep a cord tied to your wrist so you won't lose your net, and the way Papa would throw it, he'd put one lead weight in his mouth and hold the net in both hands. He'd twist his body back ever so lightly and then all in one motion, he'd twist forward, release the lead weight from his teeth and fling the net out with a snap of his wrist. That net would go sailing out, *whooooosh,* and the whole thing would just open up and land on the water. Then it'd sink down fast and catch some fish, if there was any fish there to be caught.

Papa must have planned it just right to catch the tide and go fishing and come back, because Papa caught fish. He caught a bunch of mullet. Mama cleaned them, she loved cleaning fish, so she cleaned fish, fried enough to feed Papa breakfast and packed some for his lunch. She cooked him some fry bread to go with it, and he got back on the road by five o'clock and walked back to work at the South End, which was seven miles.

When Asberry and Michael and I got up, Mama fried us fish too. We had fish and grits for breakfast, oh, yeah, golden fried mullet.

When he got home, I said, "Papa, you didn't get no sleep?"

"No-ooo. I didn't catch no sleep. But it had to be done, gal, so I did it."

So Papa had himself a long night, he had no sleep at all that night. But we had plenty of fish that afternoon for dinner too, fish and rice and cornbread. Papa slept good that night and we made it through the lean part of winter.

◆

Chapter Nine

Moving Day

PAPA WORKED FOR THE BUCKRA MAN, THAT'S THE
white man, the kind of white man who tries to mess in your business
and control your life. "Buckra" came from a West African word used
to describe a white man who surrounds or governs. But we never saw
the buckra man at Belle Marsh. We were up on the North End of the
island on our own property and no buckras came around here. They
didn't have any reason to. No reason at all.

Now, I did see some white men every once in a while. There
were white guys working for the timber company, and they would
pass by in a truck occasionally and wave or stop and come to the
house and get a drink of moonshine from Mama. But they worked
just as hard as Papa and the other men, their clothes were just as
dirty and they smelled like pine tar, and I didn't think of them as
white. They were just like us.

So I never remember any bukra men coming to visit Papa until
he started to build us a new house. That's when the trouble began.

It was a warm weekend in 1949, back when I was four. Papa was
wearing his denim overalls like he usually did and he was cutting

down pine saplings and shrubs when this white man pulled up in a company Jeep, a Reynolds Jeep that is, stopped and got out. I didn't know who he was. I'd never seen Cap'n Frank before. But all of a sudden here was a different sort of white guy than the ones that came around with the soot still on their face. A whole different sort of white guy, with his khaki pants, khaki jacket, his white shirt and his hair all slicked back. He was *really* clean.

"Well, Hicks, I see you're working hard," he said. "What are you doing, making a new field?"

Papa stopped what he was doing and propped up on his ax, right near the road that goes through the property.

"No, sir, Cap'n Frank, this is where I want to build my new house."

Asberry and I looked at this man we didn't know for a little bit, then went back to playing in the sand on the edge of the road. We knew better than to listen. We weren't allowed to listen to adult talk.

Cap'n Frank didn't stay too long anyway and I guess he didn't say anything that made Papa mad that day because Papa just kept on clearing off the place for his new house.

Our house was so old that Papa didn't want to live in it anymore. Well, actually it was that we couldn't live in it anymore. When it sprinkled rain outside just a little bit, it *poured* on the inside. The rain gathered up under those wooden shingles and would find a weak spot on the roof and come down, *whoosh*, right through those shingles.

We had to stop whatever we were doing right then, hop to it, and gather pots and pans. Mama and Papa would grab the cotton mattress off their bed, roll it up and put it in a corner that wasn't leaking. They'd move anything they thought could get wet and we'd all be watching for leaks.

Everybody would stand there looking up at the ceiling.

"I got one, Mama. Mama, there's one over here."

Asberry or I would run to put a pot under the leak.

"Put it right, now put it right," Mama would say.

You'd wait till the first drip hit the floor before you put the pot down to make sure you got it just right. Otherwise, you were gonna have to move that pot.

At first there'd be just a few leaky spots in that ceiling. Then it would get worse. The water would spread, there'd be a wet line all across the ceiling and you'd hear the drops going *splat*, *splat*, *splat* everywhere. Pretty soon every pot we owned, the chamber pot, all the jelly glasses and everything else that could hold water was under a leaky spot.

Asberry and I made a game out of it. We'd sit there and watch, we'd lay down near the pots and pans and we'd count the number of drips falling in a particular pot.

"I got more drips than you got," Asberry would say.

"Mine dropped fifty times," I'd say.

And you didn't want your roof to leak, but you were actually praying for one more drip so you could beat the other one's count.

But while Asberry and I were having fun, Mama and Papa weren't. Papa *sure* didn't like it when he was sound asleep and it would start raining and all of a sudden, the water was falling on him. He'd wake up grumpy then.

"*Hettie, Hettie, Hettie*. Wake up. Wake up. Wake up! The roof's leaking. We need some pots and pans."

Instead of him just getting up and getting them, he'd call Mama first.

"*Wake up*! It's raining outside, it's leaking on the bed."

He'd call and she'd jump out of bed and go get the stuff.

It was raining and *she* had to go outside to the kitchen to get the pots and pans. She'd throw a shirt or something over her head if it was really raining hard and she'd dash outside the back door, run into the kitchen and dash back out again. Most of the time, she'd put a pot over her head while she'd dash back in the house.

Mama would go, "Why don't you get off your behind and do something sometime? Why does it always have to be me?"

But she couldn't lay in bed and argue too much—not when the water's coming down. Somebody's gotta move. Mama knew the burden of airing out the mattress and hanging the quilts out to dry was gonna fall on her shoulder anyhow, so she was gonna be sure that they didn't get wet. They were made out of cotton and if they got wet and didn't dry, they'd stink. So Mama'd be groaning, but she'd go.

Papa would help her put the pots and pans around once she came back with them but she had to go get them. They'd get all the pots and pans set out and Papa would still be grumpy. He wouldn't cuss God but he'd come close to it.

"*Dang*! A man can't lay inside his own bed and rest. I gotta get up early in the morning, it's raining outside, the floor's hard and cold, the children' bed is wet, my bed is wet. *Dang*!"

He'd go from dang to damn, and his manners would keep going down from there. He'd get madder and madder as the roof leaked more and more.

Papa would go and sit in a chair someplace then and roll him a Prince Albert tobacco cigarette, because there's nothing he could do about the rain. Either he'd go to sleep in that chair or he'd pull out his cast net to work on to occupy his time. Papa's anger would go away when he was working with his hands. He'd start working on something and it was gone.

It was a good house when Papa's father, my Grandpa Gibb, built it back around 1900. Papa had always lived in this house. He was born in it in 1903 and he was forty-six years old now. But like I said before, the house was built out of pine, one board thick, and it wasn't sealed. Most houses over here weren't then, and Mama and Papa would line the inside with cardboard and newspaper and pages out of the Sears catalog to keep the air out. Anyway, the house was plain worn out, or at least the roof was.

I remember Papa patching that roof more than once. A whole lot of work went into it, starting with selecting the best pine tree to make his shingles out of.

Papa only used the heart of the pine, because it's firmer, heavier and doesn't get termites. He could look at the bark of a pine tree and tell you which one had a fatter, more solid heart.

Papa said the bigger and the more flakier the bark is, the better the heart, so he only used peelers, the pine trees that have real big bark, and he'd look to see if there was sap oozing on the outside, because that's another sign that it was a fat pine tree. Then he'd check how straight the tree was, because if that tree was straight, it was less work for Papa when he made his shingles.

"Yeah, that's a fat one there. We'll cut this one down," Papa would say and then he'd study what direction to make it fall.

"We'll throw it in that direction over there."

He'd block it with a wedge and he'd cut the tree with a one-man crosscut saw he always kept real sharp. In no time at all, it would fall in just the direction he wanted and sure enough, the tree he picked would have a solid inside.

He limbed the tree up then and measured it and split it in blocks, according to how long he wanted the shingles to be, and then he was ready to make the shingles. Papa would pick up his broad ax and in one stroke, *whack*!, he'd split it just right, and that shingle would be just the right size and the right length. It'd fall on the ground and he'd tell Asberry and me to stack it up so it could air-dry before he used it. We'd make a stack about three feet high and then start a new one.

When he was ready to get up on the roof, Papa would tie the shingles in bundles and take them up with him so he didn't have to keep coming back down to get more.

But Papa was tired of repairing that roof and he decided he was gonna build him a house with a different type of roof on it. A tin roof.

So Papa had gone to Cap'n Frank and told him he wanted to buy some lumber. Richard Reynolds owned the lumber mill over here, which is why Papa went to Cap'n Frank. Frank Durant was the island manager for Richard Reynolds, and he was in charge of all the men that worked for Reynolds, including Papa.

He had been the captain of a boat bringing up groceries, whiskey and ice from Savannah back before Reynolds hired him, and that "Cap'n" stuck to him like white on rice. His family had been in these parts a long time, about as long as we had, I expect. There was a Durant back before the Civil War who was an overseer for one of the Spaldings on the mainland and there was one who had been the county tax collector.

To look at Cap'n Frank, there wasn't anything special about him though. He was middle-aged with kinda blond hair that was beginning to turn gray a little bit, and he was kinda average size and average height. He was about five foot nine and next to Papa that wasn't much at all.

When Cap'n Frank opened his mouth, he had a real husky voice. That was the only thing about him that stood out. He spoke kinda slow and it sounded like he was hoarse all the time. But that didn't impress Mama none. Mama always said, "He ain't nuttin' but a straw boss. There ain't nuttin' to him." That meant somebody else was higher than him. Reynolds was the real boss.

Cap'n Frank liked to know *everything* that was going on. He didn't miss much if he could help it, and that's why Cap'n Frank came by. He was being nosy, just coming by to check on what Papa was gonna do with the lumber he wanted but that started the wheels going and Cap'n Frank started working on Papa after that.

He never came back to Belle Marsh, he just talked to Papa wheresoever he saw him, whether Papa was working on the North End or whether he was down on South End getting his paycheck.

"Hicks, why don't you move up to Hog Hammock? Your Uncle Nero has died, you're down there by yourself, you're the only family down there. The kids gotta walk so far to school. You gotta walk so far to come to work and if somebody gets sick, you have to walk so far to get help."

Papa kept on clearing his land.

Cap'n Frank acted like he was all kindness, like moving was all for Papa's benefit, but Papa said no. He was determined he was gonna build his house in Belle Marsh.

So they sweetened the pot.

"Well, Hicks, since the lumber mill is here on the island, you can get all the lumber you want for nothing if you move over to the Hog

Hammock community. All you'll have to pay for are the doors, the windows and the tin."

Still Papa kept on clearing his land.

Then Cap'n Frank told him, "We'll make it easier for you, Hicks. We'll pay you while you're building your own house. You'll be earning the same salary and you won't have to worry about going to work."

When that didn't work, Cap'n Frank said, "Well, Hicks, you know it'd be too bad if you lose your job and have to go to the mainland and your family have to fend for themselves."

When you say job and family in the same breath, that's pressure. Reynolds and his people controlled all the jobs on the island and they controlled the boat to and from the mainland.

I don't know what Papa told that man. I don't think he cursed, a black man couldn't curse in front of a white man back then, especially not in a violent tone. All I know is that when Papa got home, he ranted and raved to Mama. He absolutely did not want to move. This was *his* land. But there was a price to pay if he stayed.

Now, Papa liked traveling around. He had done some timbering over on another island, one time, but he went of his own free will then, to provide for his family. This was different. He didn't want to leave Sapelo for good.

Papa didn't have much choice, really. Finally, he said, "Okay, but if I move, you be sure my house is as far away from those Hog Hammock people as I can get."

He did not like those Hog Hammock people. He said they were mean, lying and two-faced and they liked to tell buckra everything. See, there were some people over here who had what we called high morals, who did not tattletale on their fellow man to the white man, even if they knew it was something he would want to hear. And there were others, especially on the South End, who would tell everything about you. Some of them had it so bad that if two men had an argument on Friday night, when they went to work on Monday morning Cap'n Frank would see them coming and holler, "What's this I hear about y'all having a fight on Friday night?"

So, when Cap'n Frank said Papa's house could be set off a little from most people on the South End, Papa started working on building him a house in Hog Hammock. He and Mr. Charlie Walker, that is. Mr. Charlie worked for Reynolds, he was a self-taught carpenter, and Cap'n Frank put him on building Papa's house too. Papa still got his little check every Friday and some days he worked on his house, some days for Reynolds. It took Papa and Mr. Charlie most of the year to build that house because they didn't have electricity, they used handsaws and they didn't work on it steady. But Mr. Charlie and Papa built it. They sure did. And finally the house in Hog Hammock was ready.

Moving day was upon us now and it was time to move. It was a gorgeous day, a Saturday in October of 1950. The sky was bright blue, the sun was shining and it was warm.

Mr. Minus came to help us move in the big old red company truck he drove that was owned by Reynolds. Cousin Dorothy was with him, they were married by then. Papa and Mr. Minus loaded everything in that truck. We didn't have much furniture. Mama and Papa had gone to Brunswick and bought a few pieces and they were already waiting in the new house at Hog Hammock. So all we had to do was load the three beds, the mattresses, some chairs and the casket that were made for me when I died, the smooth inside box and the rough outside box. We had the wood stove too, a couple of tables, some kerosene lamps and the smoothing irons for ironing.

They put everything in the back of the truck and there was plenty of room still for us. Mr. Minus and Cousin Dorothy got up front and we climbed in the back. It was a big, open-bed truck with boarded sides.

Mr. Minus put it in gear.

"Y'all ready?" he yelled.

"Yep, we're ready." Papa said.

Mama's counting noses.

"Hold it. Where's Murkel?"

There was no "Murkel"—Michael—in the truck. Papa went back into the living room and there was no Murkel there. He went into the kitchen. No Murkel.

Now where is Murkel?

Mama goes, "Now, y'all think. Think of where Murkel was the last time you saw him."

"Mama, Mama, remember he was laying on the bed with a blanket on him," I said.

"Hicks, did you take Murkel off the bed when you roll that mattress up?"

"No, I didn't see that boy."

Mama had laid Murkel on the bed in the living room. It was Mama and Papa's bed, the only one that had a real mattress. The beds we had in the back bedroom had mattress ticking, that heavy striped material, and they were stuffed with pine needles. Mama had emptied those and laundered them.

Papa and Mr. Minus had broke that bed in the living room down last and for some reason, they didn't notice Michael. I don't see how they didn't notice Michael, but they didn't. They just thought there was a blanket laying on the bed, and they rolled the mattress up, tied a piece of string around it and threw it on the back of the truck.

So Papa went up on the back of the truck and he unrolled the mattress and there was Murkel.

Mama starts yelling. "You could have killed my grandbaby, you could have killed my grandbaby."

But Michael never knew he was in that mattress. He was still sleeping, just as comfortable as he could be. I'm going, "Gee, he can sleep through *anything*."

Everybody loaded back on the truck, and Papa sat on the edge of the truck, the very back edge of the truck. We were all looking backwards as that truck pulled away from the house and Mr. Minus got out on the dirt road and start heading down to the South End, to Hog Hammock. Papa was looking backwards too, he couldn't help from looking backwards from where he was sitting on the back of the truck.

Papa stared a long time at that view. The pecan trees in our front yard were bearing, they were full of pecans that were ready to drop, and the sun was turning the marsh all golden.

Once Belle Marsh had been part of the Spaldings' land. A son of Thomas Spalding owned it and after the Civil War, it changed hands two or three times. It ended up being bought by Amos Sawyer. He was a Northerner, a white man from Massachusetts, who owned a soap company. I don't know what kind of soap it was, I never did hear, but Amos Sawyer must have gotten wealthy from making soap.

He bought land on the North End of Sapelo and tried lumbering but he gave up after awhile and he deeded Belle Marsh to the Joneses. That was in 1885, twenty years after the Union Army won, and the Joneses had owned it ever since.

Papa believed that some of his family had lived there before that, that they had always been on that part of the island, so someone in his family may have been in bondage to the Frenchmen when they were on the North End in the late 1700s. Our family always used some French words, words like "bateau" for "boat" and "toilet" for "outhouse," and Grandpa Gibb and Grandma Ada even called Papa "Frenchy."

Papa didn't say nothing as we drove away, not a word. He just looked. He was carrying all his worldly goods with him on the back of a truck. He could see the marsh edge of Belle Marsh for some distance and he kept on looking till he couldn't see Belle Marsh no more.

And that's how we came to live in the last house on the outskirts of Hog Hammock, in the *very last house* near the road leading up to the North End. Belle Marsh was the first black community on Sapelo that was closed, but it wasn't the last, and Papa was never quite right again. You move a man out of his domain and he's not gonna be happy.

Ain't Nuttin' Right with Hog Hammock

WHEN WE PULLED INTO HOG HAMMOCK, IT WAS the middle of the day and the fall sunlight was coming through the trees and casting shadows all over the yard and the house. It was absolutely gorgeous. It had started off a gorgeous day back at Belle Marsh and it still was. There were all those pine trees in front, just outside the yard, and I wasn't used to pine trees. We didn't have many pine trees near the house at Belle Marsh, we mostly had water oaks and live oaks and a magnolia tree. But it was mostly pines here, with a few oak trees in the backyard and one on the side.

The light was shining on the roof too, it was a tin roof just like Papa wanted, and it shone like pure silver in that sunlight. The pitch of the roof was like the letter *A*, like the one at Belle Marsh, but the front door of this house was on the narrow end. At Belle Marsh, the front door was in the middle of the wide side. So our new house looked totally different.

We got down from Mr. Minus's truck and went inside. I had been down one Saturday with Mama and Papa before we moved in so it wasn't a complete surprise, but this time I was here to stay. I was looking all around like I was seeing it for the first time and it was huge to a little child. I'm going, you know, this is like a mansion. *A mansion.* Because just compare. We still had an outdoor toilet, and we didn't have electricity or anything, but the house had glass windows instead of wooden ones, it actually had a tin roof, and *everything* was brand new.

But what really got me was the kitchen. Our kitchen had always been in a separate house at Belle Marsh and you were all the time walking to that kitchen. You not only cooked your food there, you would eat there. It was only when you had company that you brought the food out of the kitchen into the main house. But this kitchen was inside the house and it was the strangest thing to me. I had never been in a house on Sapelo where the kitchen was under the main roof. Grandma's was separate, Aunt Mary's was separate, everybody's was that I knew.

Papa was proud of the house he'd built, very proud, he just didn't want to live in Hog Hammock. But that didn't take away from how pleased he was with his house. There were three bedrooms now instead of two and Papa took me into the middle bedroom, and said, "This is your room. You don't even have to let nobody sleep with you if you don't want to." I was Mama and Papa's last child and the baby of the family always had a special place over here, so I was a privileged child. Besides, Papa believed I was a special child anyway.

He would go out of his way to have a piece of sugar cane for me, he'd take me to church and he'd take me with him to visit someone. He'd say, "You want to go with me? I'm going to Cousin Annie's house." Or, "You want to go with me? I'm going fishin'." So Papa was gonna let me have my own bedroom, but Mama put a stop to that. It would have meant that Asberry, Barbara, Michael and Elise were all in one room together, so she put Asberry in with me right then and there.

After we got everything moved in, Asberry and I went outside. The house faced the road, the dirt road we called the highway. It went up to the North End of the island, or down into the community, if you were going that way. There were children walking down the road and that was a big surprise to me, since Asberry and I had been the only kids at Belle Marsh.

Phillip was with them and we knew Phillip, because Phillip's mama, Cousin Anna, was Uncle Nero's daughter. She had lived at Belle Marsh before she moved to Hog Hammock. Cousin Anna and Mama were good friends and she and Phillip used to come back and visit. So we remembered Phillip, but he was the only one we knew. We didn't know Miss Mildred, Miss Mildred Grovner, who lived just a little bit away, and we didn't know Miss Mildred's kids. She had three children then, she had Maggie, Mary Lee and Caesar, Jr., and they were with Phillip. Mantee was there too, he was a little older than them, and he was a first cousin to Miss Mildred.

I didn't even know there would be kids at Hog Hammock. I hadn't even thought about it. Really, I didn't know much about Hog Hammock at all. I had only been in what we called "the community" one time before the Saturday I'd seen the house, and that was to go to the store with Mama and Papa. Mama said, "Do you want to ride with me over to Mr. Charles's Grab-All?" which is what Mama called it because you could get anything from your staples to a bottle of liniment there.

This was back when we still had Bully so Mama, Papa and I rode to Hog Hammock in the wagon to Miss Beulah and Mr. Charles Hall's store. I remember walking around the store and seeing cookies and candies in jars and canned goods and grits and rice and flour and sugar, and the Clausen bread with the little white girl on the label. A little girl with pigtails and a blue ribbon in her hair and a slice of butter bread in her mouth. Mama got some Clausen bread and a jar of peanut butter and on the way home she got a knife from Papa, spread some peanut butter on a piece of bread and gave it to me, because I was hungry and it was gonna be a slow journey back home. But we went straight to the store and left and that was it. I didn't know much about Hog Hammock.

So Asberry and I looked at those kids like, "Who are you? Who are you?" They looked at us the same way and we all sorta sized each other up, and we were a play group in no time. We got to know Ned and Marian later, they were Cousin Annie's grandchildren and they weren't there that day, but Asberry and I played with Phillip and Maggie and Mary Lee and Caesar and Mantee that afternoon. So it was an exciting moving day. I kept thinking, "Is all this actually happening to us? This big house with glass windows? And new kids to meet to boot? Naw, it can't be."

Early the following Monday, Papa went back up to the North End to work. Papa's job at that time was clearing new roads on the North End, cutting the passes and keeping the grass in the open fields down to the right level for the cattle, so they could graze. It was a huge area. Papa, Cousin Luke and Cousin Randolph were all on those tractors five days a week, spring, summer and early fall.

So Papa went up to the North End, like always, except that this day he walked out to the road and he caught a ride with Mr. Minus when he came to pick up men from the community who were going up to work on the North End. Asberry and I walked to Raccoon Bluff to school, just like always, except that we were coming from a different direction, so it was a whole new walk. The first day, Mama went with us to show us the way, and then she visited with Grandma like she usually did. So we had a new house, yes, in a new community, yes, but to us, everything still centered around the Bluff and the North End.

Hog Hammock is on the southeast side of Sapelo, not too far from the ocean, and about three miles inland from the Big House. The legend is that Sampson Hogg, Mama's great-great-grandfather, founded Hog Hammock.

When freedom came, black people got to pick their own names for the first time. A lot of people didn't want to take the name of their former slaveholder and some of them named themselves based on the task they did during slavery. According to the story, Sampson Hogg was in charge of raising hogs for the Spalding family. After the war, he used the name "Hogg," with two *g*'s.

Sampson Hogg and his wife, Sally, lived in Hanging Bull after the war, then they moved to the Bluff, and then they moved down to what became Hog Hammock. There were already black landowners in the area, but somehow the place wound up being called Hog Hammock.

The family kept the name Hogg until after Sampson died, but they must not have liked it, even with those two *g*'s. They rowed over to Darien, to the other side, and petitioned the court to change their name to Hall, and that was the end of the Hoggs. They were just Halls from then on.

In 1950, when we moved to Hog Hammock, there were about three hundred and fifty people, all black, living there, and it was the city to me, coming from the North End where there weren't many people. There were at least sixty houses, small, wooden houses sitting back from dirt roads that wound through the community.

The tracts of land deeded to people in Hog Hammock after the Civil War were about ten acres. Several generations of family members had built on each tract by now, so the average lot was a good bit smaller, but people had their own garden even if they had to walk miles to find a good spot. Everyone kept chickens and maybe one or two hogs, and one or two people had oxen and a few more had mules.

St. Luke's Baptist Church was there, and still is. It was founded in 1886, eighteen years after the First African Baptist Church, and because First A.B. was all the way over at the Bluff, there was a praise house in Hog Hammock for First A.B. members. It was a little wooden church, with a large bell outside, that could hold about twelve adults and a few kids, and there were regular Tuesday and Thursday night prayer meetings there.

There was also an elementary school, Mr. Charles's store, the Farmer's Alliance Hall, like the one that used to be at the Bluff, and the secret societies, the Farmer's Alliance and the Order of the Eastern Star, still used the top floor for meetings. The bottom floor was a social hall where you'd go to have a good time on Friday and Saturday night.

In the winters, you'd see smoke curling from old chimneys in Hog Hammock and in the summers, you'd see people out sitting and talking on their porches, and that's the kind of place Hog Hammock was when we moved in. But I didn't wander far from home at first.

In the coming days, Papa started fixing up the house. The outside wasn't painted yet, so Papa whitewashed the house from a mixture of lime and water and painted the window trim green. Then he went to work building us a front porch.

He had torn down our old house at Belle Marsh for lumber and he used the flooring for our new porch. Then he used some of the other lumber to build a potato house to store sweet potatoes in, and he gave the rest to Grandpa to use for repairs on his house. Lumber was precious and you didn't have any to waste. We used every piece. Papa had even saved a door from Uncle Nero's house too that he used on the inside of our new house, though that was partly so he'd have something that was his uncle's.

After that, Papa got to work clearing a field so he could plant a crop in the spring. He cut down the pine trees that were out front and that was a lot of pine trees. Then he limbed them up and cut them into lengths and took his log roller and rolled them off. He saved some for firewood and some he let dry and burned later, but he got all those pine trees cleared off.

A log roller is a wooden pole with a hook and once you stab the hook into a log, you can roll it away. Papa would have the logs cut and laying out there and sometimes when he was at work, Asberry and I would both get a log roller and get to work. We were little, but heck, we could roll a thirty-foot log with that thing.

Papa would come home and we'd go, "Papa, see what we done did? We moved all the logs for you." He'd look and say, "Sure did. Good job." So he didn't have to worry about that, because we did it while he was away.

It wasn't long before it began to get warm. At Belle Marsh we would have been smelling the fresh smell of the marsh and the orange blossoms from our trees would have been making the air all sweet. We were far from the marsh at Hog Hammock and we couldn't smell it or much else either, except for the pine trees and some wild honeysuckle. Mama was missing all those spring smells she loved at Belle Marsh. She'd say, "The plum tree's putting out blossoms now. The pear tree's putting out blossoms about now."

Pretty soon I was going, "Yeah, there ain't no orange trees here. We don't have anything here but pine trees."

So, Asberry and I started in fixing up the yard. We went to an old house spot where nobody was living anymore and we dug up some Seven Sisters roses and took them home and planted them in the front yard. The Seven Sisters rose has got small rosebuds that come in clusters of seven or more, and they're called the Seven Sisters, for the seven daughters of Bilali. The roses aren't pale pink and they aren't red, they're more what you think of as actually rose-colored, and they're the prettiest thing.

We got some crape myrtle from another old house spot and planted that. The old people called it the watermelon flower because it blooms when the watermelons are first coming out, it's still blooming while the watermelons are ripening and the flowers are a deep rose color, kinda like the inside of a watermelon. So it's the watermelon plant. We also put in a grape arbor, though we called it a grape tree, and after the grapes grew, you could walk under the poles and pick yourself some delicious muscadine grapes.

One night Papa took a break and took Asberry and me to the beach that's close to the community, Cabretta Beach, to see the moon coming up over the water. It was my first time at the beach. Belle Marsh is a marshy area and the waterfront at the Bluff just had a little, narrow strip of sand, so while I'd been on an island all my life, I'd never seen the beach. The air was warm, the breeze was warm, and *that sand*—there were miles and miles of nothing but beautiful white sand and sand dunes with swamp myrtle and other plants growing on them.

Papa said, "Take your shoes off," so I took my shoes off and I walked barefooted in the sand and the water and it felt so good, so different from anything else. There was more water than I'd ever seen, and you could hear gentle waves coming and going.

The moon rose up over the water, shining on that water. It was a full moon, a giant yellow moon that seemed to fill up the whole sky. I said, "It's so huge, Papa, *so huge*."

He took us to see the sunrise too, because, you know, we never could see it rise at Belle Marsh. We went early, somewhere before four and five o'clock, before day, what we called "for day." Papa was going to go fishing with his net in the mouth of Big Hole, off Cabretta Beach.

Asberry and I went walking on the beach and then we took a little nap. We didn't have blankets or anything, we just lay down on the beach and went to sleep and stayed there until Papa said, "Wake up. Wake up, y'all. You see the sun coming up?"

The sky was a beautiful pink and lavender and the sun was coming up slowly over the water, and I wondered, "Okay, should it be wet?" Because there was nothing but water out there, all you could see was water, and here comes the sun, a big red ball, coming up from someplace behind that water.

So, a whole new world was opening up to me but Mama and Papa weren't gonna be happy in Hog Hammock. It wasn't long before Mama started in complaining. She liked the new house, she just didn't like Hog Hammock, even if it was named for someone in her family. There were Halls at the Bluff as well as Halls in the community, but her family was from the Bluff. She had grown up not liking Hog Hammock. When she was a young girl, Howard Coffin had an oyster factory at Barn Creek on the South End, in the 1920s. An oyster factory is a place where you shuck the oysters and can them so they can be shipped off and sold. A lot of women from the

Bluff would walk down and work there and Grandma did, and Mama came with her sometimes.

The oyster factory lasted awhile and then it closed. The ladies weren't told why it closed but Mama blamed it on the Hog Hammock women. She said the ladies from Hog Hammock would cheat, that they'd put oyster shells down in the bottom of the containers to make it look like there was more in it and then put the oysters on top, and when the oysters were shipped off to other places, those shells were discovered. Working at that oyster factory was hard work, she said, but it was a good living for people, and she'd tell Asberry and me, "Don't trust the people from Hog Hammock. They can't be trusted."

Really, I didn't know it yet, but we had our own little civil war going on Sapelo. It was the North against the South all over again and we even had our own Mason-Dixon line at Aunt Lena's ditch.

Aunt Lena's ditch divides the North End of Sapelo from the South End. It's a *deep* drainage ditch running across the island and it probably was built so that the rice in nearby fields wouldn't be underwater at harvesttime. No one remembers who Aunt Lena was, but she fell into that ditch one day and she had to be rescued, and from then on, people talked about Aunt Lena's ditch.

On the North End, people were very independent and they wanted to have as little to do with buckra as possible. They wanted to keep their own identity. They'd worked hard for it and they held onto it. On the South End, people were used to being around the white man because the Big House was there and all the white people who worked for Reynolds were there. So, they were inclined to pick up some of their ways quicker—even something as simple as switching to Ivory soap, "sweet soap" we called it, instead of sticking with

Borax for washing your clothes and yourself—and a lot of South End people pretty much accepted the idea that being around the white man gave you more prestige.

It wasn't too different from what took place in slavery days, when the black people working around the slaveholder and his family in the Big House grew to think they were more important than the people working in the fields. That pattern was still going on, based on the fact that the people on the South End lived nearer the Big House so they were the ones who usually would get the jobs as maids and cooks in the mansion house or would work in Reynolds's mechanic shop, carpentry shop or dairy, and meanwhile, a lot of the people on the North End did hard, physical work like maintaining the roads on the island.

Over time, the folks in the Hog Hammock had begun to call the people on the North End backward and ignorant, and the people on the North End didn't want anything to do with the people in Hog Hammock. And when I came around, the divide between us was as deep as Aunt Lena's ditch.

Mama liked the new house but before long she started in complaining about Hog Hammock. She didn't complain all the time, she was too busy doing her chores. But when she did, she said the people's not right in Hog Hammock, the soil's not right, it's got no shells in it and it's too shifty, the fields won't grow the same, and even the oysters don't taste the same. "There ain't nuttin' right about Hog Hammock," Mama said.

Papa didn't complain all the time either but he was more unhappy than Mama. After a few drinks, he'd cuss about the men he worked with. He'd rant and rave about them telling buckra everything, trying to get a few extra bucks in their paycheck, and them stealing things. Now, Papa would get bent and rusted nails from the job, he'd take those because they were scrap, and he'd bring those home and we'd hammer them out and put them in a can and save them to use later. But a lot of the other guys would just steal new ones or help themselves to tools.

So he'd rail about the dishonesty of the men, but what he was really angry about was having to move from Belle Marsh. And to make things worse, the Reynolds people, when they was trying to get him to move, told Papa that his share of the family land there was four acres. They told him they'd swap him land in Hog Hammock, that they'd provide the lumber free, and all he had to pay for was the tin and the windows and the doors. But when we moved to Hog Hammock, they took two acres for payment of the lumber and traded him two acres in Hog Hammock. So it wasn't an even swap.

They went back on their word and Papa lost two acres in the trade, besides losing his family place. We had to pay on what we owed, every month or as often as we could, and we had to take the money down to Frank Durant knowing all the time Papa got cheated in that deal. A black man couldn't yell at a white man back then, not on Sapelo, that's for sure, so Papa was stuck. He was just plain stuck if he wanted the privilege of living on the island. So he railed against everybody else instead and was angry.

He didn't just walk off, like his father did. Papa could have just taken that boat to the other side and be gone forever, and we knew it, but Papa wasn't gonna leave and stay gone. He was too much of a family man for that.

He kept on working all day for a few bucks, and getting up to the North End as much as he could, but he never forgave Reynolds for taking his land. He sure didn't.

Chapter Eleven

The Jack-o'-Lantern

MAMA AND PAPA WOULD ALWAYS TELL ASBERRY AND me when we were going out after dark, "Okay, now. Be careful goin' down the road 'cause you might see a jack-o'-lantern."

We had the jack-o'-lantern over here, see, and by that, I don't mean the jack-o'-lantern we saw pictures of in books at school, the pumpkin with a cutout face and a candle down in it that became a light. That one was like, "Who they trying to kid?" Because we had the real thing. The *real* jack-o'-lantern. It was a real living being, a mysterious ball of light that could get you hopelessly lost in the woods at night.

Mama had seen it, Papa had seen it, a lot of the old people had seen it, and not long after we moved into Hog Hammock, Charles Walker saw it.

Charles Walker was the son of Cousin Annie and Papa's first cousin Ned, and they were living near us in the community. Cousin Annie was full of spunk and determination, just full of spunk and determination, but her son Charles didn't have any spunk at all. Not at all. Cousin Charles was in his thirties and he was well over six foot six or six foot eight. He was so tall that it seemed like he loomed up seven feet in the air or more. But tall as he was, he was meek as a lamb.

Cousin Charles never did anything harmful to anyone, he wasn't that type, but he was good at drinking, now. He would drink that booze and it's like he totally changed when he did. He'd make all kinds of brave noises then and he'd have nerves of steel and he'd go around from house to house talking up a storm.

He'd come to our house and go, "Hello, Cousin Hettie."

"Well, Cousin Charles. Why don't you come in."

"I don't mind if I do," he'd say and he'd come in. Then he'd go, "Well, I see you're cookin' dinner there. I'll jis' set a little and then I'll be on my way." And he'd be telling you stories and you'd be cracking up and your dinner's done and after awhile you'd say, "Charles, you wanta have a little dinner?" and he'd eat dinner with you and keep telling stories, and if you let him, he'd just spend the night in your chair or lay down on your cot and go to sleep. Because he didn't want to go home after dark. He was scared of the dark. At nighttime his nerves of steel went away and he wasn't worth a hoot. "He wasn't worth shit at night," the old people said.

But you couldn't just let him stay. My brother Gibb, back when he was living on Sapelo, beat his butt one time because Charles peed on the cot rather than get up and go use the outside toilet, so you couldn't let him stay.

One night when somebody didn't let him stay over, Cousin Charles set out walking home late at night. Cousin Charles knew the road like the back of his hand, he knew that road now, even to where the mud puddles were, but it gets real dark over here, and there aren't any street lights or nothing, just the moon and the stars, and the dark black of night. And since no one was there but Cousin

Charles, nobody ever knew, really, but I think what happened next went sorta like this.

He'd had a few drinks like he always did, so he probably was a little foggy, and he was walking home all alone, going past tall, straight pines and huge, live oak trees towering over him with long, gray moss dripping from them. He was whistling to himself to keep up his nerve, when he saw a light up ahead, a little ways up ahead of him, and he went, "Aah, that must be Cousin Jimmy. He set off just a little while before me and he got a light." That light was a welcome sight to Cousin Charles, so he started walking faster, to catch up with his relative.

The light turned off the path all of a sudden, so Cousin Charles turned too, and then it got off the path too, so he did too, and it went over a ditch, so Cousin Charles went down into the ditch and through some low-lying water in that ditch, and up over on the other side, saying, "Now where is Cousin Jimmy goin'?" But he kept following that light, just following that light that was glowing like someone was holding it and walking in the woods. The light kept glowing up ahead, and Cousin Charles kept following the light. It was leading him deeper and deeper into the woods, past short, scrubby trees that were covered with twisting vines and had all kinds of odd shapes in the dark and shadows. Trees that were about his height and could be a man, an animal or some wild, devilish creature he didn't want to know about, if they moved in the wind, *just* enough.

Crickets were chirping a hundred times louder than they usually do, because the woods were so very still and quiet at night, and frogs were croaking a terrible lonesome sound, and there was this loud squawk, this *awful* squawk, and his heart pounded hard and he jumped in fright. He heard the sound of something rising up and large wings flapping quick-like and a po'jo', a blue heron, flew away.

Every step he made was a bit timid then. He didn't know what he was gonna step on or what he was gonna come across. He heard a snake slither across the leaves, right near his feet, and he stopped dead still because that meant he had an enemy out here, a deadly enemy, on his trail, and he was pure afraid of snakes, so afraid that he was just about trembling in his shoes. Before he could collect himself, a bat flew right by his face and his hand flew up too, to protect himself, and he cried out in the dark, "Cousin Jimmy, where are you? Cousin Jimmy, oh, Cousin Jimmy. Help me."

A cloud came up over the moon and the stars got dim and it was darker yet and Cousin Charles was as scared as he could get. It was so dark and he was so turned around from following that light that he didn't know where he was or what was happening to him. He must have started running then, crashing through the woods to catch that light, running to save his life.

But that ball of light was always up ahead of him, no matter how fast he ran. He was gasping for air as he leaned up against an old oak, and what did he see but an owl staring down at him, not blinking at all, those big, yellow-and-brown owl eyes just staring into Cousin Charles's own eyes, down into him like he was the King on Judgment Day. Then the owl hooted, *whoooooo—whoooooo— whooooo* and that *whooooo* cut right through him and his skin got wet with fear, because you know and he knew the owl hooting at night is a sign of death. A sure sign of death.

The owl swooped down off the oak tree then and Cousin Charles thought it was coming for him, but it went on like he wasn't worth fooling with and flew off into the brush, hunting for its dinner, but that was it for Cousin Charles. His wits were absolutely gone. He staggered after that light, real slow now, just able to keep on his feet, and the light led him on in circles in those woods till his legs gave out and he couldn't stand up no more.

The sky was getting a little pale, it was dayclean now, and the first rays of light were beginning to streak across the sky, and that glowing light vanished. That ball of light that tormented him all night was gone, but it was too late for him.

The sun rose all golden, like always, and back in the community, Cousin Annie was worried, real worried, because her son Charles hadn't come home that night. No one knew where he was, there was no word that he had stayed at anybody's house, and everybody knew he was afraid of the dark, so the menfolks set out looking for him.

They found out what house he'd been to last and they went off in the woods from there, searching and searching until they found him. They found him laying down right by a bunch of briar bushes, all curled up with one hand covering his mouth and face, and with red welts all over his skin, because the mosquitoes and gnats had been eating on him all night, they had themselves a regular feast on him, and Cousin Charles was talking out of his mind, just jabbering and muttering to himself, and he didn't know those men at all. He had known them all his life, but he didn't know them now.

The men got him home and washed him off, dried him down, got clean clothes on him and gave him a little drink of whiskey and then Cousin Charles began to come around.

The news got around the community that they'd found Cousin Charles and what bad shape he had been in and Grandma and Mama and all the old people chawed on that bone all day. "Charles need to stop some of that foolishness, going out drinking and coming home late at night, and following anything he see," they said.

"That's God's way of teaching him a lesson," they said, and they meant every word.

And God's way must have worked. Cousin Charles didn't leave home at all for days, not until he got his nerve back up, and after that he always tried to get home before dark.

◆

Chapter Twelve

Make Sump'n of Yourself

THE OLD PEOPLE HAD A LOT OF WISDOM AND THEY had signs and beliefs to guide them but they didn't get a chance to get much schooling. They knew you had to be able to read, write and figure, though.

To me, the one who said it best was Ronnister Johnson. I always loved listening to Ronnister. He was *the* storyteller of the island and he also was our Santa Claus at the Christmas program every year at the church. At the point where we were all singing Christmas carols and we broke into "Jingle Bells," you'd hear this jingling sound from outside the church and *Sandy* Claus, as we called him, would come bursting in with a sack on his back.

You'd never find another Santa like Ronnister. He said "Ho, ho, ho," like every Santa, and he had a red suit, a long cap and a long white beard, but unlike the Santas in the Sears catalog, he was *black*. And he didn't come in *walking*. He came in with his stick, an old broom handle, like you'd use for a ring shout, a special form of dance we had over here, and he'd *pound* that stick on the wooden floor, he'd twist his body and gyrate his hips, he'd take a few steps forward and a few steps backward, and he'd dance his heart out.

"More, Ronnister, more," the adults in the back, the ones who were two cups of gin to the wind, would yell, and Ronnister would roll his shoulders and his stomach and push all that stuffing in his suit up. He was hilarious. The audience was wiping their eyes with handkerchiefs they were laughing so hard.

Miss Jessie Mae Moore, my favorite teacher, ran the program and one year after Ronnister had changed back into his regular clothes, she said, "Mr. Johnson, would you like to say anything?"

He said, "Um, no, not really, but I tell you what. You young people? Y'all stay in school. In my day when we went to school, we didn't go to school very much. Me and my brother, every time we got dressed and figured we were goin' out the door to school, Mama'd come and say, 'Son, y'all can't go to school today. You have to stay home and help kill grass in the field.' Lemme tell ya', Mama been dead and that grass ain't dead yet. Yessir, we still hoeing that same grass today."

He said it in jest and everyone laughed, but to hear Ronnister, who couldn't read and write, stand up and say, "Y'all stay in school and make sump'n of yourself," it stuck with you.

In slavery times it had been illegal to teach any black person considered to be a slave to read and write, so afterward there was a great desire to learn. The Freedmen's Bureau got a school for black students up and going on Sapelo just two months after the war. Sixty students turned out for classes, including children and adults, and one of them was a grandson of Bilali's, who named himself Liberty Bell.

Any schooling they got would have been exciting to them but they probably didn't get to stay in school long though: it was a luxury. They were on their own for the first time and they had to work the land or starve. Over the generations to come, that same pattern was followed. You got some education, but if your family needed you to work in the field, you stopped going to school and pitched in, because your work counted toward your family's survival. And when I came along, we were still struggling to get an education.

Papa went to school through the third grade and he could write his name, Sapelo, and the county we lived in, but that was it, and that was more than Mama could do. Mama didn't go as far as the second grade but somehow she knew her ABC's. She hadn't learned to connect the letters to form words, so she couldn't sign her name, but she could do simple figuring like counting money and getting her change back from a dollar. You couldn't fool her on that, and that was about as much as she needed to know. But she wanted us to learn the three R's and she taught me my ABC's before I started school.

I would watch Barbara and Asberry leaving in the morning with a look on my face like where are they going that I can't go? Mama could tell I felt left out so she'd take me outside, get a stick and draw an "A" or a "B" or a "C" in the sand.

"Okay, you make it now," she'd say, and I would copy the letter and she'd have me say it after her too so I would know what it was. Then she got Barbara to write the numbers from one up to ten on a piece of cardboard and Mama would point to the numbers and I would say them. She taught me the Lord's Prayer too, so I knew things a lot of kids didn't when I started school.

When I got in school and began to see how the letters formed words and how the words formed sentences, all of a sudden the realization hit me, "I can read!" Once that realization set in, nothing could stop me. I *loved* reading. I was just like Grandpa. I read everything I could put my hands on and wanted more.

So, in January of 1951 Asberry and I bundled up and went to the school in Hog Hammock for the first time. We had waited until after Christmas because our teacher at the Bluff, Mr. Govner O'Neill, thought that starting a new school would be easier for us if we came in when everybody else was coming back fresh from the holidays. He was probably thinking about me. We didn't have kindergarten on Sapelo, you started school in the first grade. Most kids were six years old when they started and I was still five. I had started school in September, we moved in October, and I wouldn't be six until June.

I had on my best school dress, a little plaid dress, but I wasn't looking forward to the new school. Mama had told me, "Now, there gonna be some other chirren you haven't seen before," and that was enough to make me hear alarm bells. I was still shy and I still stuttered when people's eyes were on me. But I had my big brother by my side and that kept me from feeling too intimidated.

When we got to the schoolyard, it was just amazing to me. I had never seen so many kids in my life, I didn't even know there were that many on Sapelo. There were over a hundred kids here. I looked at the big ones and they looked so much older and bigger than me.

The schoolhouse itself wasn't a surprise. It was a white, wooden two-room schoolhouse, about like the one at the Bluff. It had a wood stove for heat and a small kitchen and apartment for the teachers to stay in because most of the teachers were from the mainland.

Both the school at the Bluff and the one in Hog Hammock were Rosenwald schools, built in the 1920s. You may not know about Rosenwald schools but they meant a lot to black people throughout the South. Julius Rosenwald was the president of Sears Roebuck, and he got inspired after meeting the famous black educator Booker T. Washington and set up a foundation to build schools for rural black students. The lumber and other materials for the schools on Sapelo were provided but the men over here built them. Everyone was proud of that.

Asberry and I looked around the schoolyard a little and then the principal came out and rang a little hand bell and everybody lined up in orderly fashion to go in. At the Bluff, there were only about twenty-five kids so everyone filed into one classroom, but here, the first three grades went into one classroom and the second three grades went into the other one.

I was in the first grade and Asberry was in the third so we were both in the same classroom, but in different areas of it. Each grade was grouped together in rows and everyone sat in an assigned seat, a brown wooden seat that was constructed so that the back of your seat was the desk for someone else. We sat facing the teacher, Miss Bloodworth, and the blackboard and the America flag with forty-eight stars on it.

People think you don't learn as much in a two-room schoolhouse but, really, we learned more. The teachers were good, they were strict, and they kept you busy every minute. When it was your turn to recite, you'd better have done your homework and know your lesson, or the other kids would laugh at you.

When school let out for the lunch recess that first day, I stayed close to the schoolhouse, with my back up to a big oak tree, a good distance away from where everyone was jumping rope, swinging on swings and playing ball. I didn't want to mingle. If I could have played without opening my mouth, I would have been fine, but I knew if I had to say something, I'd stutter. So I stood and watched and the kids left me alone.

On the way home from school, two boys picked a fight with Asberry though. They wanted to see what Asberry was made of and he whipped them both and they were good friends after that.

Now, girls size you up a little differently than boys. The girls waited a little while, and then some of them started picking at me. There was a certain group of Hog Hammock girls who thought they were special because their parents had the "better" jobs on the island and got a little extra money in their paychecks. They would make sure I could hear them and say things like, "Oh, look at that one there, she's one of those dumb people from Belle Marsh."

Those girls didn't know me. They'd never even been to Belle Marsh, so that was stupidity on their part, but they'd talk that way about anybody from the North End. "That's alright baby," Mama said. "You go ahead and keep your head high and you get your learning." So I did.

I ignored them when they called my hair old-fashioned because it was long and full and plaited. Their hair was short, in a modern look, and some of them keep it straightened. Mama didn't believe in straightening hair except on special occasions.

I ignored them when they'd say, "Where'd you get that old dress from?" about the homemade dresses that Mama stayed up at night to make me. But it made me angry that some people could be so cotton-picking mean.

One day when the weather was beginning to get warm, we were walking to school and Asberry had our book bag and I had a big navel orange that was a special treat Mama had given us to share at lunchtime. We hadn't gone too far before Asberry said, "Here, hold this a minute, sis. I gotta go in the bushes." I held the book bag and he went across a little ditch in the bushes and I waited and waited and waited. Asberry sure was taking an awful long time to come back out of the bushes.

"Asberry?"

There was no answer.

I went across the ditch and looked around and there was no sign of Asberry. "Girl, go on ahead, because he ain't gonna go to school," something told me. But I was five years old and I had never been anywhere without Asberry. All I could see was this long road ahead of me and it was scary. I could go on or I could go back home and I stood there and made up my mind I was gonna go to school no matter what. I was gonna learn things.

I started on down the road and all of a sudden, I stubbed my left foot, and that was a sign of bad luck. If you stubbed your right foot, that's okay, you'd just keep on your way, but if you stubbed your left foot, you had to stop right there and reverse your luck before you could go on your way.

I had never stubbed my left foot before but I knew what to do. I picked up a stick and drew a circle where I had stubbed my foot, put an X in the center of it, spit in the middle of the X, and turned counterclockwise in a complete circle.

It was an old, old ritual. An X is the same thing as a cross, so to us, it was powerful. It would get rid of whatever evil had entered the circle. You spit in the middle of the X so your good luck would come back, and you turned counterclockwise in a complete circle to finish it up. Then you didn't have to say, "I stubbed my foot. I'm going home. I'm not gonna have no good luck all day."

I got to school and I didn't have a bad day. I didn't get called on to read in front of the class so I didn't stutter, I got to eat that whole orange by myself, and nobody begged me for part of my orange or tried to snatch it from me and run. They left me alone at recess.

I walked home feeling proud of myself and Asberry popped out of the woods and joined me like he'd been with me all day. But I didn't need my big brother by my side after that. That day was my solo. I knew I could do things on my own then. I had been in school getting my education while he was playing in the woods. I had reversed my luck and gone on my way. I was gonna make sump'n of myself.

◆

Chapter Thirteen

The Old Man

THE WINTER I WAS ELEVEN YEARS OLD, GRANDMA'S arthritis had gotten so bad that Grandpa was taking care of her around the clock and Mama told her, "Come give Papa a break. Stay with us awhile." So she stayed with us a few months and that's when I began to learn about slavery days on Sapelo and my ancestors.

Grandma had the crippling type of arthritis and she couldn't walk much. She'd sit in her rocking chair and hold onto its arms and swing her weight toward the left and then to the right and that rocking chair would go *zip-zip-zip* across the floor.

She could go anywhere in the house she wanted, but mostly she stayed in front of the fire in the wood stove in the living room because the heat felt good to her. She was there the day I came home telling Mama how my teacher, Miss Jessie Mae Moore, had brought a book into school and read to us about plantation days on Sapelo and Thomas Spalding.

Miss Moore was always making us privy to things that weren't in our regular textbooks and that was the first time I had heard of Thomas Spalding. He wasn't the only plantation owner on Sapelo during slavery times, but he was the biggest and the best known. He and his family wound up owning most of the island and he had about five hundred slaves to grow his rice and cotton and other crops.

Spalding was a wealthy man, a state legislator and one of the first of the Sea Island planters to get a special kind of seed from the Bahamas and cultivate what became known as Sea Island cotton. That cotton was *famous*. It was long-stapled, so the fibers were extra long, and it was the finest and softest cotton there was. But the thing that interested me in what Miss Jessie Mae Moore read was what is said about the way Thomas Spalding treated his slaves. It said he was much kinder to his slaves than most slaverholders and that everybody said the slaves on Sapelo had it good.

So, I came running into the house saying, "Mama, Mama, guess what I learned today? Miss Jessie Mae read to us about Thomas Spalding and how the black people over here were treated good in slavery times."

Grandma looked up and she got hot under the collar right then and there. "Baby, don't you believe everything you hear," she said. "I remember my Mama and Grandma telling me things were so bad over here that they actually had to *catch rats* to eat. They almost starved to death. Those people had it rough."

When Grandma got mad, you kept quiet. You kept your mouth shut, or she would start in, "Yeah, the chirren these days ain't got a bit of manners. They just listen at your conversation or look right in your eye when you' talkin', those no-manners little wretches, them. Back in my day they couldn't do that."

When she was a child, all the women chewed chewing tobacco. They would chew it until it got nice and mushy and if they caught a child listening to adult talk, they would take aim and spit right in that child's eye, *p'tui!*, she said and, "That chile got a eyeful of tobacco and he ain't botherin' your conversation no more. He's gone where chirren are supposed to go."

I disappeared as quick as I could because I could just see a wad of tobacco flying across the room and hitting me in the eye. I wasn't about to ask her any questions about anything, including slavery days, but I was curious and I listened every chance I got. I just became very good at pretending I wasn't listening.

To me, slavery was this whole mysterious thing no one talked about. I did hear talk about how old man Lincoln freed our people, but shoot, that was common knowledge in every black household. You didn't have to go to school to learn that. Our textbooks didn't define slavery too much. They talked about the Civil War like it was this great thing that helped the blacks but they didn't say anything about what life was like back then for black people. I was totally ignorant of any facts.

Grandma would say little snatches of things that started with "when buckra owned us," so I knew my family had been slaves once, and I knew the kids back then didn't look any different than me, except in dress, because sometimes the old people would laugh and say about a dark-skinned child in ragged pants, "Yeah, you look just like them little chirren in slavery days."

I had to rely on the little bits and pieces I got from Mama and Grandma, and mostly they talked about "The Old Man." The Old Man from back in slavery times.

I could tell by the way they said The Old Man, that it was a term of respect. There were other men that Mama and Grandma called "old man," including Sampson Hogg who founded Hog Hammock, but they used his first name as part of the title. He was "Old Man Sampson." They didn't simply say "The Old Man" about anyone but this one person and I could tell by the way they said it that he didn't need a first name. He was someone of *great* importance. He stood by himself. He was *The* Old Man.

I knew he must have been someone in our family because Mama and Grandma were always talking about the family members who had gone before us. They spoke of them in the present tense, they kept the memory of them alive by talking about them and they gave them honor. Really, it was a lot like the way people in Africa traditionally have had reverence for their ancestors. I just didn't know about that tradition until I grew up. But I couldn't miss the fact that the ancestors were important and besides, it wasn't like they were gone anyway. If you tell the spirits of your family to move aside before you throw water outside after dark, the ancestors are listening and hearing all the time. They're still with you, even if they're just a spirit.

Then I learned The Old Man's name. I read everything I got my hands on, just like Grandpa, and somebody showed me an article on Sapelo. I picked it up and was reading it and all of a sudden, there was someone called Bul-Allah who had worked for Thomas Spalding. I said, "Hold it now, who's that? This isn't right. I've never heard of him." When I asked Mama about him, she said, "Oh, that's The Old Man we've been talking about. He used to work for the buckra man."

The Old Man and the guy in the article were one and the same, and it felt good to know his name, except he was not Bul-Allah to us. He was *Bilali*. That was a name that had been passed down over here. We had a Mr. Bilali Bell alive and kicking right then. He lived at the Bluff and was a deacon of the church. His name actually was William but everybody called him Bilali, and he was a descendant of Bilali's too.

The first Bilali was the head driver for Thomas Spalding, and he was an African and a slave too but he was over all the other slaves who were working in the fields. He had become a legendary figure over the years but he was real and he was my great-great-great-great-grandfather.

Bilali had a lot of children, and one of them was Hester. Hester was the mother of Sally, who was the mother of Harriet, who was Grandma's mother. Grandma didn't ever know Hester, but Grandma knew Hester's daughter, Sally, and Mama remembered Sally a little too and she definitely remembered Harriet, because that was Mama's grandmother. So there was a direct line down from Bilali to us.

I could kinda imagine what Bilali looked like because Uncle Shed was supposed to have looked a lot like him, only Bilali was a little taller and a little darker skinned. Uncle Shed was Harriet's brother and Bilali's great-grandson. He was born in 1856, he lived to be well over one hundred years old and he was still around when I was a little girl. So when the old people said Uncle Shed had the same features, the same narrow nose and lips that Bilali had, my ancestor came alive in my mind.

Grandma said The Old Man talked different, he and his family spoke in a funny tongue to each other, and he believed different and prayed different, and even some of the foods he and his family ate were prepared differently. He carried himself different too, and he kept his family apart from almost everybody else. So he was different. Quite different.

Bilali was Mohammedan, a Muslim, and he had a little mat that he used to kneel on, and he would bow to the sun and pray three times a day, when the sun came up, when it went directly overhead and when it set. He had a special string of beads too. It was a long string and he and Phoebe, his wife, would pray on those beads, and then she would say "Ameen, Ameen."

On special occasions, Phoebe must have fixed a special little rice cake, because Ma'am said her Great-Grandma Hester always did. Hester would wash the rice the night before, pour off the water and let it sit all night so the rice would swell up, then she'd beat it and make a paste out of it and add honey and make it into little, flat cakes. She'd give one to each of the children and they'd eat it and then they'd say, "Ameen, Ameen." So it may have been a thing she did on a certain religious day.

We didn't have rice cakes like that over here anymore, but we did have something Mama and Grandma called the rice cake. So the tradition of the rice cake got passed down, it just changed over time. The rice cake to us was the crusty part of the rice down at the bottom of the pot. It was golden brown and crunchy on the outside and soft on the inside and very tasty. Everybody wanted the rice cake. And when Mama would cook oysters and rice or peas and rice, that rice cake tasted that much better, and boy, you had trouble then.

It was said that when the British were invading the islands off the Georgia coast, back during the War of 1812, Thomas Spalding decided to arm his slaves. He wanted them to be able to fight off the British if they came. He gave Bilali firearms and told him to train the slaves how to use them. Bilali did, and the British never came, and some people say that's why, because they did take some other islands, like Cumberland Island, which is to the south of us.

Most slaveholders would have been scared stiff to give their slaves firearms because their slaves could have easily used the firearms against them. Bilali must have been absolutely trustworthy. Spalding must have respected him.

Slavery was horrible in and of itself, so life on Sapelo wasn't easy for black people even if Bilali was the head driver and even *if* Spalding was a little better slaveholder than some. And who knows about that? The view of Spalding as being "strict but fair" was passed down by his descendants and friends, not by black people here. And there were other, smaller slaveholders here anyway, so not everybody would have been under Spalding's so-called good treatment blanket.

Grandma and Uncle Shed said some of the slave masters were the devil from hell. They didn't mention any names, but the old people didn't ever deliberately bring up anything bad from slavery. They locked those memories away in their minds and didn't talk about them. It was only when they got angry that they'd let a little bit slip out.

Every time Grandma or her cousin, Cousin Annie, would hear of a terrible injustice against black people anywhere, they would start in on how evil buckra was and say, "Yeah, we had something like that happen on Sapelo when they hung that young man down at Hanging Bull." They didn't say who he was or why he was hung, just that it happened during slavery days. A large, strapping black man was sometimes called a bull back then, and according to that story, that's how the old slave community of Hanging Bull got its name.

So Bilali was an important man over here, but just because there was a black driver on Sapelo, it doesn't follow that life was easy for the people who were slaves. The Africans were forced into slavery and brought here against their will and didn't want to be slaves to anyone. Grandma was dead serious when she said those people had it rough Cousin Ronnister had a story about that, Cousin Ronnister Johnson who was always telling stories. This particular story was about a rebellious shipment of slaves over here. A *highly* rebellious shipment.

The people on a certain slave ship didn't want to be slaves, they were *not* going to be slaves and they ran off into the woods and stayed there. And they wouldn't come out. The old slave master said, "Just let them stay inside that woods until they're ready to behave themselves. Don't bother them, just take them out food and water, just leave them alone."

Every day it was the job of the other slaves to take food and water to the edge of the woods, until those people in the woods made up their minds that there was nothing to do but come out and join the others—when they were ready to behave themselves.

Cousin Ronnister made a joke out of it, but it was actually a true story that had been passed down to him, that he'd paid attention to. The area where those rebellious slaves lived was called Behavior from then on. It was a slave community and it disappeared after slavery, but it was probably near the cemetery, the one I almost was buried in, that's named Behavior Cemetery. So the name "Behavior" got carried on, and in a way, it honors those people. They had a independent streak in them, a definite independent streak.

Mama said that Grandma told her that them old buckras were nasty and that they would catch us and drag us on that ship by tricking us. I asked, "Mama, how they trick us?" She said, "Grandma and her people said that they waved a piece of bright red cloth and we would get curious, like, what is that thing. And they'd keep waving that red cloth and when we get close enough, they grabbed ahold to us and then they would throw us inside the ship and that was it. We would find ourselves over here in this country."

Red was a hated color, and when somebody was wearing it, Grandma would say, "I don't know why she don't take that red thing off, it make her look like a monkey. Where she think she at? She needs to stop wearing that." See, the buckra man enticed you with it, which means you were weak or silly enough to go for a piece of red cloth and get yourself caught, so you looked silly with that red on. Mama said that red cloth especially attracted young children.

So there were pieces of the slavery-times puzzle everywhere. There wasn't much about slavery itself, just a little about the people, but I knew they were real people, they weren't just beings you can dismiss with the label "slaves"; they were people who had all the same fears that we would have in their place, the same hopes and the same need for love. Grandma would laugh when she'd tell us about one old lady from slavery times. The old lady didn't have a man and she wasn't getting any younger. When the other ladies asked her why she didn't have a husband yet, she said, "I'm waiting on a *fresh* batch."

She didn't want an African that was already here. For some reason, she hadn't found what she was looking for. She may have wanted a man who hadn't learned American ways yet, but whatever it was, she was waiting on a fresh one from Africa. I can imagine that it would have been a big time when a ship came in with a new batch of slaves. All the people over here would have been looking to see who came, with a mixture of hope and fear. They wouldn't have wanted to see their brother or sister or anyone in their family step off that ship because it would have been horrible for them to have been sold into slavery too. But at the same time, they must have been saying, "I wonder if there's somebody I know on that ship," and looking at the people's faces for anything that said, "Yes, you are from my country, you speak my language, you are like me."

Grandma wasn't born a slave, she was born right after that time. Ma'am was born into slavery and she was a slave for a little while, and Sally and Hester lived a lot of their life during slavery times, but they were still alive after slavery was over. Hester was old then, she lived into her nineties, and she got to see the coming of freedom. But when freedom came, they put the stories of slavery behind them. They sealed their lips on that and didn't look back. They wanted to go forward.

"Those were *those days*," Mama would say, like that was all you needed to know. "Those were those days." She didn't explain things in detail. She left some things deliberately hanging. She'd tell me sometimes. "That's alright. You figure it out yourself. You know exactly what I mean. If I give you all the answers, you'll never be as smart as me." So I was gonna have to figure it out myself if I wanted to know.

The Hag That Rides You

I GREW UP BELIEVING IN THAT MYSTERIOUS BEING of the night, the hag. The old people called it the "haint" and the people my age said "hag," but it was one and the same supernatural being whatsoever name you gave it. The hag was always here on this island. Always. As far back as anybody can remember.

The hag came in the absolute dark of night, when you were least suspecting it, while you were asleep in the bed, and it would jump on you and ride you, ride you and ride you, and you'd wake up the next morning and you'd be so tired you don't know what to do.

If it bothered you every night, it would take a toll on you. It would do you bodily harm. The hag could ride you till there's nothing left of you, till you got weak and weaker and weaker, till the sap is all gone out of you and you were dead and in the grave. That's right.

That must have happened over here, before my time, because the old people would say, "Chile, that hag almost ride me to death last night." They said it like the memory was deep down in them somewhere. Like someone that was always complaining about the hag almost riding him to death was found dead in the morning, and what else killed that person? It was the hag.

At some point in their lives, everybody had been ridden by the hag. Everybody. Grandma, Mama, Papa and Aunt Mary would say, "Yeah, we know what it feel like, 'cause we have been haint ridden a number of times."

Mama said the hag was an evil old lady turned inside out, an ugly old lady turned inside out. Now, that didn't mean the hag would be oozing all over you, or was all slippery and slimy when it jumped on top of you. What "inside out" meant was that the hag had changed from one thing into something else, like by day, the hag was a little old lady sitting in a rocking chair shelling red peas, and at night she became totally different. Totally different.

Her manner turned inside out, her shape changed and she turned into the mysterious being that could fly through the night air, fly like a bird to your house and sneak in. There was always someplace in your house the hag could slip in whether it was through a crack under your door, your window or the floorboards. She would make herself real small and slip right in, and then would magnify herself and get big again. The hag would light on your back and ride you all night. She would ride your backside like you were a horse.

Winter or summer, she would come when she wanted to come and she would ride who she wanted to ride, and wasn't at all picky if you were an adult or a kid. Mama would say, "Sleep on your back, sleep on your back," because that was the only way you could protect yourself from the hag. If she caught us laying on our stomach, she'd make us flip over.

But there was only one way you could stop the hag from visiting altogether. You could put salt in an open bottle and leave it near the bed and the hag would fly into that bottle with the salt. The salt would hold her there and she couldn't get out. In the morning, you'd put a cap on the bottle and you'd say, "I gotcha now," and you could actually hear the hag screaming in the bottle, "Let me out, let me out." You buried the bottle in the ground then and the hag wouldn't bother you no more.

I listened to Mama and Grandma telling me about destroying the hag, about enticing it into that bottle with salt in it, because that's what Mama would do when she was little, and Grandma too, and I listened with my mouth wide open. I believed. I had no reason not to believe, because it was as real as daylight to them.

There was only one hag, not a whole group of them, but somehow, another hag must have always flown in then, because the hag was still here during my time. And Asberry and I just had to know who the hag was.

See, it was never said whether the hag was a living person who changed into the hag at night, or if she was a dead person who rose up from the grave after dark, just that she was an ugly old lady. So what popped into a kid's mind was a witch, like the one in the books at school. We went around looking for women that looked like that, and Cousin Alice looked just like that.

Cousin Alice was a Hall, and she was from Grandma's side of the family. She was a sister to Miss Katie, the midwife, and to Mr. Charles who owned the store. Cousin Alice grew up on Sapelo, but she was living over in Brunswick, and she was not a good-looking woman. Not at all. She was a tall, lanky woman and her front teeth kinda protruded and her eyes were small, and her mouth twisted toward the side.

She'd come to visit her family and if you saw her, you got a little fright and you thought, "Oh my goodness, it's her. She's the one that turns into the hag at night and flies over and rides you." We put all the blame on Cousin Alice then, and actually, I found out later when I was older that Cousin Alice was a very nice woman. But at the time, we didn't hang around long enough to tell if she was friendly or not, and Asberry and I weren't the only ones who thought she was the hag. Asberry and his friends whispered about her. They all believed she was the hag, and one of those kids was even her grand-nephew, and here he was talking about his own aunt that way.

Mama told us, "Y'all quit picking on Cousin Alice. Leave grown people alone." But she didn't say it wasn't Cousin Alice, and that didn't help at all. It was like, "Gee, does she think Cousin Alice is the hag too?"

Now, I was never scared of the night. I liked it, I liked the moon and the stars and everything about that mysterious time of day, and when it was time to go to bed, I would sleep and dream, and nothing interrupted that sleep until morning, except for Papa on the week-ends. Until the night the stories of the hag came true, that is.

I was going off to sleep, just like normal, and all of a sudden, I woke up and this weight was pressing down on me. I could feel the weight from my head down to my thighs. It was like somebody dropped this one-thousand-pound weight on me, very s-l-o-w-l-y. Something was on top of me, it was pinning me down, it was on my back riding me, and then I knew. "The hag is riding me. Uh-oh, the hag is riding me!"

I was going, "Why is it bothering me? I ain't done anything to it? Asberry, yes, but I ain't done anything to it." But it was squeezing down, down, down on me. Slowly squeezing the air out of me, like squeezing a balloon till the air is all gone. I was being suffocated right there in the bed.

I was crying out, "Mama, Papa, somebody! Come help!" I was yelling my heart out, I was screaming my lungs out, and nobody came. Nobody was gonna come. It was like they had left me, left out of the house. They were sound asleep in their beds and there was nothing but darkness and this thing holding me down.

I was struggling and thinking, "Maybe if I kick the wall, someone will hear me. Mama's a light sleeper, she'll hear me." But I couldn't move. My voice wasn't working, my arms weren't working and my legs weren't working. Nothing was responding, but I wasn't asleep. My senses were too sharp.

My brain was still working and half of it said, "You can move. You can move," and the other half was saying, "You can't move. It's too heavy. You can't move."

The two halves of my brain argued back and forth and I held on with all my might to the one that said, "You can move. You can move. If you can move, you can throw it off," and I moved and the hag rolled off onto the floor and *poof*! It was gone. It was gone. And it never came back and rode me again.

◆

Chapter Fifteen

The Bolito Man

MAMA DIDN'T DANCE, MAMA DIDN'T DRINK—SHE didn't even taste her moonshine when she was making it, she just eye-balled it to see if it looked right—and Mama didn't play Bolito. But Mama didn't mind telling Aunt Mary her dreams so Aunt Mary could see if she could find a number in them for Bolito.

Bolito was *big* on this coast, child, not just on this island, when I was growing up in the 1950s. Everybody knew about the Bolito Man: the numbers man, the numbers racket man. It was illegal, just like moonshine was, but the numbers game was important to people. If you took a chance on one piece at ten cents, you would get a seven-dollar return if you won. If you spent a quarter and your number won, and you got twenty-five dollars, well, heck, your salary wasn't even twenty-five dollars for the whole week on Sapelo. So you picked a number and you took a chance.

Bolito hadn't been around too many decades, at least not in this area of the world, though I suspect some form of gambling's existed since the beginning of time. The Bolito Man was definitely newer than God or Dr. Buzzard was on Sapelo, which is why the expression is "God, Dr. Buzzard *and* The Bolito Man," but all three used your beliefs in the supernatural, dreams, signs and magic, all three helped you reverse your luck, and all three worked together on your behalf.

We believed God's hand was in everything, but that there were certain things you didn't ask God for. Just like you didn't ask God for revenge, that's what Dr. Buzzard was for, you didn't ask God for money, because money, according to the preacher, was the root of all evil. You did a hard day's work to get your money. Now, you could pray to God and ask him to better your *condition*; that was okay, you hadn't said "money," and if God saw fit, he'd send you a dream you could use for Bolito. Then if you won, you could say, "God gave me that number," and that justified it.

Dreams were taken seriously on Sapelo. Nobody laughed at dreams. They gave you signs of everything from upcoming deaths to births on the island, as well as a Bolito number now and then, and all of them came from God, just as your dream did that allowed you to join the church when you were twelve years old.

First thing in the morning, as soon as Mama woke up and remembered, she'd tell one of us what she had dreamed and that way she locked it into her memory. Then when she'd get together with Aunt Mary or some of the other ladies, she would repeat her dream word for word, exactly the same way.

The ladies on the island always got together and deciphered their dreams. Whether they were washing clothes, visiting the sick or just visiting, if you got more than one lady together, they'd start talking about their dreams. One lady might say, "Girl, I dreamed about you last night and you were sick, *God*! you were sick." The lady she dreamed about would say, "You watch my words, some-body's bound to be sick in the family," because the dream meant that illness would strike in her family, not at her necessarily. They'd sit back and wait then and when someone got sick, they'd say, "Chile, remember that dream we talked about last week? We already knew that."

A dream of fish meant you were in the family way. If you were a young lady and were married, then the ladies would say, "That's good, baby. I know you're gonna have good luck." But if you weren't married, a young lady was afraid to get up in the morning and say, "Mama, I dreamed about fish last night." She'd look at you like, "What have you been up to? What have you been doing?" You'd be in hot water then. You'd better keep that dream to yourself.

If you dreamed about a dangerous snake like a rattlesnake, it was a bad sign if the snake got away. If it turned and ran in your dream and you didn't kill it, then it meant that you had an enemy, a very dangerous enemy, out there prowling. But if you were able to kill it in your dream, you had conquered your enemy. Your enemy was gone, and that was a sign of good luck then. So the old people always said, "Don't let that snake get away. Don't let that snake get away," and they carried that over to real life. They would get in a frenzy almost to kill any rattlesnake they saw.

A lot of dreams meant just the opposite of what you dreamed about. If you dreamed about an old woman, not a particular old woman, just an old woman, then your dream was about a young girl. If you dreamed about a young boy, then your dream was about an old man. If you dreamed about someone dying, it meant someone was going to be born. Then when a child was born, the woman who dreamed about it would say, "I knowed somebody was gonna come into this world."

So they picked their dreams apart for news—and for signs for Bolito, because everybody knew that dreams gave you the best numbers for Bolito. Almost all the ladies played Bolito. The men didn't much. If they had any extra money, they probably spent it on moonshine, but the women sure did, and the dreams for Bolito worked like this: If one of the ladies dreamed about me or you, she'd think nothing of asking you what your age was. She'd say, "How old are you now?" You might say, "I'm forty-nine. Why?"

"Well, I dreamed about you last night." Then she'd play Bolito. When they dreamed about you and played your age, *bam*! Very seldom did that number fail. If you were forty-nine, they'd play forty-nine. Then they'd play ninety-four. You could also break it down and play single fours and single nines, as many as you could afford.

Every week Aunt Mary would pick a number to play and after she did, she'd say, "Hettie, you want to play the numbers with me?" And Mama would always say, "No-no-no, that's alright."

Mama made her moonshine. She knew that was illegal, but the money she got from that was her way of helping her family. Her thinking was, "Well, I'll do that one. That's not too bad." But she drew the line at Bolito. Mama didn't like taking chances. She didn't have any money to waste.

Aunt Mary was the complete opposite of Mama. She liked drinking, she liked arguing, she kinda thrived on it, and she liked taking chances. Aunt Mary decided what was right for Aunt Mary. She didn't *not* do something just because someone felt it was wrong. She had Grandma's temperament.

Aunt Mary was one of the children Grandma had before she married Grandpa, and her father had been a Walker. She was tall and dark skinned with high cheekbones, and she had the Walker stomach; a stomach that all the Walkers had that sat up high on them. She carried it well and she stood straight and she stepped high like a thoroughbred horse. Mama didn't dress up if she wasn't going out, but Aunt Mary was always well groomed, even at home. Every hair was in place and she'd have little gold earrings on and a blue dress. She always wore blue. She liked all shades of blue but she *loved* royal blue and I think she thought she was royalty anyway, the way she held her head up and she stepped so high.

Aunt Mary's favorite way to pick her numbers was through dreams, but there were other ways to get numbers, and one of them was through a black newspaper called the *Pittsburgh Courier*, from Pennsylvania. Porters and bellhops carried it all over the country by train so it became very popular. Black people everywhere got that paper, and Aunt Mary and Uncle Joe would buy it from someone on the mainland. It had news of the black community and world news but what Aunt Mary paid the most attention to was a cartoon right in the middle of the newspaper called "Sunyboy," and Sunyboy was a black character.

Sometimes, we'd go to Aunt Mary's with Mama, and Aunt Mary and Aunt Annie Mae would be looking at the Sunyboy cartoon. Aunt Mary would have her magnifying glass out and they'd go over the cartoon. Aunt Mary would say, "Umnn, Sunyboy's talking to that guy over there and if I'm not mistaken, that looks like a six coming out of his mouth. A whole lot of sixes coming off his tongue." Or, "You notice Sunyboy's shoelace? How it's tied like a eight?" Aunt Annie Mae would say, "Gosh, he's wearing three hats on his head. Why's he wearing three hats?"

Everything was a potential number. Everything in that cartoon. Whatsoever Sunyboy happened to be doing, Aunt Mary and Aunt Annie Mae were interested, and Aunt Mary would have her dream book by her side to help unscramble those shapes she and Aunt Annie Mae found in the cartoon. A dream book is like an alphabetical dictionary of dreams with numbers beside them. It's a little, thin paperback book you could get on the mainland, in the five-and-dime or the drugstore and the ladies would buy one of those and keep it for life. For instance, if Aunt Mary wanted to find the number for hats, she would look in the dream book under hat. Then, if that number were thirty-two, she'd play thirty-two. So the dream book, the Sunyboy cartoon from the *Pittsburgh Courier* and the magnifying glass was another way to get your numbers for Bolito.

There was another way to pick a number too, and the frog played a part, the big, swarthy, warty black bullfrog. It was never a green frog, always the bullfrog. The women would be talking about the numbers and wondering what number is gonna fall, and one of them would say, "Let's catch a frog and give him a dime and see. Maybe my luck will change this week."

I never knew why they'd give a dime, it was one of those mystery things. I did find out later that on some of the islands near here, people wore a dime around their ankle to insure good luck, so it had magic to it. A dime was 100 percent silver back then, so it was a pure coin. That may have had something to do with it, and of course, a nickel or a quarter would have been too big to get down a frog's mouth anyway.

In the summertime, if it were after dark and we were at Aunt Mary's, she'd have a smoke bucket going by the big oak tree in her front yard. You put Spanish moss in a bucket and burned it and that helped chase the mosquitoes away. Then, before you'd go to bed, you'd carry that smoke bucket through the house. You'd wave it around the rooms, especially up under the bed, because the mosquitoes would hide there, and after you did that you could sleep peacefully.

One night Aunt Mary and Mama and Cousin Dorothy were sitting on the porch talking about what Bolito number was gonna fall. Asberry and me and Capus were sitting under that oak tree, not too far from that smoke bucket, and Aunt Mary told us kids, "Catch me one of those toad frogs."

I refused to have anything to do with frogs because the old people said that if a bullfrog peed on you, you'd get warts. But Asberry didn't care and there were always bullfrogs around your smoke bucket, the fire attracted them somehow, so Asberry found a frog, a big one, as wide as your palm. Finding that frog wasn't hard but a frog can hop fast, and this one went hopping all over the yard when Asberry tried to catch it. It ended up taking both Asberry and Capus to round it up and get it to Aunt Mary.

Aunt Mary took the frog and she cleaned its tummy off with an old piece of rag. She washed it and scrubbed till it was real clean and that tummy was its natural color, which is sorta a dull white. Then she opened the frog's mouth and fed it a dime. You know how you force a child to take medicine? It was like that. Aunt Mary held its mouth open and she slid the dime in the side of its mouth, then she rubbed the frog under its throat so it would relax. And that frog swallowed that dime.

Then she felt the frog's tummy. She probed and probed until she could feel that dime in there, and when she found it, she rubbed that spot some more so a number would show up, and said, "See here, Hettie, what do you think that looks like? Don't you think it looks like a six?"

Mama said, "Yeah, it look like a six to me." Mama was going to agree to whatever Aunt Mary said, because she knew if she said, "Naw, that looks like a nine to me," Aunt Mary would say, "Oh, Hettie, you just ain't looking at it right. That definitely's a six." Aunt Mary didn't need anybody's opinion anyhow. She had her own. You'd waste your breath if you tried to change Aunt Mary's mind. She was as stubborn as Grandma.

One time Aunt Mary and Mr. Charles Hall got into a heated argument and he called her something that was unbecoming to a lady. Aunt Mary got so mad she said, "You don't know who you're messing with. I'll kill you." She grabbed Mr. Hall by the balls and twisted hard and she brought him to his knees. It took two men to pull Aunt Mary off. She was Grandma's daughter alright. You did not mess with Mary Parker.

That frog got good treatment as long as Aunt Mary had it. It wasn't roughly treated at all. It's just that when she gave it back to Asberry, the frog didn't know it yet but it was doomed. When Mama and Aunt Mary weren't watching, Asberry bashed it with a stick, killed it and dissected it with his pocketknife. He had a dime then to go to Aunt Beulah's store to get ten grape jawbreakers.

Now, if a kid like Asberry hadn't been around, that frog would have been turned loose and for all I know, there could be some very old frogs with dimes in them over here. People over here were not going to even think about eating frogs like people do some places. I've heard it said that frog legs are delicious but that wasn't something we ate. You couldn't get a frog past the old people's lips. They'd go, "How can people think about eating them? It turns my stomach."

So the frog was for Bolito and it was also for calling the rain and that was it. Calling the rain was the real purpose we believed God had made the frog for. The frogs would get thirsty and you heard them making a racket calling for rain. The old people would listen for the frogs when it was dry and if they were calling for rain, they'd wish them luck. Then if it had been raining a long time and the frogs were still calling for rain Grandma or Mama would say, "Oh shut up. We got enough rain. Ain't you satisfied yet?"

Once you picked your numbers, you would take them to Miss Clara. There were other women who collected numbers sometimes, but Miss Clara was the one I knew. Miss Clara would send the packet of numbers to the mainland. If she didn't go herself, she'd send them by someone else. Then somebody else picked them up at the dock and passed them to the next person. Everything was passed secretly. Nothing was open. They didn't want to get anybody in trouble.

The same number was supposed to fall whether I lived in Brunswick or on Sapelo or anywhere in the surrounding area so there had to be a central location for the numbers somewhere. If you'd win, that money just appeared. Somebody would carry the earnings back on the boat. You'd get your money on Saturday, so you had a good day then.

The person in charge of the numbers was the Bolito Man. I always wanted to know who he was and how that winning number was thrown. I asked Mama one time, "Mama, who is the Bolito Man?" Mama said, "I don't know, baby, he lives somewhere on the other side."

So the Bolito Man wasn't on Sapelo, he was somewhere on the mainland. He could be anywhere, he could even be down in Florida near the palm trees. The old people said Bolito was a Cuban thing and there were Cubans there. A few of the ladies even had an expression, "Baby, play me a piece of Cuba." So he could have called from Florida with that winning number. He was a highly mysterious character that no one ever saw.

I pictured him as a devious-looking, medium-tall and slim brown man with fiery eyes, a goatee and processed hair. Men on Sapelo didn't process their hair much at all but somehow I thought men of the world had processed hair, so, naturally, the Bolito Man must have processed hair. He was showy and flashy in his suave suit and he had diamonds on his fingers that glittered.

His dress and appearance and everything about him was totally different from anybody I knew. Grandpa didn't look like that, Papa didn't look like that and I'd never seen any books with black men like that in them. The Sears catalog, which is what I saw the most, didn't even have black men in it then. But in my mind, I'd see the Bolito Man sitting behind a desk, very businesslike, because he had people he was bossing, like a king, waiting for his runners to come in and bring him some money.

One morning Mama woke up and she'd dreamed of Dan, Dan Gardner. Dan was the child of Uncle Joe's sister, Miss Rosa Parker Gardner. Aunt Mary and Uncle Joe promised Miss Rosa on her dying bed that they would take care of him. Miss Rosa was suffering at the time but she wouldn't go until she knew who was gonna take care of her baby. She had other children, but Dan was the youngest. He was about three years old at the time. When Aunt Mary and Uncle Joe told Miss Rosa they'd take Dan, Miss Rosa just closed her eyes and died. That was all she had been worried about, who was gonna take care of her baby.

Aunt Mary had only one child, Cousin Dorothy, whom she'd had before she and Uncle Joe married. Cousin Dorothy was grown up at that time and Aunt Mary was raising Cousin Dorothy's son, Joe Nathan, but Uncle Joe didn't have any children of his own, so Dan was like a child between them. He was their child together. Aunt Mary raised Dan and Mama helped her with him, so Dan was like a nephew to Mama. Mama liked Dan and he liked her. He looked a little like Uncle Joe and he was just as mannerly.

Dan was twenty-one years old at this time and he was overseas in the service, right after the Korean War, so it was about 1953. When Mama reported her dream to Aunt Mary like she always did, Aunt Mary instantly said, "Play that number! Play that number!" Mama broke down and played the number for Dan's age. It was the first time and only time Mama ever played the numbers and she won. She won twenty-five dollars, and she ordered a dress for herself from the Sears catalog.

It was a pretty dress, a coat suit, matter of fact, with a skirt and jacket, and it was a blue color, a light blue. Mama wore all colors, but I think she liked green the best, so why she got blue, I don't know. But it was fitting, since Aunt Mary always wore blue and it was Aunt Mary who got her to play.

The new suit came in time for Mama to wear it for Anniversary Sunday, the first Sunday in May. That's a church occasion, the anniversary of the founding of First African Baptist Church, but it's like a holiday. The weather was warm that year and people were fanning themselves, and there was a whole collection of people. Everybody who was over on the mainland at the time came home for it, and then there were all the people from the guest church on the mainland too.

The elders always invite a church from the other side to conduct the service to whip up some excitement, because people will come just to hear a guest minister. If that guest minister's any good at all, he gets everybody in an uproar and some of the ladies will be jumping up and screaming and praising the Lord.

The guest church sends a letter back saying they'll come and then the minister, the choir and half the congregation comes over on the boat. The company boat back then was the *Tarpon*, an old shrimp boat that didn't hold more than about twenty-five people at the most. So the Tarpon had to make a lot of trips for Anniversary Sunday. There were also black people on the other side who owned their own shrimp boat, and they brought more people over.

Everybody stood outside the church and talked that day, like they always did, and the ladies were watching who was coming to church and whispering, "My Lord, I haven't seen her in ages. What brings Arlene on Sapelo today?" Or, "Did you see Hettie? She even got a new dress." That's what they said about Mama. "Hettie's got herself a new dress." Mama hadn't had a new store-bought dress in years.

Mama was all dolled up, she had her hair down long in a pageboy with bangs, like the little Dutch boy on the can of cleanser, and she had on her light blue suit, some white dress shoes, a white hat and a white purse. She was color coordinated.

No one on Sapelo ever got arrested for *playing* Bolito. The law always went for the big guy, for the guys in the houses that collected the money for the numbers and those people didn't live on Sapelo. We would hear talk of people getting busted. I'd hear someone say something like, "Chile, you know that numbers house that Uncle Bernice goes to in Brunswick? That's my cousins Sadie and Harry's. They got busted last night." But being on an island away from the mainland, you felt safe from the law. So Mama didn't have to worry about anyone taking her blue suit away. She wore that suit till it wore out. She was *proud* of that suit. Dan gave her that suit, she said, Dan, and God.

Aunt Mary tried to entice her to play again but Mama held her ground. "No-no-no, that's alright. That was a stroke of luck," she said, and she never played the numbers again. She left it alone from then on.

Chapter Sixteen

God Resides in the East

WHEN I'D GO TO SAY MY NIGHTLY PRAYER, I'D BET-
ter not, I repeat, I'd better not let Mama catch me with my head
turned to the West. I was up for a good fussing at if she did.

"What do you think you're doing? Get off your knees," Mama
would say. "Do you know where you're lookin' at? You're lookin' at
the West. Do you know who sits in the West? You better turn your
butt around this way."

I mean, "Whew." I'd better find that East direction quick.

Mama and Papa and all the old people always said, "God resides
in the East and the devil resides in the West." They firmly believed
that.

The first thing I learned when it came to directions, was East
and West. Forget the South and the North. I knew at an early age
that the sun rose in the East, so it was easy to pinpoint, and I knew
the West, because the sun sets there and the darkness begins. So I
knew my directions and who I was supposed to be praying to and
who I was supposed to be avoiding. It was God resides in the East.
Pray to God, not the devil.

We had Muslim and Christian beliefs blended in our religious rituals and praying to the East was the most important Muslim one. Bilali was Muslim and he believed in his faith. It's said that during the War of 1812, when Thomas Spalding gave Bilali firearms so the slaves could fend off any British that came, he asked Bilali if the slaves could be trusted. Bilali answered, "I can only account for my people. I cannot account for the Christian dogs that you have."

Even if that isn't a true story, Bilali wouldn't have had much regard for them. He prayed to the Islamic God and he would have believed he had the true faith. There were Christians here, though, and while Bilali was already Muslim when he got here, we don't know how the people who were Christian got their beliefs.

On some plantations there were churches, and slaveholders would have their slaves sit up in the balcony and pray because they thought it had a "civilizing" effect on them. There's no record of a church on Sapelo in slavery days, though. The Spaldings went to church over to Darien on the mainland. So did some of the Africans get introduced to Christianity by the British before they got here? Did traveling ministers come to Sapelo, as they did some places? All I know is that Grandma said that people had to sneak out into the woods at night to pray. But were they Muslims or Christians? Or did they follow African religions? Most people probably had held to African ways. Grandma didn't say.

When freedom came, Bilali's children and grandchildren formed the First African Baptist Church. Some of them would have been Muslim still and some likely were Christians by then, and they wanted to go to church together. So they patched things up, and they used Muslim traditions in a Christian church. There must have been some resistance, though, because there were about five hundred people over here after slavery and eight people were baptized the first year. The next year a few more were baptized. So there weren't any mass baptisms. It was a gradual thing but eventually everyone joined. You prayed to the East, and the congregation faced the East. You were buried in the cemetery with your foot stone to the East. Your feet were pointed to the East, and your head was looking that way, so when Judgment Day came and you rose up, you'd be standing looking toward the East when Gabriel blew his horn.

Everybody went to church on Communion Sunday. We call it First Sunday, the first Sunday of the month. Whether you went to church in between times or not, you went then. Only a couple of the ministers we had were born and raised on Sapelo. The others came from as far away as Savannah and they would ride the company boat over for First Sunday.

We'd walk up to the Bluff and there'd be people coming by truck, by horse and wagon, or by foot, and everybody was wearing their Sunday best. The men always had suits on and the women had on dresses, but those dresses weren't sleeveless. You couldn't come to church with bare arms. Never. That's right. You had to have your shoulders and upper part of your arms covered. It was disrespectful not to, and the women also had to have their heads covered by a hat at all times.

The First African Baptist Church was a big whitewashed church that had a steeple and a bell, *the* bell. In fact that was the bell that rang when I died. The church also had a tin roof that was shiny when the church was built, but when it started to rust it was painted a dull copper-looking red.

The church had pretty lavender stained glass windows with veins of white running through them like somebody took a stick and swirled white paint in the glass.

Surrounding the church were trees with benches where people

would sit before and after church and talk, gossip and catch up with any news.

We'd walk into the church together and then we'd separate, and that was another Muslim tradition. The men didn't sit with the women. Papa would join the men on the left side of the church and Mama would join the women on the right. There was a third row of benches too, a short row in the middle that was mostly for young adults and children. Asberry and I were big enough to sit there now and we had asked Mama, "Can we sit in the middle row? Can we sit in the middle row?"

The deacons and the choir would be up front, with the deacons on the left and the choir on the right, and there was an arch above the pulpit and a small hand-lettered sign that said First African Baptist Church, Organized May 2, 1866. The preacher sat in the pulpit in a high-backed chair that was simple, but it looked so regal. All the cloths on tables and the pulpit and the carpet were a wine-colored red, a holy red for the blood of Jesus.

First Sunday would start with Sunday school and when it was over, the men would go outside for a breather, but the ladies very seldom left their seats, and a few minutes later, church would begin. Two deacons would get up and begin the service and one would tell you to open your hymn book to a certain song and he'd read the first stanza, and then you'd sing it behind him. As soon as that last note was out of the congregation's mouth, then the deacon picked it up and read the next stanza, and then the congregation would sing it right behind him, and so forth. And that's called raising the hymn.

The second deacon gets down on his knees and leads the congregation in a prayer then, and there would be a song, an uplifting song like, "We Are Climbing Jacob's Ladder." That song would bring the spirit into the church, so things would start out lively and the whole service would be lively. Then, after the Lord's Prayer, and that was usually sung, it was time for the minister.

When the minister would start to preach, you were ready. We had a minister that sometimes would start off mild. He'd start teaching the text he wanted to get into, and all of a sudden, he'd start the preaching, and the tempo started going up, up, up, and the ladies started tapping their feet and the men started saying "Amen" and stomping their feet, and hands started to clap, and heads started to nod, and it would keep getting to a higher pitch. And then the minister would cut off, *bam*, and there were still some little old ladies in the back screaming, "Hallelujah! Hallelujah!"

The pianist would strike up a chord and then the music would start and the congregation and the choir would fall in line with each other like they'd been practicing for weeks, and everybody would be singing, say, "Amazing Grace." Everybody was in the same mood, they knew exactly where to come in without anybody leading the song and the whole church was rocking then. The whole church was moving. Even the building seemed like it was swinging gently with you.

The collections were taken up and prayed over by a deacon, and then the head deacon would get up and he'd talk about the text that the minister talked about. He'd say what a nice service it was, and why y'all should pay attention to what the preacher said. And sometimes, he'd go on and on. Finally the snow white cloth over the communion tray was lifted and communion was served and there were more songs and more prayers.

The kids would be getting fidgety, and grownups sleepy, and we never would have gotten out of there if it wasn't for Miss Clara. Miss Clara Hillery. She would listen for awhile and then when they'd go on too long, she'd start up. "Shut up, shut up, shut up, people wanta go home. All that long-time talk. *Sit down, sit down, sit down.* People wanta go home."

We kids couldn't say "yeah" but we were hoping they'd hear her, and her voice would go all the way up to the front. Most of the time they'd cut it off a little short because once she started, Miss Clara wasn't gonna stop. She'd say it again and again. "*Shut up, shut up, my Lord, my Lord, shut up. Shut up, now.*"

Miss Clara's son, Mr. Jimmy, was a deacon, and he'd be up front and that was his mama back there doing that, but if it bothered him, he didn't show it. He had his own thing. He had a series of musical grunts. You'd watch him and if he disapproved of what the preacher or one of the deacons was saying, he'd shake that head and go, "*Uh-uh, uh-uh, uh-uh-uh-uh.*" Then if he approved, he'd go, "*Uhm-uhmm, Uhm-uhm, um-um-um-um.*" So he and his mama were quite a combination.

One morning after my twelfth birthday, Mama told me that it was time for me to go join the church. Twelve was an important age to us. When you turned twelve, you were no longer a child. You were supposed to be responsible for your own sins and actions, and the old people would start referring to you as a sinner if you didn't get baptized then.

I couldn't just stand up and profess myself. There was a whole ritual to joining the church. Depending on your teacher, that ritual took you two or three months, and a long period where you study with a teacher may have been another Muslim tradition. You *had* to have a teacher to guide you and you would pick one of the elders of the church to be your teacher.

I picked Mr. James Spaulding, who was a deacon from Raccoon

Bluff, but he was living in Hog Hammock by then, right down the road from us. He was a tall, light-skinned guy with gray hair. He was nice-looking, all the Spauldings were—and he was from a family over here who had taken the Spalding name after the Civil War, but spelled their name with a *u* in it usually—and he was nice to children. You had no fear of Mr. James Spaulding.

I went to Mr. James Spaulding's house and the first thing he said was "Alright, there ain't gonna be no more playing with your friends no more."

"Yes, sir."

"You must be good, because good dreams don't come to children who misbehave, and I want you to read, every day you come, a Bible verse for me."

So you started the process of cleansing yourself. You'd study and you'd pray, and everything led up to your having a special, spiritual dream that meant you were ready to become a member of the church. You had to prepare yourself to receive that dream.

For the first two or three weeks, you'd go to your teacher every day, and he watched you carefully. He wanted to make sure you understood what you were learning. I'd get a Bible verse from Mama or find one myself, and I'd read it to him, and then he'd explain it to me. Like, Genesis, Chapter One, Verse One. "In the beginning, God created the heavens and the earth." Mr. James Spaulding would say, "What the Bible means is that this was the beginning of time. God created the heavens and the earth and everything. The earth belongs to God, not man. We were created later to take care of the earth, and to obey him."

After awhile he told me, "Do exactly as I tell you, now. You must do exactly as I say. You have to find your own place now, a secret place, and when you go seeking, that's your own special place.

Nobody must know about it but you. You go by yourself out there to pray and talk to God."

I picked a pine tree off in the woods, and I made it my tree. It was the tallest tree around and it was in an East direction, to the East of the house. Nobody went there but me. I'd go to the tree three times a day, like Mr. James Spaulding told me. Morning, noon, and at night.

When your teacher decided you were ready, you had to get out of bed at midnight and go out to your private place to pray. If I wasn't awake, Mama or Papa would wake me up when midnight came. "Okay, baby, time for you to go outside and go seeking. You go ahead out, I'll be right here when you come back." So I'd go out in the dark into the wilderness and go seeking.

I was never afraid of the dark, it was just that I had to stay by myself, and I got used to that after awhile. Papa would say, "Girl, there ain't nuttin' to be frightened of. Just go out there, nuttin' will bother you. I'll be right here when you come back." So you'd figure that God would take care of you and you weren't going to step on a snake or something. You had to believe that.

I'd go out to my pine tree and kneel down and pray for an hour, or if I didn't feel like kneeling anymore, I'd sit there with my back to the tree. I'd hear frogs and cicadas chirping and a hoot owl hooting sometimes and out in the dark by myself, the sounds were louder than they've been before, but I did not abandon my purpose. You were not supposed to let anything take you away from your purpose. If a mosquito bit me, I'd brush it off and ignore it. I went outside at midnight every night for almost a month, and then I'd go back home, and clean my feet off before bed.

I had to recite my dreams to Mr. James Spaulding too. When I first started, my dreams would be things like, say you and I were playing down the road and I'd throw a stick at a cat. Mr. James Spaulding would listen and say, "You doin' everything I tell you?"

Gradually, my dreams started changing and finally, one night I dreamed about angels. There were angels flying around in my dream, and there was one angel who wore a yellow robe. The rest wore white robes and I could understand that because we believed white's for purity, see, so they were in white, all except for that one angel in a yellow robe. I told my dream to Mr. James Spaulding and he said, "You're ready to go before them now," and I became a candidate for baptism.

I had to repeat that dream before all of the deacons, hoping I did it right and they'd give that final nod of the head that everything is okay. I repeated it as best I could and they all nodded their heads. It wasn't traditional at all, having an angel in a yellow robe, but they all nodded their heads. I never knew what it meant, but that yellow robe was pretty, and it was happy-looking. Maybe that's why I dreamed it or maybe it was just that I was a little different from most kids. Some people elsewhere believe that the color yellow can be for inspiration or quickness of mind, but I'd never heard that then. But I passed.

I was baptized in June, on the Saturday before First Sunday, which is how we always did it at that time, and the sun was warm and the water was cool but not cold. Mama made a white robe for me out of a sheet and a white head rag tied in the middle of my forehead. Mama used a white string and tied the robe around my ankles so it wouldn't fly up when I got in the water.

That day there were five of us for baptism and we marched down to Blackbeard Creek singing "Shall We Gather at the River," with the elders following us, and half the congregation was standing up on the landing watching because baptism was a big occasion. Mama and Papa were there watching and Asberry was there and Grandpa had come down to the landing too. Grandma hadn't because her arthritis was bad, but we were to her house before the baptism. The deaconess and the deacons were watching and my playmates were watching, and I'd get condemned or blessed by the elders and teased by Asberry and my friends if I didn't do right. Your friends came just so they can tease you at school on Monday.

A lot of kids were scared when they went in the water to get baptized. You didn't know how to swim, usually, and your parents had been telling you, "Stay out of that water, stay out of that water, y'all drown, messing around in that water." Then they'd tell you it was time to join the church and get baptized and all of a sudden they were saying, "Go in the water, go in the water." And it was like, "Oh, my God, I'm gonna drown."

Some kids came out of the water screaming at the top of their lungs and the ladies on the bank would be saying, "They're acting like someone gonna kill them in that water. No one's gonna kill them." And one girl panicked and knocked down the minister and the deacon one time.

I was last in line in my baptism group. I made it my business to be last in the line. I wanted to see how the other kids did, so if they made a mistake, I'd know how to behave differently.

The other kids did okay and my time came. A deacon came and got me and led me down into the water. The minister was standing in the water and he read something from his Bible and then he recited the Twenty-third Psalm, with the part that you shall not fear evil because the Lord is with you. And then he was ready to dunk me.

The deacon got on one side of me and the minister was on the other and I was facing the East. One held my head and one shoulder and the other held the other shoulder and held my nose shut and they both at the same moment tilted my head back in the water and when I came out of the water, my eyes were facing East.

So it was, "I baptize you in the name of the Father," and they dunked me in the water. I'd had my head in the water before, when I was playing, unlike some kids, but this was different. Someone was *holding* me under this time and I wasn't so sure whether to trust them.

They brought me back up kinda quick. "The Son." I was down in the water again, and this time the dunk was a little longer. "And the Holy Ghost." They held me down a little bit then. It was faith-testing time. They were testing my faith, and I knew that's when everybody was judging me. From the way I behaved, they'd say what kind of Christian I was gonna be. If I fought and sputtered, the ladies would say, "You see how she act when she came out of that water? You watch, she will be a little devil the rest of her life. Mark my words."

If I was frightened, it was just a little bit. I didn't let anybody know about it. The deacons said I was ready, so I had to be ready. I was saying to myself, "I don't care if it kills me, I'm coming out of this water with a smile on my face." And I did. All they could say about me was, "That Cornelia was ready to be baptized, alright."

The deacon led me out of the water and up to the shore and the ladies of the church dried me off with a big towel. Papa said, "I'm proud of you. You did good." Mama said that too, and then everybody dispersed and went home to get ready for the morrow.

Sunday was the big day. I wore a two-tone white dress, an organdy dress with flowers on it that Mama ordered from National Bella Hess. I had white pumps to match my dress and I had a white slip too, and that strap kept slipping off my right shoulder. I was supposed to be looking dignified and not pulling my strap up, but it'd slip off my shoulder and I couldn't stand it. I kept pulling that thing up and hoping no one saw.

The elders led the five of us who had been baptized up before the pulpit and one by one they shook our hands and the minister told us to pick an elder to guide you the rest of your life. It didn't have to be the same one who had been your teacher, but I picked Mr. James Spaulding again. Then we were led back to our seats and for that day only, we were on the first row up front with the adults.

At communion time, for the first time, those bread and wine trays did not pass me by. The deacons came down the aisle with a tray of bread, regular white bread, broken up in pieces; then they brought the wine. It was in glasses, tiny, little glasses that didn't hold much more than a thimble did, and it was sweet. After you were baptized into the church, from then on you would be able to have communion unless you were in trouble with the church. They'd refuse communion to someone who had not obeyed an order of the church. A deacon would keep an empty glass on the tray then, and when he stopped before you, he'd pick up that glass and turn it upside down, so everyone would know you had refused a direct order of the church, and that told you right there you'd better do what the church said.

At the end of the service, it was fellowship time. The congregation always marched up front and shook hands with the minister, the church officers and the deacons. Then everybody would shake hands with each other, and church was over then. This day the five of us had the honored position up front along with the ministers and other church staff. Everybody filed by and shook our hands first and congratulated us. It was the moment I had been waiting for. I was now a bona fide member of First A.B. Church. I sure was.

The Dog Finger

I HAD JUST STARTED TO LIKE GRANDMA THE WINTER she was staying with us, when *bam*. Everything changed. See, Grandma had a mean side to her and she did curses. I'm not talking about cussing, plain ordinary cussing. I'm talking about *the curse*.

Miss Nettie placed curses, she lived over at the Bluff, and she was kin to Grandma. Miss Sara Bell used the curse and she lived at the Bluff too. All the women in the Bluff that I knew did curses. Mama said the men used the curse also when she was growing up, but they didn't use the curse anymore. It was the women who put the curse on you.

The women would curse a person that was bad or ill-mannered, and they'd curse kids that would continue to do something they told them not to. They didn't think nothing of cursing their own kids or grandchildren either. And Grandma put a curse on me.

One day my brother Asberry came in the house after school and Grandma was in the living room. Asberry yelled, "Good evenin', Grandma."

"Good evenin', son."

I came in a minute or so behind, and as I was coming through the door, Grandma noticed me coming in, and I couldn't get the words "good evening" out fast enough to please her. I stuttered, sometimes, not bad, like when I was a kid, but I'd still stutter sometimes.

Grandma looked at me out of her good eye and said, "You no-manners wretch, you pass by me without speakin'. For that you'll never have no good luck, you'll have bad luck the rest of your days."

Mama came out of that kitchen charging like a she-bull, saying, "Mama, whatcha say to Cornelia?"

"The little wretch passed by me and wouldn't speak."

Mama said, "Well, you know she stutter and she can't get her words out as fast as other people. She did not mean not to speak to you."

I was crying my heart out and going, "Why she do that, Mama?"

Grandma cursed me for no good reason. I had all the intentions in the world of telling her "good evening." That and the way Mama came charging out of that kitchen probably canceled the whole thing, anyway, but Grandma didn't take it back. She mumbled something, but she didn't take the curse back.

Papa couldn't stand Grandma and Grandma couldn't stand Papa. Every time Papa would make Grandma mad, she would curse Papa and wag her finger at him. And it wasn't just any finger either—it was the pointer finger, the one next to the thumb, and we called it "the dog finger"—the finger you used to curse somebody. The dog finger is the finger the old people used for cursing. You didn't point any other finger, you pointed the finger right next to the thumb. I don't know why it was called the dog finger, but that's what it was called. And if someone pointed that finger in your face, you'd better watch out.

Papa and Grandma started out liking each other, but something went bad along the way. I think it was early on, because Papa would get mad and tell Mama, "Yeah, your mama's the one that told me when you was carrying all those chirren that I should go and get a girlfriend and not wait on you. What kind of mom would tell a son-in-law such a thing?"

Mama would get angry then and yell at Grandma, "What do you mean, my own mama, telling Hicks that? You think I don't know, but I know." Grandma was half deaf and she'd sit there and hum to herself like she didn't hear a thing, or she'd say, "Hicks is nuttin' but a liar. I didn't tell him nuttin' like that." And Mama would say, "Hicks' not a liar. I know he's telling the truth."

So that's probably what it was that made Papa not like Grandma, but whatever it was, they'd battle back and forth. God, they used to go at it. Grandma would call him all kinds of names and go, "God is gonna shorten your life for treatin' an old person like this and carryin' on the way you do." Papa would go, "Old woman, shut up. You'll die before I do." She'd be yelling at him and Papa would sass her right back. He was just as mean as she was, or meaner.

Mama would try to get in the middle of it and she'd lose, so she'd be sitting there begging Grandma to hush. "Hush, Mama. You got no reason to talk to Hicks like that." Grandma would act like she didn't hear Mama, and Mama would yell at Papa then. "That old lady is older than you, Hicks. Have some manners."

Papa didn't pay any attention. Grandma's curses didn't shorten his life any. When she placed the curse, she was usually already half drunk, and that probably weakened it right there. God wouldn't send it through.

Some people's curses were stronger than others and Miss Frances

Grovner was supposed to have one of the strongest. Miss Frances was very fair skinned with freckles and wavy hair, and she was short. She lived at the Bluff.

Asberry and I would stop by her house sometimes and get us a snack when we were little. We knew she'd have something good for us to eat, because Miss Frances was Asberry's godmother. She would say, "Come in, chirren," and according to the time of year, she'd give us grapes off her vine, or sweetened bread or watermelon. In the summer, it would be watermelon. She had them graded by size, and even if five or six children came up, everybody would get a fist-buster. A "fistbuster" is a small watermelon. They're the ones that stay out in your field and don't grow. You hit them with your fist and they bust open and that's why they're called fistbusters.

She and Mr. Reuben, that's her husband, would go all over the island selling watermelons. You'd see them coming in their wagon and they'd have big melons for fifty cents, medium ones for twenty-five cents and small ones for a dime. They would give away quite a bit too.

Miss Frances was Asberry's godmother, yes, but he didn't like her much. He sure didn't, and she didn't like him too much either at that time. See, Asberry hadn't joined the church. When Mama first told me it was time for me to join the church, I went to Miss Clara Hillery's to study, and Asberry did also. Then Ada wrote and invited us to come over to St. Simons for awhile that summer, so we thought, "Okay, we'll join the church later." But the next year we weren't going back to Miss Clara. That was the fussiest woman on God's green earth and she'd have a fit that we'd stopped in the first place. So I picked Mr. James Spaulding, but Asberry didn't go on with his studies, and to the old people, that made him a rank sinner.

The Dog Finger

Miss Frances was the mother of the church, and I don't think sinners and mothers of the church blended too well. The mother of the church always had an eye on young people to make sure you were behaving right. No leg crossing, no turning around, no talking in church, and they'd give you a signal when it was time to stand or sit. Holding their head up meant stand, lowering it meant sit. You learned the ways of the church from them after you became a member, and Miss Frances's own godson wasn't baptized.

Now, Miss Frances was a fun lady, but she didn't stand no stuff. You didn't want to cross Miss Frances. People talked about Miss Frances in hushed tones, like she had extra powers. And she did. She was even called in when it took someone a long time to die. When the person was suffering, but they couldn't go, Miss Frances would ease that person's path and make them pass over quicker. There were other women before Miss Frances that they'd call on, but Miss Frances was the one when I was young.

Once Miss Frances got in that room, she'd stay a little while, then she'd come out, and not too long after that, that person was gone. They didn't linger any longer. Some people said Miss Frances had a magic potion, some people said it was a prayer, but nobody knew exactly what she did, because nobody other than Miss Frances was allowed in the sick person's room. Prayer was involved, I'm pretty sure, but what else, I don't know.

Everybody knew she was good with the dog finger too, and the legend goes that one time Miss Frances had a few hard words with Mr. James Spaulding. They were about the same age and friends as far as I know, and Miss Frances was a mother of the church and Mr. James Spaulding was a deacon, so they were both elders of the church. It happened in the churchyard, as a matter of fact. They were standing there talking and something sparked them off. I never knew what it was, but they had an absolute good argument.

She started talking loud to him, he called her a few choice names that she didn't like, and once it turned personal, that was it. She ended up putting a curse on him. A harsh curse. The old people said Miss Frances wagged her dog finger at Mr. James Spaulding and said, "You will never have any good luck the rest of your life. You will go from piddle to post, like a fish in the sea, with no place to call home again."

To Mr. James Spaulding, it must have been almost like the hand of God striking him down right there in the churchyard. He must have felt that curse all the way to the bone. Mr. James Spaulding believed in the curse, he believed in the Bible, he believed in everything. And he totally believed in the power of curses, and Miss Frances's curses, and she'd just put a complete curse on him. She spelled out what was gonna happen to him, and how he'd never have a home of his own again.

As soon as it happened, the news went around quick, because if Miss Frances put a curse on you, everybody knew it was gonna happen.

Not long after that, Mr. James Spaulding's house burned down. He wasn't home at the time and Mr. Bilali Bell and some of the others at the Bluff saw the smoke and they tried to put it out, but the fire was too big. He lost everything when his house burned down. The old people said it was the curse and they felt sorry for poor Jim Spaulding.

I was pretty young when Miss Frances put that curse on him and I didn't think much about it until his house burned down. Then, it was like, uh-oh. All of a sudden, I gained respect for that dog finger. Before it was like, "Aw, there's nothing to that." Then it was like, "That curse is really working. I can see it working."

The Dog Finger

The night his house burned, he came up this way to the community and stayed with his sister-in-law, Miss Josephine, for awhile. They didn't get along too well, so he moved into a house across the road that her son had and that's where he was when I decided to join the church and he was my teacher.

I knew about the curse on Mr. James Spaulding, but that didn't stop me from picking him as my teacher. You'd hear the old people all the time saying about somebody, "Chile, that one had a curse put on him when he was young." Those curses were long lasting too and they'd follow you all the rest of your life. You couldn't pass your curse on to someone else, it wasn't contagious—the curse remained just between two people. You didn't stay away from someone just because he was cursed.

Mr. James Spaulding stayed in the house in Hog Hammock for about a year or two, two years at the most, and a little after I joined the church, he left the island. He went to Darien, to one of his daughters. He'd come home for church sometimes, but I didn't get to see him too much. So the elder I picked to be my guiding influence was gone. When he left that was it. You weren't asked to pick somebody new.

From Darien, Mr. James Spaulding went to Cannon Bluff, that's on the mainland too, to another one of his daughters. He moved to Savannah next, to a third daughter, and then he moved in with a grandchild. From there, he went to a nursing home and that's where Mr. James Spaulding died.

So after Miss Frances put a curse on him, Mr. James Spaulding didn't have no place to call home. He went from "piddle to post," as the old people called it, from pillar to post, just like Miss Frances said. From one place to another for the rest of his days.

One or two people said you could pray a curse off you but I don't know. It doesn't look like Mr. James Spaulding could, and I had such respect for that man that always I called him by his full name. I didn't ever say "Mr. Jim," I always said "Mr. James Spaulding."

I kinda think the only way you could lift a curse was not to believe in it in the first place, and on Sapelo, you believed, because you were raised up that way. You believed in the curse, and if you believed in it, then it was gonna be. It had power over you.

It didn't have anything to do with whether you were religious or not. Nothing at all to do with that. That's right. Matter of fact, Mama and Grandma and Aunt Mary told a story about Christ and the curse that went like this:

Jesus was quietly riding down a path with his mule. All of a sudden, the mule reared up and threw him off. He heard laughter and he looked round to figure out what it was. A dove had frightened the mule, so he told the dove, "For the rest of your life you will fly no higher than the top of the grass." And the flounder was the one that laughed, so Jesus got mad and said, "For the rest of your life, you'll always be looking at the sun, you'll never look down anymore." And he slapped the flounder so hard, he slapped both eyes on one side of the flounder's face.

So the old people said that's why the flounder has both eyes on one side of his face. It's because Christ put a curse on him. That story was about as familiar around our house as Brer Rabbit.

When I first heard that story I thought to myself, "He did? Christ did that? Who would think that Jesus would do something mean spirited like that?" I asked Mama, "Why'd he do that, Mama?" "Because he was mad," Mama said. I figured the sun was

A sand dune on Sapelo.
Looking east toward home.

There's no "welcome" on our Hog Hammock sign. If we feel you're part of us we will make you feel at home.

Me and Mama.

*Before 1967 everyone
on the island had an outhouse.*

*After the open well came
the hand pump. After the
hand pump came the spigot.*

The back of the Reynolds mansion.

The ruins at Chocolate. No one knows what they were used for.

The Sapelo lighthouse, built in 1820, guided many ships into the harbor, including slave ships.

Saw palmetto.

The youngest cast net maker on
Sapelo. Grandson of Hicks Walker.

One of the
baskets made
by my father,
Hicks Walker.

*Papa and his
cast net.*

*Allen Green
the basketmaker.*

Papa on his porch swing.

An herb we call Life Everlasting, and silver grass.

An oyster roast in honor of President Jimmy Carter's visit to Sapelo in 1979.

The Sapelo ferry.

My son Maurice leads wagon tours of the island with his mules, Pat and Mandy.

Me and Mama.

*Me and my
grandson, Gregory.*

Waiting for services to begin at St. Luke's Baptist Church.

hot and he was tired and Christ slipped one moment, and the next moment he was probably going, "Oh, what did I do?"

So even God's son made a mistake, and God didn't think less of his son for doing so. It kinda let me know that nobody's perfect and that maybe I could get by without Mr. James Spaulding being the guiding influence for the rest of my life.

C h a p t e r   E i g h t e e n

◆

The Buzzard Lope

FRIDAY NIGHTS WERE GAIETY TIME. PAPA AND HIS buddies would get their little bit of pay and they'd get together at one house or another and drink and have a good time. But there was more to it than that, because once they really hit the bottle, their anger at buckra for all they'd put up with that week would spill out. Then they'd go home and take it out on their families.

They were fun-loving men and they'd start off joyful but by the time the men would get up and do the Buzzard Lope, Papa would have tears in his eyes. Now, the Buzzard Lope is what everyone on Sapelo called a shout, and Geechee and Gullah people on some of the other islands called a ring dance shout. By "shout" I don't mean a loud or unruly shout from your mouth. It's more like a celebration, an organized celebration, done in a circle, to the beat of a stick, a broomstick.

I remember a Friday night when I was eleven and it was Papa's turn to have his buddies come to his house. Papa and his friends were sitting in straight-back chairs, eating roasted peanuts, drinking whiskey from little two-ounce glasses, and laughing about the old days when they were courting the girls and going to hot supper nights.

After a couple of drinks, they started berating and cussing their bosses for being so mean and hateful that week and the more they drank, the more they remembered all the hard times they'd been through and the sad things their families had told them that happened over here, and a sadness came over them. By that time, one of them picked up a harmonica and said, "That's enough of this mess, let's have some fun," and they started tapping their feet, clapping their hands and jumping up to dance, and that's when I saw Papa wiping his eyes and pretending he hadn't shed a tear.

They started with the Charleston and other dances that had been popular when they were young and after they felt brave enough, because it's not easy to do, they did the Buzzard Lope.

Sam Dixon grabbed the broomstick, and Papa threw a work handkerchief, a blue bandanna, down on the floor. He threw it just right, it had to be thrown just right, so it would have a peak in the middle of it, because that handkerchief was gonna be the buzzard's prey. Then Mr. Minus, Cousin Luke and Pete, that's Isadore Wilson, who later became my sister Winnie's husband, joined in and they all formed a circle around that handkerchief.

Asberry, Michael and Elise and I were laughing and cracking up because we were getting a free floor show. I was watching every move. You didn't get to see the Buzzard Lope every day. Papa learned it from his father, my Grandfather Gibb, and the other men learned it from their families. A lot of men on these islands knew the Buzzard Lope once, but it wasn't done much by the time I came along. So it was a special thing.

The buzzard was a big part of life over here. It was a bird that was both respected and hated at the same time. We were taught that the buzzard had a purpose for being here, that God put the buzzard here to do its natural thing of cleaning up the earth. Because if there was nothing to remove a dead horse by the road, it would be quite unpleasant to the eyes and nose.

I'd seen buzzards working on a dead horse, so I knew that's what the buzzard did. But if you were a kid who was kinda squeamish and you asked, "Why is the buzzard doing that? That's nasty," the old people would say, "It's doing its job, baby. It's doing its job."

Papa and the others were in their work clothes, in their bib overalls and their heavy, cut-off work boots, their brogans, and there was rhythm in that circle. You could hear the beating of the stick good on the wooden floor. That sound can fill up a room, now, and the men were moving around in the circle. Their arms were stretched out wide, gliding like a buzzard, because a buzzard can glide on that air current a long time, soar in that sky a long time, without flapping its wings.

Papa and the other men kept their arms out in that open, fluid way, flapping their wings once in awhile, moving their feet in a certain way, and going around and around in that circle, like a buzzard circling its prey. I was just amazed, I was going, "How can they be in their rough work clothes and be so fancy at the same time?" They were acting just like the buzzards do in real life.

They would hop forward a little, and hop back, forward a little, and back, getting close to their prey, but waiting to see if it's dead or not, before moving in for good. Because that's how the buzzard does. After the buzzards circle a good while, they will land close to that prey, to see if it's dead, and they will start hopping forward a little, and then they hop back, and they go forward a little, and then back, till one of them breaks away and goes in to check out the prey.

Then one of the men separated out, it was Papa, because he was one of the best dancers of the Buzzard Lope over here, so he got to imitate what the buzzard would do, the head buzzard, the turkey buzzard we have over here, the big black bird with the head that's as red as the thing under the turkey's neck. Papa was dancing that part, so he was the head buzzard, the king buzzard.

The head buzzard tastes the prey and sees whether it is worth eating or not, sees if it's poisoned or not. He has the power to check it out, to determine if it's poisoned or not. If it is poisoned, see, he's immune to it. That's the way the legend goes. That poison would kill all those other buzzards, but not the head buzzard. He was just like Dr. Buzzard, the root doctor you could find on some of these islands who's got these mysterious powers that make him immune to that poison. Then, if that prey isn't poisoned, the head buzzard signals the other buzzards, and they can move in and eat. They can feast on their prey.

Papa was moving forward and back, doing his solo dance, and the other men had stopped where they were in that circle, waiting on the head buzzard to go in. They kept moving their arms like wings, but they were staying where they were, and the rhythm of the stick was picking up. It was like a drum beating, because those shouts came from Africa, now. They got changed some over time, but shouts came over with us from Africa.

The beat of the stick was faster, the sound was louder, it was bouncing off the walls and vibrating back in the room, like it was alive. Papa had his arms out straight and every time he went forward, he was bending down a little, toward the floor, and getting back up. He was bending a little bit lower each time, getting himself ready. One knee was bent forward, the other leg was straight back, and he was going lower and low, until he was sure of himself. Until he could bend down almost to that handkerchief on the floor, but not quite, and then he knew that with his next bend, he could pick it up. Then he bent lower one more time, like the head buzzard going in, and he picked that handkerchief up with his teeth. He picked that handkerchief with the peak on it up off the floor, with his teeth, and he never fell on the floor.

I was going, "Whew! Papa can do that? How can those old guys do that?" Because they were all up in age. Papa was forty-two when I was born, and he was in his fifties now, and his friends were in their forties and fifties too. But they worked hard, they were in good shape and they could do the Buzzard Lope.

The stick stopped beating, the dancers quit and they were clapping their hands and congratulating him, "You did it well, the best you ever did." Asberry and I and Michael and Elise were clapping our hands too and laughing, and we were proud of our papa.

There's a story that goes with that dance and it is from the days of slavery. From a time when the people who were enslaved had a hard taskmaster, a very hard taskmaster, and they were working in the fields, in the sun, in the summertime, and that heat got to someone. It got to him bad, or maybe he was feeling poorly already, and the heat made him that much worse, and he fell over, dead in the field. The master wouldn't let the workers stop. He wasn't going to let two or three people stop to bury their family member until it was dark and they couldn't work any longer. But a whole day in August was a lifetime, and the buzzards came, and they circled around, and the head buzzard came in and checked out the prey and the other buzzards joined him, and they started their natural thing of cleaning up the earth.

If you're in a group and you hear a story like the one that goes with the Buzzard Lope, everyone instantly feels the same thing.

Your heart goes out. This awful feeling comes over you and you become one for that instant. That's how it was with Papa and his buddies. The men had a camaraderie out of this world when they were together, a sharing from the soul. They knew what it was like to work outside in the cold and not be allowed to stop and build a fire to warm themselves. They knew what it was like to have someone from the mainland come home and say they were making fifty dollars a week, and they were making twenty dollars a week, "and Reynolds has all that dang money." They knew what it was like not to be able to reach in their pocket to buy their child a new pair of shoes, to have to tie their kid's shoes together to keep the soles on.

They might take turns out acting the part of the buzzard in that dance but they weren't the buzzard. They were the prey. Black people had been bossed around and shoved around and picked on ever since we got here, and now, buckra wanted our land.

The community of Lumber Landing had just been closed the year before, in 1956. It had been owned by the Samses, a black family, since 1885. The Samses and the Bankses, nearly twenty people in all, had lived there when I was younger. When there was just one family left, they had been moved, just as Papa had been in 1950. Like us, they hadn't had too much choice about it, and that hurt. So, Friday night was rebellion time.

It wasn't until they would break up and separate from the group and go home that they would raise holy hell. One old lady over here would say, "The devil's gonna get in them this weekend and they're gonna rant and rave," and she was right. That devil got in them, for sure.

On Friday nights, we knew that Papa wasn't coming home till late. That if he and his friends weren't at our house, he had stopped by somebody's house, and he was drunk. He wasn't much of a big drinker back when we were at Belle Marsh, but things had changed.

Since we moved to Hog Hammock, he'd started coming in cussing and fussing and going, "I break my back and I don't get nuttin' for it, nuttin' but a hard way to go," and he'd be angry at the men who didn't pull their share on the job, because a lot of them didn't, now, and then he'd get angry at Cap'n Frank. He could not stand Cap'n Frank. He just could not stand him. He'd call him a damned cracker, and when Cap'n Frank's hair got white, he'd call him a white-haired bastard, and he'd say, "That white-haired bastard passed me driving a Jeep and it was raining and he wouldn't even give me a God damned ride."

Mama knew why he was angry. She just didn't like his drinking and she'd say, "Oh, you smell like an old mash barrel. Look at you," and if he lit into her, she'd start telling him how mean he was, and soon she'd be saying, "You got mo' mouth than a po' horse got behind," and Papa sure wasn't going to stop then.

He'd go to sleep for a few hours and then he'd get up. If there was something he had to do on Saturday, he'd stay around and do that first. But if there wasn't, as soon as he waked up, he was going back down the road someplace.

Come Saturday night, I would go to bed early, because I knew by the time he came home, I wasn't going to get any sleep for the rest of the night. I was going to lay in the bed and listen to an argument.

People always say don't argue with a person who's arguing and they'll soon shut up. But not Papa. He would argue all by himself. Mama could be perfectly quiet and not say anything, us kids could be quiet, and he would keep on cussing and fussing. He'd pick a topic and argue about it all night long. He'd tell Mama how whorish her mama was before she got married to Grandpa. He'd pick on Barbara. He didn't like her boyfriend, he'd say her boyfriend didn't mean her any good, he wasn't going to marry her; and Papa was right. He didn't marry her.

He'd pick on Michael and Elise and talk about not wanting any bastard kids in his house, especially if they belong to a married man. He loved Michael, he loved Elise, he just didn't like the facts of their birth, because Ada hadn't been married when she had either of them. He wasn't too hard on Michael, because Michael's father had been a single guy. He could accept that the man didn't see fit to marry his daughter, but at least he was single. But he couldn't stand it that Elise's father had been a married man. That was a different thing. Every time he looked at Elise, he saw that married man and he was off in a flying tantrum, and Elise wasn't to blame at all.

Sometime on Sunday, it would get quiet again, and Papa would bathe and shave and get ready to go to work on Monday morning, perfectly sober. Perfectly sober. Papa would become a perfect father and husband again on Monday. He wouldn't drink then, because he took his job and stuff seriously. He wouldn't take a toddy unless he was out in the rain and got a chill.

He would bring us kids persimmons or wild grapes that he found while he was working, or whatsoever happened to be ripe. He would work on his cast nets and do his regular things, he would tell us stories, and we had this perfect Monday, Tuesday, Wednesday, and Thursday, and Friday morning wasn't too bad. Then on Friday afternoon, we were visited by this man we didn't know. The one that was angry at buckra and took everything out on us, because he couldn't tell it to buckra. Papa wasn't the only one. A lot of the men over here were raising holy hell on the weekends, so they could face another week on the job. Some of them would hit their wives, to show her who was boss, though the women usually put a quick stop to that. Papa wasn't like that but his ranting and raving was almost worse.

When Papa couldn't take things no more, when he had to leave or he was gonna open his mouth at buckra and get his whole family in trouble, he would pack his grip, his little black grip that looked like a doctor's bag of old, but was a little bit bigger. He'd put his clothes in it, wipe his eyes and blow his nose and he'd say, "Okay, now, y'all take care of things," and off he'd go.

We'd stand and watch him go down the road, and he never turned around and looked back. We were sad then. We knew that Papa was coming back but he was gone now.

Papa would find a job on the mainland and he would be gone about three months, till he worked that anger out. Then one day he would just show up. We kids would see him coming up the road and we'd yell, "Mama, Mama, Papa's back!" And pretty soon things started all over again.

It made me stubborn. It made me determine that I didn't want life to be this way for me when I grew up. I didn't want a husband who would raise holy hell every weekend like clockwork. I wasn't going to put up with that the way Mama did. I wanted more out of life than that,—and I wanted to be stronger-willed than Mama, more like Papa, minus the drinking.

I asked Grandma about the Buzzard Lope once. "Grandma, did that happen over here?" and Grandma said, "That was a long time ago." She didn't dwell too much on things that were ugly. She didn't want to pass those things on to the next generation. She just got a faraway look on her face and said, "That was a long time ago," and that was all she said.

◆

Chapter Nineteen

In Come Dr. Buzzard

WE'D GO TO CHURCH, WE'D SHAKE HANDS AND WE'D
sing spirituals when I was growing up, but we believed in God, Dr.
Buzzard and the Bolito Man. I've told you about our belief in God
and in the Bolito Man already and now it's time to tell you about Dr.
Buzzard.

The church was a *huge* part of our lives. We went there to wor-
ship and to settle disputes. People were called before the elders for
adultery disputes, stealing disputes, fistfights, name calling and to
try and prove who was the rightful father of a child if a man denied
he was or if any woman other than Grandma had the nerve not to
tell.

But we had Dr. Buzzard too. Let's say I tried the church and that
didn't work. I'm still angry so I need to do something a little more
drastic. I'll try Dr. Buzzard." And *in come* Dr. Buzzard.

Dr. Buzzard was the root doctor. The conjurer. The worker of
black magic. He could put a spell on you and do you bodily harm. He
could lift a spell off you. He could even turn a spell around and
throw it back on the one that put it on you to begin with. Some

places people called that voodoo or hoodoo but over here we mostly said "root" or "mojo" to refer to the mysterious roots and herbs Dr. Buzzard used.

No one was safe from root, absolutely no one, and the old people had a hard time believing in natural illness. It was hard for them to take the word of a doctor about anything. Even if someone persuaded them and said, "Take them to the doctor, take them to the doctor," if the doctor didn't find an instant cure, then the illness was blamed on something different. *Entirely different.* Root. Somebody "fixed" somebody.

When my Aunt Della got breast cancer, Grandma refused to believe it was cancer. She said those doctors removed Della's breasts for nothing, that somebody worked root on her daughter. She went to Brunswick and got Aunt Della out of that hospital and brought her back over here. Aunt Della died at home and after that, Grandma didn't believe in hospitals anymore.

If people suspect someone of doing some evil thing to them, they get wary. I'm thinking of one man over here in his eighties who believed that someone tried to put root on him once. It happened forty years ago. But from that day on, he always has been on the watch for anything that's not normal and he will not eat any food he didn't cook himself, because you might put something in it and do him harm.

He was sick with pneumonia in the hospital once and the whole time he was there, he refused to eat. He didn't know those cooks. Those cooks didn't have no reason to do him harm, but he didn't trust them. The doctor had to let him go early because he would not eat. He went and stayed at his niece's house in Brunswick then, his own niece, now, and he would not eat anything from her either. It's that deep-seated in him.

In Come Dr. Buzzard

When I was growing up, I was completely surrounded by people who believe in root. Everybody over here believed, and I especially believed because Grandpa was known for doing some root.

Now, Grandpa was a religious person. He prayed to God and he read his Bible every day. But he fit into the category of believing in God, Dr. Buzzard and the Bolito Man. See, the old people didn't put their faith in God alone. God had his place, but so did Dr. Buzzard and so did the Bolito Man and it was almost like they didn't believe in one form of the supernatural any more than they did the others. It was like they said, "I'm gonna pray to God but God takes his time to answer, so I'm also gonna consult Dr. Buzzard and use this magic potion which will bring me faster results."

I can also see some of the old people thinking, "Maybe God intends for me to use this magic potion anyway. He granted me that knowledge, so it must be okay." Because they knew and the Good Lord above knew too that they needed some extra luck.

Grandpa dealt in white root mostly. Like if a man came and said, "Can you help me with somethin' so I can get a job? I'm down on my luck," he would give him something for good fortune. If a woman came and said, "I got a sore foot that's botherin' me. Will you help me?" Grandpa would give her a root to ward away illness. It was just like it was with the amulets he handed out. He did the kinds of things that give people hope and bettered their lives so he was well regarded.

Some of his roots grew on the island. He got other roots and powders mail order, from an outfit in Chicago and one in Atlanta. I know he got his High John the Conqueror root and Little John by mail. These two roots are pretty popular because they're for love problems; High John is the bigger and the more potent of the two.

Some people said that Grandpa helped them turn root back onto somebody they suspected of doing evil to them. He may have reversed the root if he figured there was no rightful reason for that evil spell to have been cast to begin with, but I don't think he made a practice of it.

I have a suspicion that Grandpa could have even conjured up the initial spell—the evil one—himself if he wanted to. He did have a mean streak in him. But he never did anything that I could see and Mama never said a word about her papa. So, all I know is that he was known *mostly* for good root.

The knowledge of root came to Sapelo and all the Sea Islands with our ancestors. In Africa voodoo was "wudu," "juju" was an evil spirit, and "wanga" was a charm. The first Dr. Buzzard in the Sea Islands got off the boat and began practicing root in St. Helena, South Carolina. He was said to be as powerful as a buzzard and to have the patience of a buzzard, and that's how he got his name. Ever since then, root workers in the Sea Islands have been known as Dr. Buzzard and it always has been said that the ones in South Carolina have the strongest root of all.

Sapelo was not ever really known for its root the way the South Carolina islands were, or even the way some places in Georgia, such as Savannah, were. We always had at least one or two rootworkers on Sapelo though. When Papa was young, old man Scipio Bell worked root and was good at it.

Old Man Scip Bell had a little store and he kept a "fix" around the door, a spell, so that if somebody broke in when he wasn't there, he would know. And sure enough, one day a little boy broke in and helped himself to some Red Bird crackers. He started eating them and when he went to leave, he got out to the front porch and he froze. He just *froze*. That little boy couldn't move for trying.

Mr. Scip got back and got him a switch and he gave the little boy the switching of his life and that little boy didn't ever bother Mr. Scip's shop again.

Mr. Scip had passed on by the time I came along. Mama Lizzie—I'll call her "Mama Lizzie" because I don't intend to use her real name, since there's no good reason I know of for all of our secrets to come to light—and plenty of reasons for this one not to—was the one that worked root then, the very woman at whose house Papa fell asleep after selling his ox, Bully, and lost all the money he got for his cow.

There were so many legends about Mama Lizzie, and a lot of them happened before I was born, that how can I say which ones are true or which ones are partially true? I can only tell you some of what the old people told me. And one thing is for sure, I never heard of her doing good root.

If you wanted to put an evil spell on somebody, you'd go see Mama Lizzie and she would mix you up a magic potion, the old people said. She would tell you how to slip the potion into somebody's drink or food and it would turn that person completely crazy or worse.

Her potions would poison you but they weren't any of the normal kind of poison that you could get your hands on. "Yeah, chile, I think that one may have been pis'ned," people would say, but they believed that poison had to be conjured up and put together by someone of stature. A root doctor could do it and get away with it because root doctors could do anything. They had strange powers the rest of us don't have. If you or I tried slipping poison in someone's drink, we would get arrested and put in jail, but with the root doctor, no one would ever be the wiser.

The old people thought that people with real dark complexions must be workers of root. The darker your complexion, and the redder your eyes, the more people thought you were a conjurer. I don't remember Mama Lizzie's eyes being red, that would have been unusual for sure, but she definitely fit the first part. She was a very dark woman, one of the darkest women here.

Mama Lizzie had been around a long time so she was kinda old when I got to know her. You could tell she had been quite pretty when she was young, though, and she still was a good-looking woman, with strong features and long hair. She liked wearing dark clothes so she had her own look, a mysterious look, and the air that hovered about her seemed charged. She stood erect as a person can stand and she looked straight at you and she demanded your total respect. You *had* to look at her when she looked at you, even if you were a kid and you weren't supposed to look an older person in the face. She compelled you almost. She had a certain power and she wasn't afraid of anything. Nothing intimidated her.

She would always have moonshine to sell so her house was a regular stop in the community. The men would go there and sit and talk and drink and some women would too, but the menfolks couldn't stay away. She drew them to her.

I knew that it was her house that Papa had stopped by the time he sold our ox, Bully, and the money he got for Bully was stolen. I heard Grandma and Mama and the other ladies talk about her doing root when they thought I wasn't listening, because root wasn't a subject that they talked to kids about. That was kept secret till we got a little older. I knew there was something about her, something powerful, but I didn't think much about any of that. She could be nice to little children and she would give us snacks to eat when we went to her house, just like the other ladies did. She made a delicious pound cake and that was enough right there to get me to stop by her house.

One day when I wasn't any more than six years old, I was over playing in Mama Lizzie's yard with some other kids and I saw for myself that Mama Lizzie had a mean side to her. A very *mean* side.

Mama Lizzie was in the yard and a neighbor lady came over to tell Mama Lizzie that her puppy had killed one of her chickens. It was a young chicken, a biddy.

"I saw you' puppy inside my chicken house killin' my biddies. You have to do sump'n about that dog," the lady said. She probably expected Mama Lizzie to tie up her puppy and whip it to try to break it of the habit because that's what most people did. That may sound cruel but you simply couldn't have a chicken-eating or egg-eating dog. Everyone on Sapelo kept a few chickens and those chickens and their eggs were food. You needed them for your survival, just like everything else you raised.

Mama Lizzie turned and called the puppy to her and this cute little black thing with a long tail came running to her, and when it did, she grabbed hold of its back legs and she swung it up against a big oak tree and she killed it. She did not hesitate a minute, she just swung it up hard against the tree and killed it. It was the most horrible thing I'd ever seen. It was her puppy alright, but it wasn't her puppy to bash up against a tree. I was going, "Gee whiz, if she did that to that puppy, what's she gonna do to me?" I stayed away from that house for a long time and I began taking the stories about Mama Lizzie more seriously than I did before.

Everyone on the whole island was afraid of her, including Cap'n

Frank. She had to be the only black person on the island he was afraid of. Most white people on the coast did not believe in root at all and so it had no power over them, but Cap'n Frank's family had been in these parts for a *long* time. He was totally entwined in a world where he knew that people practiced root. He would have seen peculiar things happen that he couldn't explain away except for mojo and he had the fear of root in him.

Cap'n Frank must have thought that she could put the evil hand on him if he didn't watch out, because he would stiffen up if he saw Mama Lizzie coming. His body would actually stiffen. If he was going out the door of his office and he saw her, he would turn around and go back into the building and close the door behind him. He was absolutely afraid of her and Mama Lizzie knew as much and she was proud of it. He was a power in just about everybody else's life but she had him in the palm of her hand.

Some folks said Mama Lizzie had killed a man once with her root. Cap'n Frank had heard the talk but he didn't have any proof whatsoever of it so he couldn't do a thing about it. He had to live with her being on the island every day, and the way he did it was to make sure he didn't cross her or do anything that would make her angry. That wasn't so odd, really, except for who he was, because the rest of us weren't gonna tangle with her either. Not lightly anyway.

The incident that raised everyone's suspicions took place a good while before I was born but people were still talking about it when I was growing up. One of the things I've learned from living on a small island where our roots have been for two hundred years is that our traditions get passed down, yes, but so do our hurts and angers. They can be handed down from generation to generation too. This particular hurt came about when Mama Lizzie's sister got pregnant and the word spread over the island that "Thomas," I'll call him because that was a common name here, was the one responsible. He denied it in no uncertain terms and he said, "Well, if she is, it's not mine and I'm not gonna marry her."

Some people said that a certain other young man was really the father, but Mama Lizzie's sister said Thomas was the father. Mama Lizzie believed her own sister, naturally, and when Thomas refused to marry her, Mama Lizzie said she was gonna do something about it.

His family was frightened by that and told Thomas that he absolutely shouldn't go by Mama Lizzie's house again—under no circumstances should he go. "But if you do go," they added, because they knew he stopped by there a good bit, "don't eat or drink anything from her house." They warned him that Mama Lizzie was angry and Thomas should have known what she was capable of, but what did he do? He went anyway. He was a smart fellow but there was something within him that wouldn't let him stay away.

He went to Mama Lizzie's with some other guys late one afternoon, believing that if he was with them, she wouldn't do anything to him and Mama Lizzie treated him so nice that he figured, "Well, she can't be that mad at me." The others were eating and drinking Miss Lizzie's stuff so Thomas did too, because there again, he thought he would be safe as long as he was eating and drinking the same things that they were.

Eventually, night fell and it was time to leave. Mama Lizzie was still being nice to them and she said, "C'mon, c'mon, take a drink, you can carry more with you." She went into the back room where she kept her whiskey and some little half-pint bottles and she filled their bottles one at a time while she was back there, and then she came back out and sent them home with their individual bottles.

Thomas started walking back to the Bluff, and that's about a seven-mile walk, and after awhile, he decided to sip from that bottle. He opened the whiskey and took a drink or two and right away he started feeling sick. He threw the rest of the bottle away and kept on going, slowly now because he wasn't feeling too well. He would have had plenty of time before reaching the Bluff to know how wrong he was to think Mama Lizzie was gonna forget her anger that quick. He made it home to Raccoon Bluff but he was sick as he could be. His brother took one look at him and asked Thomas where he'd been and what he'd had to eat and drink.

"At Mama Lizzie's."

"Are you a fool? You' not supposed to go to that lady' house. She accusin' you of gettin' her sister pregnant. Where's the bottle?"

Thomas told his brother where he threw the bottle at and his family went and found it and their worst fears were confirmed. The rest of the whiskey in the bottle was as green as gall. When Thomas had been drinking from that bottle, the whiskey was crystal clear. But now that whiskey was *green as gall*.

Thomas was ill from then on. His head hurt like crazy; all of his complaints were about the pain in his head. His family took him to a doctor on the other side but the doctor couldn't find anything wrong with his head. Thomas bounced back and forth for a while. Some days he would feel good and some days he felt like his whole head was gonna burst wide open and he got worse and worse. He lingered but he suffered until he died.

After he died, his family said that Thomas would still be living if he hadn't stopped by Mama Lizzie's. They believed that firmly and I don't think there was a soul over here who didn't believe it also. They didn't know exactly who the child that Mama Lizzie's sister was expecting belonged to but they were angry and they would tell you openly, "Mama Lizzie shouldn't have picked on our brother. We're gonna turn that spell back on her family."

They went to see a root doctor on the other side and I don't know how it was done but the hand of evil was turned back on the girl who accused Thomas of fathering her child and she developed the same complaints and the same illness. That was proof to his family that Thomas did not die a natural death, that his death was caused by root, because you were not supposed to be able to turn root back on a family unless someone in that family was guilty of having cast the first spell. It was Mama Lizzie's sister's turn to suffer then and she got worse and worse and she died when her baby, a girl, was eight months old.

The whole thing happened in about fourteen months. Mama Lizzie's sister sounded the alarm when she was three months' pregnant. Her baby was born six months later. Two months after that, she died. It was all over, for both her and Thomas. They were gone. Just like that. So Mama Lizzie took the baby girl and raised her.

You've probably heard how history repeats itself? Well, it came very close this time. That baby girl grew up and when she came of age, she got pregnant. She told Mama Lizzie who was responsible, just like her mother did, but at least her accusations were known to be right. She set her sights on a young man on the island and he was going with another young lady, and according to talk on the island, Mama Lizzie's niece threw herself at him, she enticed him and he gave into temptation. He might have told himself that he was just doing what any normal young man would do but he was caught because he didn't mean for it to happen but she got pregnant.

He didn't want to marry her and he didn't want to marry into that family. He tried to think how he could get out of it, but his father said, "No, you better do the right thing because you know what happened to Thomas. You better stand and face the music." So out of fear that Mama Lizzie would put root on him or someone in his family, he reluctantly gave up the lady who he loved to marry the one who had enticed him.

Thomas and the girl got married and had the child (and some others too) and he loved his kids out of this world but it's kinda a sad story. He always regretted the fact that he had to break the heart of the girl he loved to marry the other one and I think he resented being made to do that. Mama Lizzie's niece was trapped in her own way too. She got the man she had her eyes on but she spent the rest of her life hungering for true love, that real true love she could have had.

The legends continued to weave around Mama Lizzie. There was always something else to talk about, always another juicy morsel to chew on. Some of the men from the community were fishing down at Big Hole off Cabretta Beach one day and they saw some flames inland. They rowed their boat back to shore and rushed in because we didn't have a fire department. You had to reach the scene quick to put out a fire of any kind and this was totally different from any kind of fire they had ever seen. The flames had the weirdest colors. There were blue flames and green flames and red flames. Mama Lizzie's house was burning down.

The flames had just started shooting up all of a sudden and they got big so fast that there wasn't much time to haul water from a well and throw it on them Mama Lizzie's house was a regular little wooden house like all of us on the island had, and within minutes, that house was gone.

This was one time that everyone on the island felt bad for her because to lose your house is an awful thing, but Cap'n Frank put words to what everybody else was thinking. He had seen the strange flames but even if he hadn't, people would have come running to tell him and according to legend, Cap'n Frank said, "I'm sorry Mama Lizzie's house burned down but I sure hope her damn root burn' up with it."

That house was long gone when I was a kid and Mama Lizzie lived in another one but I knew where the first one had originally stood. Grandma said they never found any good reason why Mama Lizzie's house burned down. Maybe she was doing too many evil things just for the sake of doing evil and maybe the evil spirits from that stuff she was messing with had turned on her and burned it down.

There was a pecan tree right by the house site and people said that Mama Lizzie had buried her bottles of poison under that tree. The pecan tree never bore good pecans after the house burned and the old people took that as proof that Mama Lizzie had put her poison there. I heard the talk of course and I was a curious kid so when the pecans fell one fall, I went by and picked pecans up off the ground and tried them and you couldn't eat them for nothing. They were bitter, very bitter, like they were cursed.

There's a lot we don't understand about root and black magic and all beliefs in the supernatural, really, all the things that you can't prove and that I call the "unseen." And it was that way with Mama Lizzie too.

School would get out every afternoon at 3:15 P.M. and Asberry and I would walk home. I was in the third grade at this time, so it would have been about 1952 when we were walking home from school. We were just beginning to get fairly close to our house when I noticed this *big* black bird walking down the road. It was bigger than a crow, and the only black bird we have on the island bigger than that is the buzzard. I could swear it was a buzzard. It was big like a buzzard, it was black like a buzzard, but why was a buzzard walking down the road instead of flying?

We slowed our pace to watch it and it kept walking down the road. That big black bird never got off the road. We were just behind it and we kept walking and that bird kept walking. It never flew.

I began to get a little funny feeling inside. The buzzard kept walking down the road just like that was a natural thing to do but it wasn't. The bird stayed on the road until a little after it passed where we lived and then it went off in the woods and Asberry and I ran into the house.

"Mama, Mama, this big black bird was walkin' down the road in front of us and it never flew."

Mama looked up from her mending and said, "Mama Lizzie died today."

Just like that. No explanation offered and none needed.

"Mama Lizzie died today."

◆

Life Everlasting

THE OLD PEOPLE KNEW THE SECRETS OF ROOTS AND herbs. We had roots and herbs growing all over Sapelo, and we used them for everything. Grandma used them, her mother used them before her and Grandpa had a vast knowledge of all things natural, being one-half Creek and one-half African American, and everyone on Papa's side of the family relied on things from the earth too.

Say you got a swollen ankle. Grandma would tell you, "Baby, go ahead now, you go home and you get yourse'f some mullein." Mullein, that's a plant with big, light green fuzzy leaves, and you'd make a poultice and put it around that leg. You'd sit there and apply it and change that poultice kinda regular and the swelling would go down. Or Mama would say, "I'll soak some collard green leaf in vinegar for you and we'll put it on your forehead headache." You'd keep that collard leaf on your forehead for an hour or so, and your headache would go away.

Uncle Nero Jones, Papa's uncle that I keep telling you about, believed in the wisdom of the old ways. He lived by them, he followed all of the old ways, starting with the herb—he'd brew some and drink a cup every day. Life Everlasting.

He was born a few years after slavery ended, six years after the Big War, to be exact. His family had been living in an old slave cabin. When freedom came, they moved over to the North End, to Belle Marsh. They wanted their own land and they didn't want nothing to do with the old slave community, but they weren't gonna throw everything out. They weren't gonna throw out their belief in the old ways. Not at all.

Grandma and Grandpa raised Mama on Life Everlasting tea, and Grandpa never gave it up, even when he could afford coffee. Papa drank Life Everlasting too and he drank it more than Mama did. That's probably because Papa was practically raised by Uncle Nero. His uncle was the only relative still around after Grandma Gibb left Sapelo and went off to Florida.

Papa would come across Life Everlasting growing in the woods while he was driving his tractor and he would bring home these huge bunches of it tied to his knapsack, and hang them up outside in the corn house to dry.

Life Everlasting's got tiny, little leaves that turn kinda silver-gray in the fall, when it's ready for you to pick it, and little white blossoms on top. So when he wanted some tea he'd go out back, break a piece off and boil it up.

We had other teas too. We boiled blackberry root and made a tea for diarrhea, we used sassafras tea for measles, and we had mint tea for the stomach. Pennyroyal tea was for women's problems, and we had moss tea, tea made from Spanish moss, for asthma.

You'd have to get the moss from up in the tree because chiggers get in the moss when it hits the ground. So you'd take a pole and stick it up in the big clumps of gray moss hanging from those big live oak trees we have over here, and you'd twist your pole around, and then you'd pull down some moss. Then you'd shake the moss around to get rid of anything that's in it, like spiders, and you'd take it home and rinse it off, and put it in the pot, and boil it in some water, and pour the tea off, and you'd be feeling better in no time.

We used those teas for remedies, and you could use Life Everlasting as a remedy too, for a bad cold. Mama would give it to me with lemon in it and Papa would put a shot of moonshine in his, if he was feeling bad, but mostly you'd drink Life Everlasting in the evening. It was the poor man's Lipton, with its own stimulant, and it got you up and going just as good as store-bought tea.

I grew up on Life Everlasting but as a child I always wondered about the name—like, does it mean if you drink this tea, you would live forever? Or did it have something to do with what the preacher said at church: "If you are obedient to God, you'll have everlasting life"? Could you get the same thing from Life Everlasting tea, without going to all that trouble? Maybe it meant you'd at least live a long life. Because most of my family did live to old age. Uncle Nero had lived into his eighties, Grandma was in her late eighties and Grandpa was too, Uncle Shed lived to be over a hundred, and Hester and her sister, Minto Bell, lived into their nineties.

Uncle Nero's daughter, Cousin Anna, that lived near us in Hog Hammock, drank Life Everlasting too, and she followed the old ways the same as her father did, except for one time. We'll never know for sure but it may have really cost her.

It happened back when Cousin Anna and her father, Uncle Nero, were living at Belle Marsh. Cousin Anna had a baby daughter then, Ophelia, and Mama said Ophelia was a normal little baby, a beautiful little girl, until she was almost a year old.

Ophelia was cooing and crawling all around and had started

making steps and trying to walk and all of a sudden, she stopped. She started stumbling, she started falling down, and she didn't try to walk no more. She just sat down mostly and then she quit doing even that. She just lay there in her crib and her limbs started drawing up.

Cousin Anna was worried and Uncle Nero was too. That was his grandchild, so Uncle Nero said, "Let me bury the chile. I will bury her for three days in the earth, and I'll build a shelter over her and you can stay with her."

He believed in the power of the earth to heal—just sand, doing its work, just like Mr. James Spaulding did. Mr. James Spaulding, when he was my teacher, said the Creator created us from sand from the earth, so the earth was special, it had special healing properties. That's where you came from and that's what you were gonna go back to.

But Cousin Anna refused. She refused to bury Ophelia in the sand. She wasn't gonna have nothing to do with that. "I'm not gonna bury my child in the sand!" she said. In those days that was something, to say no to one of the old people.

Uncle Nero said he would dig a hole straight down and he would put Ophelia in there and he'd straighten out Ophelia's legs and he'd pack sand around them, and that sand would keep her legs straight.

He would keep packing sand around her, just up to a certain point that was high enough, but not up to her head, so there wasn't gonna be any danger to Ophelia, she wasn't gonna suffocate or anything. Ophelia would just be in a hole in a standing position for three days and three nights.

He said all Cousin Anna had to do was give Ophelia a little bit of water and a very little food, just enough to sustain life. "You just stay wit' her, and that sand pull the affliction out of her limbs."

Cousin Anna still refused. She said no in no uncertain terms and she wouldn't do it, and Ophelia never got better. She just lay there in her crib with her limbs curled up. Her feet never touched the end of that baby crib.

Ophelia was ten years older than me, but she was still in her crib when I was growing up and Mama used to tell me about Uncle Nero trying to get Cousin Anna to bury Ophelia. I'd think about that sometimes, because the old people would bury dogs, too. They'd get something we called "stamper" and their legs would get weak and they couldn't walk, and you buried the dog. Matter of fact, Asberry and I tried it.

We had a dog named Spot and Asberry and I loved that dog. Spot was one of three puppies in a litter, and the old people were harsh in a lot of ways. Papa didn't want those puppies. He said they were gonna be chicken-killing, egg-sucking dogs and you couldn't have no dogs like that around the yard.

He told Asberry to tie the dogs out in the woods, so Asberry went out and he tied them to some trees and he left them. For days we could hear the dogs hollering and yelping, like "I wanta come back home, I wanta come back home." After a while it got to Asberry and me and we went out there. Two dogs had twisted the rope around their necks and strangled themselves. Only one dog was a smart dog, smart enough not to twist himself up in that rope but since he had been in the woods so long he was hungry, and he needed food and water. Asberry and I looked at the dog and made a decision—we were gonna take him back home, we didn't care what Papa said.

Papa let us keep him and we named him Spot. And in all the

time we had him he didn't bother no chickens, no eggs, or anything. But when Spot got sick, he got weak in the spine and couldn't walk, it was like, okay, it's the second trial in his life, and we wasn't gonna let him just die. All Spot could do was drag around, pulling with the front legs, and it was hard to watch that.

Mama and Papa told us to bury the dog leaving only its head out, and we did it just the way they said to. We put a little shelter over Spot's head and we'd give him water—and that's all—two or three times a day. He didn't like being stuck in the ground but we'd go out and talk to Spot and I guess he knew that we were trying to help him. So we left him in the hole, packed firmly in the sand, for three days and nights.

After three days, we dug Spot up, and low and behold, he could walk. We fed him a stomach full of food and water and he laid down and rested, and in a couple of hours' time, he was charging around the yard like he'd never been sick. Spot lived for nine years after that and died of old age.

Cousin Anna took excellent care of Ophelia. She did everything she could for her. She kept her clean and neat at all times and washed and combed and plaited her hair. But I don't think Ophelia ever saw a doctor, because the old people didn't go to doctors much, and back then, a doctor probably would have said, "Put her in a home," and Cousin Anna wouldn't have considered sending Ophelia off to an institution. She loved her daughter.

Ophelia had long hair and her complexion was brown, kinda like Cousin Anna's and mine, and if her limbs had been straight, she would have been short like her mama, and she would have been pretty. Her face was kinda distorted, but I could tell she would have been pretty.

When Cousin Anna needed to go somewhere, she'd sometimes

ask me to come sit with Ophelia so I would go sit by Ophelia's crib until her mama came back. Ophelia was alert, she knew people, she knew me. But except for a few words she couldn't talk, because whatever disease she had, it affected her speech as well as her limbs. Ophelia could say "Mama," "hungry," "food," and "wet," and that's about it. She didn't know much else.

Sometimes as I sat with Ophelia I felt like there was a older person locked up in there someplace who wanted to get out but couldn't. Life for Cousin Ophelia must have been frustrating and every now and then she'd pitch a tantrum. She had one arm that she could move a good bit, and she would flail that arm around and mumble to herself, and Cousin Anna would say, "Have a little patience, Ophelia. I'll get to you in a minute." Ophelia would calm down because she knew her mama had heard her, and Mama would soon come to feed or change her.

Ophelia lived in that body for twenty years and finally pneumonia set in or something like it. Ophelia couldn't say she was sick, but Cousin Anna knew her daughter, so she knew she was sick. Ophelia stopped eating and got a high fever and Cousin Anna knew it was just a matter of time. The women in the community came and helped Cousin Anna sit with Ophelia day and night and bathed her face and kept her dry and as comfortable as possible. They all took turns sitting with Ophelia until she died.

Cousin Anna buried Ophelia in my casket, the one Papa helped build for me when I was three years old. Mama had used that old casket for a blanket chest until Cousin Anna finally needed it. At twenty, Ophelia fit in that casket made for a three-year-old and she was buried near Uncle Nero in Behavior Cemetery.

So that was Ophelia. She didn't get a chance at long life. I always wondered (and I'm sure I'm not the only one) if she had been buried in sand, could it have helped her? Could she have gotten well? We'll never know 'cause that secret went to the grave with Ophelia. Try as he could, Uncle Nero couldn't get Cousin Anna to follow the old ways, to try the most powerful one of them all, the power of the earth itself to heal.

The Cusp

THERE WAS A CHANGE COMING. YOU COULD ALMOST smell it in the breeze sweeping the island. It was not at all like the way Mama used to go outside at Belle Marsh and say, "Smell that marsh, it smell so marshy." That sniff of hers brought in all the goodness of the marsh and the fish and the crabs and the oysters in it. She loved that marsh smell and the sun shining on the green sea grass and the beautiful white egrets flying overhead.

This was something altogether different. Something that made you stand still for just a second, the way a deer freezes when it first scents danger. It made the old people say, "It ain't gonna lead to no good." Richard Reynolds had invited the scientists over to live on Sapelo and study the marsh.

We were used to white people being here, but it had always before been Reynolds, his family and friends and the white people who worked for him. There were a few hundred of us and not more than about twenty white people. There were no outsiders here and hadn't been many to speak of since Geechee people first came to Sapelo.

The scientists were less threatening than the men Reynolds had working for him, and that was good. They were not here to meddle into your business and tell you how to live, and we liked that. We were respectful of them too, to a degree, because they were well educated. But still, it was not like they were Christopher Columbus and we were the native people running down to the water to welcome them.

"Good lord, more buckra coming over to the island," Grandma was saying. "Every time I look, I see more of them coming to the island."

We tried to ignore them, but they were riding around in Jeeps and digging holes in the earth to get their soil samples or standing out in the marsh getting all muddy. You couldn't help but see them. "Why those crazy people digging holes all over the place?" the old people said.

At first, just two scientists came over and set up housekeeping, and after awhile there were seven scientists full-time, some part-time ones, visiting scientists and students, so they got to be a real presence over here. Richard Reynolds turned over the dairy barn and some other buildings to them for office space and labs and the Marine Institute, affiliated with the University of Georgia, was born.

The scientists who were here full-time worked on projects for an average of five to seven years but they didn't ever explain what they were doing or try to interest young people over here in marine biology. Some of the scientists were kinda standoffish and Aunt Mary and others would go, "Oh, those people don't want to bother with people in the community here."

But a few of the scientists handled it just right, and didn't treat us like we were just here to service them. Those were the ones some of us got to know while taking care of the lab to keep it clean, working with them in the marsh, building things they needed or going with some of them on the ocean. If we felt we could trust a particular one, we'd talk to them then, and sometimes we'd tell them our lore.

First, it was the jack-o'-lantern we told them about. The scientists took away all the mystical, magical things about the jack-o'-lantern by saying that what we saw as a floating ball of light was something that naturally occurs over a low-lying damp area. What causes that glowing effect was gas, they said, and that's what we'd been looking at. It was never a jack-o'-lantern at all. And we said, "Aah, that's what it is."

Once the scientists explained it, nobody ever saw a jack-o'-lantern again. Because once you put magic to a spotlight it disappears. When you explain it away, it goes away. It's never there anymore. So, Cousin Charles Walker, who got hopelessly lost following that mysterious ball of light when I was a kid, was the last person on Sapelo ever to see the jack-o'-lantern.

Then the scientists explained away the hag, the one that sometimes would fly from Raccoon Bluff to Lumber Landing and Shell Hammock and ride three people all in one night, and then the old people would say, "That hag was *busy* last night."

That was probably a case of poor blood circulation, the scientists said. Your blood was circulating in your body poorly. "Who the hell they think they are?" Grandma said. "What do they know about the hag?"

The teachers at school also started telling us there wasn't any such thing as the hag, and the kids my age looked at each other and said, "Gosh, everybody is saying the same thing. There's no such thing as the hag."

Being in a culture where you didn't disbelieve your elders, it was hard to put aside what they believed. They taught you well, so you couldn't totally stop believing. But there were two worlds—the text-book world and their world of believing in the unseen and the unknown—and you were caught in between.

My favorite teacher, Miss Jessie Mae Moore, was trying to prepare us for the modern world and she had a saying, "White man die and leave money. Black man die and leave signs." She was right that we didn't have any money. We had signs that had been passed down for generations on Sapelo, that told our parents everything from when to plant to when a storm was coming. People over here relied on those signs.

Were we supposed to throw out the hag and all of our signs and beliefs? And if we threw out some, which ones did we keep?

While all those thoughts were whirling around in our heads, the hag went, "Uh-oh. Time to go. Too many people coming over," and it flew away. All of a sudden, the hag didn't come visit anymore. Nobody had the sensation of being in bed and waking up with this *heavy weight* on top of you, being ridden all night by a mysterious hag and being so tired in the morning you couldn't move. It was just *gone*.

But where did the hag go? Did it fly off somewhere where there was less modern know-how? Was the hag ever coming back? And did that many people have poor blood circulation? Adults and children alike?

Soon the old people said, "Chile, I remember when the hag would come ride me all the time. Things sure change." It was the beginning of the end of magic as we knew it on Sapelo and nothing would ever be the same.

◆

Mama Gets Conned

THERE'S ALWAYS A TRICKSTER IN REAL LIFE, AND Asberry was it in our family. Just like Brer Rabbit, Asberry was *it*. Kids in my generation were beginning to question our beliefs in root and magic and, of course, the scientists had explained away haints and jack-o'-lanterns by now so things were beginning to change over here on Sapelo. It would have been absolutely unheard of in Mama's time but Asberry wasn't at all afraid to play on someone's beliefs.

One day he heard Mama and Grandma talking about some mysterious white powder on Uncle Glasco's pump that gave him the shooting pains in his legs. He knew that Mama believed wholeheartedly in root and that gave him an idea.

Grandma always looked for root in everything. Mama did too, and it was almost her downfall. Mama *believed* in root. She believed in seeking it out, and she believed in trying to protect her family from it, even though she didn't have a frizzled chicken in her yard.

We had had frizzled chickens over here as long as anyone can remember and it's a special breed of chicken that looks like its feathers are all standing up, like someone ruffled them all over. A few people on Sapelo still had frizzled chicken when I was growing up and that frizzled chicken was good to let scratch around your yard, because if anybody put anything evil in your yard, they were supposed to search it out and pick it up and eat it.

Like I said, we didn't have a frizzled chicken, but Papa had a horseshoe over the door, with the ends pointing up so his luck wouldn't run out. And we had the lucky weed that grew inside the yard. That weed was *lucky* and we learned as children to respect it. So wheresoever it grew, we kids knew not to touch it. Cut down a lucky weed and you're on the verge of a spanking. Some places it's called a coral bean and it's a plant that lives in tropical and subtropical areas but I didn't know its name at that time. I just knew that it was deep green and bushy, it grows about four feet high or better, and it's got bright red seeds and it's pretty. But that lucky weed wasn't strong enough to save Mama from Asberry the time I'm thinking of.

Asberry got up early in the morning one day, early in the morning so Mama wouldn't see him, and he snuck into our kitchen and got some of her flour. He sprinkled that "white powder" on Mary the mule's gate and he pretended that he stepped in it and that he was struck by pain immediately. He stood in the yard and yelled for Mama and she came running out to see what was wrong. "Mama, Mama, I stepped in some white powder and all of a sudden, pains started shooting up my leg."

Asberry was not very original, but Mama believed him. She believed him hook, line and sinker and Asberry milked it for all it was worth. Mama got Papa to take her to a root doctor all the way in Savannah. The root doctor told them to bury red pepper at the back and front steps. Mama and Papa did just that—they dug a hole and buried that red pepper into the ground precisely six inches, because it was supposed to keep away evil spirits.

The root doctor told them to burn sulphur in the four corners of the house to get rid of the evil spirits already in the house. So Mama put the sulphur in tin cans, old lard cans, and she even had Papa helping her burn that sulphur.

I didn't mind drinking that artesian well water we had over here that tasted like sulphur. I was used to that. But I couldn't stand the smell of sulphur burning in the house. I hated it. I absolutely hated it. It smelled like rotten eggs.

I'm thinking to myself, "What they doin' that for?"

"Mama. Mama, Asberry's fakin' it. He's conning you."

"No, no, no. Somebody' fixed my boy. I know somebody' fixed my boy."

Asberry pretended the pain was hurting him all up his leg. Sometimes he'd put his head in his hands and pretend he was crazy and start tearing up the house. Mama would grab ahold of him and she'd pet him and rock him and talk to him and he'd go get the Sears book out.

"Mama, will you buy me this? Mama, will you get me this?"

And Mama would say, "Yeah, baby, I'll get it for you," and she'd order whatsoever Asberry wanted. And Asberry was just as happy as a clam in deep water. He was getting what he wanted and he was missing school and that's what the whole thing was about. Asberry didn't like going to school at all so he played that root thing to the hilt.

He'd wake up all times of night and yell for Mama. "I can't sleep, Mama. Mama, the spirits' botherin' me. See 'em, Mama? See 'em Mama?"

Mama would run and get the sulphur and put hot sulphur in the corners to chase away those spirits Asberry said he was seeing that nobody else could see but him. She'd spend sleepless nights sitting by his bed. When Mama would go out of the house to visit Grandma or go to the store, Asberry would do all the things he'd normally do, climbing trees, shooting Papa's .22-caliber rifle at targets and playing with his friends. But as soon as he'd see Mama, all of a sudden, he was sick again.

Money was so tight I was wearing old clothes that people gave us. We always wore hand-me-downs, but these were just darn ridiculous. I had Grandma's old shoes, with the heels cut off and they were old lady shoes. I would get mad and go to school barefoot, because I didn't want to wear those things. The kids laughed at me. Asberry had cowboy boots from Sears, and a ship in a bottle, and cowboy jeans and a shirt. Anything he wanted, he got.

Papa was working at Blackbeard Island then. Just about every two weeks when his check came, Mama would be heading off to Savannah to carry Asberry to the root doctor. I was left to take care of my nephew Michael, who was two years younger than me, and my niece, Elise who was five. So Mama would go off to Savannah, chasing some whim of Asberry's.

For some reason, Mama believed that a family over here "fixed" her son. She asked the root doctor to take that spell off Asberry and turn it back on them. There was a young lady in that family, and all of a sudden, the daughter started acting very funny. She started having sick spells and talking out of her head and having some of the same symptoms that Asberry had. Her family couldn't figure out what was wrong with her but Mama knew that the spell had been turned back on that girl and she took it as proof that the family was the one that put root on Asberry to begin with. "Okay, we got 'em back for what they did to Asberry," she said.

Then one day the young lady showed up at our house all confused and everything, like, "What am I doin' here?" and Mama had to walk her back home. She said her root doctor drew that girl to our house as proof she was the one that had "fixed" Asberry.

While my brother was faking it, that girl was for real and to me, it was like, "Hold it there, did Mama's root doctor really make this girl ill and if he did, where is the justice in this thing?" Because her family had to watch her, they had to go with her everywhere or keep her locked up around the clock so she wouldn't get hurt. They had a hard time with her.

Asberry kept it up for almost a year until either he got tired of it or maybe he realized, "Here my fakin' is actually causin' somebody to be ill." One morning he woke up and said, "Mama, I feel better." And that was it. He didn't have a relapse or anything. He was done with it, just like that.

As soon as Asberry got better, the young lady started getting better too. She got better and she had a normal life. She went on to have children and a husband and the whole works, so things worked out for her. But I stayed as far away from root as I could from then on. I had gotten too experienced with it and I knew right then that unlike Mama, I wasn't gonna seek root out. I was *never* gonna ask anybody for root and I never have. But Mama kept on believing in root and as far as she knew, she had saved her son from the spell that was ruining his life.

◆

To Skin a Cat

WHEN OUR NEW SCHOOL OPENED IN 1953, IT WAS expanded so that the classes went through the eighth grade and we would have a combination school closing and graduation ceremony in late May. Miss Jessie Mae Moore would put it together.

Miss Moore combed and styled her hair kinda like a pompadour on top and it sort of frizzed down in the back and she was always immaculately dressed and her shoes were always in perfect condition. Her fingernails were painted a maroon-looking color and I would look at them and wonder, "Where does she get that color fingernail polish from?" I had never seen a color like that before.

She would breeze into a room with her cat's-eye frame glasses and a smile that showed one gold tooth and every child would instantly jump to attention. We knew Miss Moore could laugh and kid around, but when it was time for business, she was *all* business. I think even Richard Reynolds sprung to attention around her, because she would get more for the school from him than she did from the county school system. If she needed new textbooks or dictionaries, she'd go directly to him with her no-nonsense attitude and just-right manners and he would give her the funds. It was a confidence thing that she had. I wanted to be just like her. Matter of fact, I wanted to become a teacher.

Miss Moore would play "Pomp and Circumstance" at the graduation ceremony *fast*, not slow and solemn like you usually hear it, and the girls in their white dresses and the boys in their blue suits would come marching down to the front of the church and get their diplomas.

The church would be full of people coming to see their kids graduate. It was a very big thing to get your kid all the way through the eighth grade. Up to 1953, you had to go to the mainland for school after the sixth grade and the only boat that went back and forth on a regular basis was the *Tarpon*, the converted shrimp boat that Richard Reynolds owned.

It had a captain's house up top, with benches for the white people, and the black passengers rode on the deck or down below in the engine room if it was real cold. (You'd go out of there talking *loud*, it was so noisy down there.) For awhile, the *Tarpon* carried up to twenty-five people and then the coast guard said it could carry only seven people safely. You could have a hard time getting a ride even if you had a doctor's appointment on the other side. There wasn't an afternoon ride back for the kids anyway, so you had to board at somebody's house on the mainland if you were going to go on in school and most families couldn't afford that. A few families moved to the mainland so their kids could go on, but those families didn't come back to Sapelo.

So, after the eighth grade was added, you could stay in school a little longer, but then that was it for most people. If anyone was going to continue their education, it was a few of the girls. The boys didn't have much alternative. They'd get a job working for Richard

Reynolds, or Howard Coffin, before him. They started pulling a man's weight and they became old men.

I never got to march down the aisle and get my eighth-grade diploma. The particular year I got to the eighth grade, the teachers weren't teaching it, so I went to St. Simons Island and stayed with my sister Ada and went to the eighth grade there. Then Mama got sick and I had to leave school before the school year was over.

In 1957, Mama was going through the change of life and she ached all the time and wasn't herself. For some reason, the change hit a lot of women hard on Sapelo. Some women went kinda bonkers and were sent to the state mental hospital until they got better, but Mama wasn't like that. She just couldn't move. She could have had a problem with her blood, it might have been anemia, because it does run in the family. But at any rate, if you were in school and your family needed you, even in the late fifties, it was just like it had always been over here: you gave up school. You did not complain about it one bit. You did not question it. On Sapelo, your family came first.

So, at age twelve, I became the woman of the household. I did everything that had to be done to run a household and remember, we didn't have any electricity. You had to pump the water, chop the wood for the fire, cook on the wood stove, scrub the laundry, hang it out on the clothesline to dry, heat the flat iron to iron it, and you had to make sure the garden was weeded too.

By the time Mama was better, the kids I had been in school with were a couple grades ahead of me, and I didn't feel like going back. I still dreamed of becoming a teacher. I didn't dwell on it but somewhere in the back of my mind, I knew I had been that special child who was supposed to have a special purpose. I also knew that becoming a teacher meant going to college, and even if I could finish high school, where were we gonna get the money for college? There wasn't any college for kids like me. I had never even heard of scholarships. So I didn't mention college to Mama and it never occurred to her that I wanted to go. She knew you needed the three R's, but no one ever said how far you needed to go *beyond* that.

To Mama, and to most people over here, if you could make out a grocery list and fill out a mail order, describe the thing you wanted and add the money up right, then you were doing pretty good. You didn't have to depend on anybody then.

They were proud of you if you went further, now. They'd say, "I heard she's a teacher now and doing well." But if that same person came home talking proper and showing off, they'd say, "An awful lot of good education did that one. She's done gone and got beside herself."

My sister Barbara was living in New York and I thought about going up there. Black people had been going to New York ever since the Civil War. Mama's sister, my Aunt Harriet, and Mama's aunt, Aunt Till, had moved there during the Depression. Discrimination wasn't as bad as it was in the South and black people could get jobs and send a little money back home to their families sometimes.

Barbara had her own place to live in New York and a job in a factory assembly line, putting stickers that said Made in Japan on trinkets that were actually made right in that factory. Why? Maybe somebody decided they'd sell better that way. That's New York for you.

She didn't paint New York as a glorious place but she'd come home and visit and tell me about all the stores, riding the subway and the bus, and all the people. We had maybe two hundred homes on Sapelo but in New York, you could see two hundred people come running out of one apartment building. I said, "Oh my goodness." It sounded fascinating. And this put me in the mood to think maybe I wanted to go up there too.

I was fourteen when I wrote Barbara that I wanted to come. It was 1959 and Barbara had a one-bedroom apartment, and she went out and rented a two-bedroom one so she'd have room for me. Then I had second thoughts about being that far from home and wrote her back.

"Dear Barbara, I changed my mind."

"You mean to tell me that I've gone and got a bigger apartment and spent that money and you're not coming?" she wrote.

"I'm sorry but I'm not coming."

Who was gonna write Mama's and Papa's letters if I went? From an early age, I was the one that wrote the letters between the family members here and the ones up north. I was the one that did all the ordering for Mama and Papa from Sears and other places too.

I never regretted not going because it turned out that a lot of people from this area didn't live such a charmed life in New York. Some of them lived in a false world pretending that everything was okay and that they had it made up there, but they didn't.

I went back to St. Simons instead and stayed with Ada. Asberry and Grandpa and Cousin Annie's daughter, Cousin Julia Mae, wrote the letters and mail orders for Mama and Papa and I was close enough that I could get home if I were needed, but I could be independent too.

Like Sapelo, St. Simons is in the Georgia Sea Islands, and rice and cotton were grown there in slavery days also. It's an island, but we thought of St. Simons as part of the mainland almost, because there was a bridge between it and the mainland that you could drive back and forth on—you didn't have to go in a boat—and it had things like grocery stores and hardware stores that we associated with the mainland. There was a pretty sizable black community on St. Simons too, with hundreds of people; much more than on Sapelo.

Ada lived in a big, yellow house on the corner of Proctor Lane. Everything on St. Simons was more modern than on Sapelo, so she had electricity. I knew all about electricity from visiting Ada over the years, plus starting in 1953, the school on Sapelo had electricity, so on a daily basis at least five times a week, I had flushed a commode and turned on a light switch when I went into the bathroom. So, when I moved to St. Simons, it was a nice thing to have but it wasn't totally new to me.

Ada was working as a maid and she helped me get jobs babysitting and working as a maid sometimes too. I was on my own for the first time and that wasn't bad. I could walk to the grocery store in the black neighborhood, I could walk to the pier and I could walk to the wharf—I had to keep in touch with the water one way or another because it'd always been such a big part of my life. So, I was always walking down to look at the water. The nightclubs were off-limits to someone who was fourteen, fifteen or sixteen, as I was when I was there, but there was Miss Hazel's Cafe, a black-run café, where I'd go to get a soda and potato chips, and I made a bunch of new friends.

I wasn't too wild. If you were wild back then, you were wild selectively. You were not wild brazenly. I didn't like smoking or drinking and when friends would pour me up a drink, I didn't want them to think I was better than them, so I'd take a sip or two and when they weren't looking, I'd pour it on the floor or slide my glass over and switch glasses. They'd wonder how come I didn't get intoxicated then, but I hadn't really had anything. Things didn't turn out quite right in one regard just the same.

I was sixteen and in St. Simons when I met the father of my first child. He was one of those guys that look a lot better at first than they are and I found that out too late. "Oh, boy, what a mistake," I told myself when I got pregnant. "What am I gonna do now?"

Mama and Papa asked me if I wanted to marry the man and I said "No." I definitely did not want to. They dropped it then because they didn't want me marrying someone I didn't want to be with, and it turned out that I was right not to marry him. He ended up marrying the next woman who came around and then running around and having kids all over the cotton-picking place, and he didn't hardly take care of any of them, including my son Stanley. I never asked him for any support and he didn't offer any. The only thing he ever did for Stanley was give him one Coca-Cola and Stanley was too young to like it, so he drank it himself.

Before Stanley was born, I came back to Sapelo and stayed here and I started going with Frank, who I married two years later. Frank's name is actually Julius but everyone called him Frank, just as they did his father, Julius Bailey, too. Frank had always lived in Hog Hammock but he was a year and a half older than me, he was born in January of 1943, and I hadn't ever paid any attention to him. We would play on opposite softball teams at school sometimes and that kind of stuff, but that was it.

I think Frank took a good look at me one night during the Christmas holiday of 1961. I was sixteen then. Frank and Minus Jr., the son of Papa's friend Mr. Minus Banks, walked me home from a party and then I began to notice him. He and Minus came to the house a couple of nights later and we sat around and chatted for awhile.

After Frank came by the house a few times, I *really* noticed him, but Minus was always with him. So, one night I said to Frank, "Are you afraid to walk down this road by yourself? How come you always got your shadow with you?" After that, Minus didn't come with him anymore. It was just the two of us and *bingo*! I chose him.

Frank was tall and quiet and smelled like Ben Hur cologne, Arid deodorant and Juicy Fruit chewing gum. If the wind was blowing right, I could smell that mixture of smells before he got to Papa's house. That was a sure thing and so was he. Frank had family ties from the North End—Miss Rosa Jean Walker at the Bluff was his grandmother and Katie Brown, the midwife, was his great-grand-mother—he was steady and I could trust him.

Frank's father had died when he was six years old and his mama taught him how to cook, how to do the laundry and how to babysit for his younger brothers and sisters at an early age. When he got to be a young boy, he worked afternoons and weekends for his Aunt Beulah and Mr. Charles at their store. He would take home what-ever money his aunt could pay him and little things she would give him like the cookies that got broken up, the end part of the bologna they sliced off or a mashed loaf of bread that Miss Catherine, his mother, could use to make bread pudding with.

Frank stayed in school until the eleventh grade and then he started working for Richard Reynolds. His job was in the green-house when we got together, and he would take his whole paycheck home every week to his mother to help provide for his brothers and sisters.

I told him I was pregnant, so he knew all about it, and I think Frank decided just to take the bad with the good. He never let it bother him at all and when my baby was born, he was proud of Stanley.

I was seventeen when Stanley was born on July 22, 1962, on a bright Sunday morning. We still gave birth at home over here so I was in my own bedroom. Mama was there, and Miss Katie Underwood—the same midwife who had delivered me and later my niece Elise when I was four—was at my side too. She was in her eighties and still sharp.

My health was fine, the baby was fine, and there was no need for any drugs or the emergency bottle of whiskey Miss Katie kept in her black bag: coaching was all I needed. Labor started about 1:30 A.M. and at 9:30 A.M, Mama and Miss Katie were congratulating me and saying, "It's a boy!"

Miss Katie counted the knots in the afterbirth like she always did after the first child and said, "Baby, you can have a few mo' chirren so be careful." She didn't give me an exact number, just said to be careful because I was gonna have a few more and time proved her right.

I had an absolutely beautiful son and I was determined to earn my own money to provide for him. I didn't want Frank to do that for me. I put that first, before anything else. I still wanted an education though. I hadn't given up on my dream of finishing school. I had even checked into correspondence courses but I couldn't afford them.

Now, people over here believed that education was important but realistically, there weren't any jobs over here for black people with degrees, so education wasn't the only thing the old people meant when they said you should "make sump'n of yourself." That included working hard, getting married, and having kids, going to church, staying out of trouble and being known for something in the community. They also said there was more than one way to skin a cat.

Why they picked a cat, I don't know. I knew there was more than one way to skin a rabbit, because I'd seen that done. You can skin it from the head down or the feet up and it doesn't matter, so I wondered, was life like that too? Could you go at it from one direction or another and as long as you got what you want done, still come out at the same place? I made up my mind it was going to be that way for me. I would do what I needed to do but when I could, I would better myself and if I had a special purpose, I would find a way to fulfill it.

Chapter Twenty-Four

God Loves You Best

IN THE EVENING, WHEN THE OLD PEOPLE WOULD leave to go back to their own kiff, their own house, they'd say "I'll see you tomorrow if life lasts, and God's willing." And that's the way it was. If God wasn't willing, forget it, but if he was willing, we'd see each other in the morning.

We had all kinds of signs of death over here. The animals would give us signs and the spirits would give us signs too. A rooster that was crowing at the wrong time of day was a sign of death, especially if he was crowing on your doorstep. Crows flying toward the cemetery was a sign there would be a funeral soon.

The spirits would come to the old people in dreams, like I've told you before. If Papa saw all of his relatives in a dream, then sure enough, it wasn't long before somebody in the family would be gone and he'd say, "Yup, I knew they were coming for someone 'cause they don't come to visit me unless they're coming for someone." The ladies were visited in their dreams too. When they were sitting around talking, they might start talking about a man who was ill, and next thing you know, you'd hear one of them say something like, "Yeah, I know what's gonna happen because I saw my aunt, I saw her spirit as plain as day. She was sitting in the corner and not saying anything and she was dressed all in white and she had this halo around her head. I know she's coming back for her husband who is sick."

Nobody would have doubted that dream. Everyone knew that a spirit dressed in white was a sign in and of itself because white was a symbol for purity. We wore it for baptism and some people wore it for funerals and it was standard practice a long time ago for the ladies who attended the body before the funeral to dress in white clothes.

The spirits could actually give you physical signs also. They had the power to do that and sometimes they did. A tree limb crashing down could be a sign from the spirits. If it was a perfectly solid tree limb and there was no rain to make it heavy, and all of a sudden it just fell out of the sky, then it was a sign of death. The spirit of someone was coming back for someone living, through that tree limb. Papa would say, "I was sitting here and all of a sudden I heard this noise and I got up and checked and there was this huge limb that fell out of the tree and I knew it was a bad sign 'cause a limb don't fall out of a tree for no reason."

The first dead person I ever saw was Mama Lizzie. I was seven years old at the time and she had been ill for awhile before she died and she'd even gone to see a doctor, which might seem strange for her. But she was probably determined to live and if root didn't help her she would have looked to other things too. I saw her being carried out of her house but only from a distance. That was as close as I got to death until Mr. Muda died.

Bermuda Grovner was Cousin Annie's brother. He lived at Lumber Landing, where his wife's family had lived for generations, and everybody called him "Muda." Mr. Muda had worked for Howard Coffin doing farming and he had done his own planting too and lots of trapping. He was in his seventies but he didn't have any health problems that anybody knew of. He could still walk from Lumber Landing to the Bluff and down to Hog Hammock, and he did that a couple of times a week. But sometimes people know when their time comes and Mr. Muda just felt that it was his time.

The week before he died, in August 1955 he paid the outstanding bills he had to Mr. Charles Hall at the store and to others. He went and apologized to his sister-in-law, Miss Frances, because they had had some hard words, so he made peace with her and with anybody else he might have done some wrong to.

His house sat right by an oak tree at Lumber Landing and there was a table under that oak tree. His wife always told him, "Muda, you need to pick up all these old shoes of yours and do something with them." That week he picked up all his old shoes, the ones we call "draggers." See, the men didn't throw out their old shoes. Shoes were hard to come by so when they got worn out, the men cut the heels off them and made them into draggers and wore them for fishing. So that week Mr. Muda picked up all his old draggers and put them in a neat line on that table, under that tree. Then he had everything in his life in order and he decided to go fishing.

He asked William Banks to go with him. The Bankses had lived at Lumber Landing for generations and William, who's in his fifties now, was a teenager at the time. He didn't want to go fishing, because it was August and it was hot, but Mr. Muda asked again, so he went along out of respect for the old man. They got out on the Duplin River and they were fishing in Mr. Muda's old wooden bateau, and he said to William, "It's so hot—let's go for a swim."

"Naw, I don't want to go," William said.

"Aw, c'mon, you're a young man. You can go for a swim."

"No, I don't want to," William said.

"Well, I'm going for a swim," Mr. Muda said and he took off his shirt, his shoes and his hat and he put them neatly on the seat of the boat and he jumped overboard.

Mr. Muda was a good swimmer and William waited for him to come up and he waited and waited and Mr. Muda didn't come. William went and sounded the alarm then that Mr. Muda had jumped overboard and that was it. He didn't come back up.

Papa and some of the other men went and dragged for his body. They had a large hook on a line on a cane pole, to snag the body, and they brought him in.

They laid him out on a cooling board in the living room of his house and they put a sheet over him. I'm not sure what they used for a cooling board because that wasn't important to me at that age but usually it was planks or an old door laid over a table or sawhorses. Basically, it was whatever you could hastily get.

Someone had sent to Darien for ice so Mr. Muda's body was iced down with huge blocks of ice, because that's what we did then. There wasn't a funeral home over here so people on the island handled all the preparations for burial themselves. By the time I came along, some people would get a funeral home in Darien to send over a casket, but even if they did that, everything else was taken care of here.

The Eastern Stars helped with burial preparations back then. That was a black order of the Masons that we had over here and they were usually the ones to lay a person out on the cooling board and they were the ones to bathe the body and dress it for the funeral too. The men would take care of the men and the women would take care of the women that died.

I had come down with Mama and Cousin Annie and some other women and their kids, because people always started coming to the house right after the person died. I was still a young child and the dead are much respected so the children were not allowed in the living room. I could see in from the kitchen, though, so this death was a lot more real to me than Mama Lizzie's had been. I remember his feet sticking out from under the sheet, and I thought, "Gosh, his feet are white."

Mr. Muda was dark skinned but it was like his feet had been bleached out by that water. And it wasn't but a few hours he was in that water, but the crabs had already started messing with him. I could see little nicks, nothing real bad, but little nicks on his feet that the crabs had made and I knew he had died before the crabs found him but it bothered me just the same. And I didn't ever like eating crab meat dishes again. That's for sure.

As people came to the house, they brought food because the grown-ups always held a wake for the person that died. Back in slavery times, people called them "set-ups" but they were pretty much the same thing—sitting up and talking all night and watching over the body. Hester, my great-great-great-grandmother told Uncle Shed once that when they had set-ups, they would kill a white chicken to keep the spirits away. I don't know whether that was to keep away the spirit of the person who had just died and might want company in death or to keep other spirits away, but she always kept a white chicken in her yard so she'd have it for that.

That tradition was long gone by the time I was growing up. People would bring food when I was growing up but that was to feed whoever was at the wake, not to ward off the spirits. At some wakes there were cakes and fried fish and other food, but your basic things were coffee, sugar, canned milk and bread. People would talk about everything they could think of, what they did that day, a death in the past that reminded them of this one, or stories about the person that died, but they tried to keep it kinda lighthearted. The menfolks would slip outside and take them a little drink sometimes, and then they'd come back in and reminisce. There was always at least one person awake at all times to watch over the body. I always wondered, did they expect the body to go somewhere? But that's the way it was done.

The funeral for Mr. Muda and his brother was held within two days at First African Baptist. That's right. His brother, Randolph, had died a couple of days before him, at the Bluff. He was old too and it was his years that took him, not something like drowning, but the two brothers died basically at the same time. And maybe that was a part of Mr. Muda's feeling that his time had come, but then again, he started his preparations *before* his brother died.

The first two people that I saw dead were both old though. It's when someone is young that it takes a toll.

In 1963 I was living at home still. Mama was over in St. Simons visiting Ada this particular day but I was there, and Elise, Michael and Papa were home, and my son Stanley, who was a baby then, was there.

As far as I know, there weren't any signs of death this time but I knew something bad was gonna happen that Saturday in May. I just knew. It was eerie. This feeling of dread hung over me and I knew that whatsoever was gonna happen was gonna happen. There was nothing I could do about it.

My nephew Michael was like a brother to me, because we were close in age and we grew up together. He was fifteen years old now, a tall and lanky teenager with a Mohawk haircut, because I cut his hair now and he had come in a few weeks before and said he wanted one. I thought about it and decided I could probably do that and I took the clippers and gave him one.

Michael went to church and he was still in school. The school over here went through the tenth grade at that time. He was absolutely a nice young man. He was quiet and mannerly and he didn't sass, so he stood out in a good way.

He was Papa's very first grandson and Papa was crazy about Michael. "That boy is gonna be something," he'd say, and he had hopes for him that he didn't have for his sons.

Papa and my brother Gibb never did get along and Gibb worked regular but he wasn't the type who tried to rise high. He held a number of jobs and his last one was working for the city of Brunswick doing maintenance work. Asberry was bright but he didn't take his studies seriously. He didn't take anything seriously, matter of fact, and Papa would shake his head and say, "Asberry ain't gonna be shit. He ain't gonna be shit."

But Michael was smart, he got along very well with people, and he had the potential to be a success at whatever he wanted to do. So Papa looked to Michael as the man in the family who would make something of himself—who would do things that black men of Papa's generation hadn't had the chance to do.

Michael was learning to play the drums and had band practice that morning and after band practice he and his friends came to the house. Michael put on old shorts because they were going clamming down at McIntyre, off of Cabretta Beach. So he changed and left and I was cleaning up the house from top to bottom the whole time. I mopped, I swept, I scrubbed. I was going, "Why am I doing all of this?" But I knew I had to. The house had to be ready.

I finished cleaning finally, and not too long after that, Buck, one of the guys who had been with Michael, came running across the road real fast. Michael was a faster runner than the others so I knew that if it wasn't Michael who was running fast, then the bad news was about Michael.

Michael had gotten clams and put them on the bank to bring home and then he decided he was going for a swim, so he went back in the water and he got caught in a riptide and he couldn't get out of it. A riptide is what some people call a real strong undertow. It can be there and you don't even know it's there until you get caught in it. What happens is that an east wind will have been pushing the water up toward the beach. The water piles up and it's got nowhere to go because the wind is holding it there. But the water's got to go some-where, so eventually it rushes out underneath the other water that's coming in and it can be so fast and strong it overpowers and that's what happened to Michael. His friends tried to get to him but they couldn't and he drowned.

Papa got very quiet. He didn't say a word but he got his large hook and his pole and a white sack and Buck went and got some of the other men and they went down to McIntyre. They got a boat somehow and they dragged for Michael and they found his body in less than an hour by the clock but still a long time out there on the water. They hooked onto him and brought him out but it was way too late for Michael. The grandson that could have died the time he was a small boy playing with Asberry and me in the marsh and Papa was gannet hunting had died in the water after all. Papa's fears for Michael that day so long ago had come true, even though Michael had gotten to live for thirteen more years.

Michael's body was taken to a funeral home in Darien, because it had been a good while since people over here laid the person who had died out on a cooling board and made all the preparations for burial themselves. By now, we sent our dead to the funeral home and the people there made all the preparations for burial, and a few days later they would send the body back in a casket by boat. So the person who had died made one final passage over the water, and came back to be buried on Sapelo.

Somebody got to a phone somehow and called Mama and Ada when Michael died and they got home as soon as they could. Ada was crying and Mama was too, because Ada was Michael's mother but that was Mama's boy. She raised him from the time he was about six months old.

At Michael's funeral, the procession song was "Nearer My God to Thee," like it usually was and the old church at the Bluff was packed. The choir sang songs like "I'll Fly Away," and there was a solo too. Most people used "May the Work I've Done Speak for Me," but I've never liked it, so I'm not sure we used it. That's a pretty song but it's sad and it brings all your emotions to the surface. When I heard it, I'd think to myself, "Did you sing that deliberately just so you could see somebody cry?" Because the families would usually be very composed until they started that song. Then they'd start crying and lots of times one of the women would scream and jump up and fall on the floor and all that kind of stuff. Then when everybody left the church, some of the people who had been there would say to each other, "Lord, that child really take it hard. She cried so much." Or, "That one didn't cry at all so she must not have cared." It was like it became a show after that song and the whole time, the ushers—it was always women who were members of the Eastern Stars—would stand by the family fanning them, because when emotion strikes, a lot of people get faint. One of the women ushers would have smelling salts in her purse too, just in case one of the family members needed them.

At Michael's funeral we cried with water coming down our faces but without a lot of noise. Mostly, my family doesn't get upset in public, except you could hear Mama sometimes because she was always a loud crier. I kept my feelings to myself that day and so did Papa and Asberry. Elise was always one to be quiet too, but not this time. Elise had screamed when she first heard that her brother had died. She screamed her heart out in church too, she screamed all over the place. She made all the noise for the rest of us.

When we left the church, we went to Behavior Cemetery down on the South End. We stopped at the old iron cemetery gate when we got there and asked the spirits for permission to enter. We have always done that over here. In the time of my great-great-great-grandmother Hester, the funeral procession would stop and say, "Family, we come to put our brother away in mother dust. Please let us go through the gate." We hadn't sought permission out loud for generations but we asked permission whenever we stepped into the world of the spirits and we did so this day. It's their home, their resting place, so we asked if we could enter, just like we would before entering your door.

Behavior Cemetery is an old cemetery, it's large and sprawling and wooded. There are headstones going back to 1824 and before, mostly simple concrete headstones that were made on this island. There's one for Bentoo, one of Hester's sisters, who died in 1890 at the age of one hundred and ten. Her headstone says Minto, so what people called her must have changed over the years. It was probably actually Bintu at first, which means "his daughter" in Arabic—the daughter of Bilali. There isn't a headstone for Hester but a whole lot of people don't have headstones.

If you were looking at the cemetery you'd say, "Oh they've got lots of space out there still," because there's no markers for about half the people buried there. Some people had had wooden markers before my time, but they were gone now, and other graves had objects placed on them. That was our custom mostly. You put a favorite object of the person on the grave to mark where the gravesite was, and that way, you could always say, "Yeah, I can go find Mama's grave 'cause I put her favorite plate on her grave." Cups and plates and things like that were used and sometimes clocks. On some of the islands, the clock would be stopped at the time the person had died but I don't know if we did that over here. There was only one clock left in the cemetery and the hands were gone, so I couldn't tell.

Over time, a bunch of the markers got stolen by outsiders as souvenirs. Others got moved by kids, as a prank, so it became harder now to know for sure that Mama's favorite plate was on her grave, unless someone had a sharp memory. Kids over here had too much respect for the dead so they wouldn't do that but there were ones that did. Some of the Reynolds kids, when they were here visiting one time, went into the cemetery and took some of the personal objects. Richard Reynolds found out about it and he got mad and made them put them back, but they were kids and wouldn't have remembered which graves they belonged on. So Behavior Cemetery looked even quieter than it really was when we buried Michael.

Michael's casket was lowered by ropes into the grave and my son Stanley was passed over the casket. That's another tradition over here. If the family has a young child, a little baby or a child up to two to three years old, the child is passed over the casket so the spirit of the deceased person won't come back to bother the baby and the baby won't be fretful. Stanley was the youngest member of our family so he was the one passed over the casket this time. Then Papa and Asberry and Gibb each shoveled some dirt in the grave. The family always participates in this. It's part of our rituals and we take comfort in them. The minister said the last prayers over the grave, including the old funeral rite "ashes to ashes, dust to dust," and a hymn was sung and it was time to leave Michael.

On Sapelo, it will come to pass that before a person is buried, rain will come to wash away the person's last footsteps, the last traces of that person on earth, or a high wind will blow them away. This always happens. Every time. Before Michael was buried, it rained. I don't remember what day it happened. It wasn't the day he died and it wasn't the day that he was buried. It was somewhere in between. But his last footsteps on earth were washed away before Michael was buried in Behavior Cemetery with the ancestors, to live on in our hearts. Sleep on, brother, we all love you but God loves you best.

One Come, One Go

I GREW UP WITH MAMA COVERING THE MIRRORS UP whenever there was thunder and lightning. She would grab a piece of old cloth or whatsoever she could get her hands on, and rush to cover those mirrors up, because she believed that the mirror draws lightning. She believed that the shiny surface of a mirror can draw lightning, just like water does, and that a flash of lightning you see in the mirror can strike inside your room. That's right.

But this was 1964, and I didn't rush and cover my mirrors up anymore. I didn't see any need to do that, but I wasn't gonna stand outside and smoke a cigarette and directly challenge lightning, either. I knew it was a powerful force. I knew it could burn the woods down, it could burn your house down and it could maim you for life or flat out kill you. So I respected it. I would sit by the window and stare out at lightning, but that was as close as I would get, and that's exactly what I was doing one day in June.

Frank and I were married and we were living over in St. Simons. It was a Saturday morning, so we were both home, and I was by the window watching the rain come down. It was beginning to clear up and I happened to glance over in an easterly direction, toward where Sapelo is, and this long, sharp bolt of lightning, this yellowish, reddish bolt of lightning, came shooting down from the heavens. Then, that was it. There was no more thunder, no more lightning, it just became a calm day.

"Frank, that look like it strike something on Sapelo," I said. He was in the room, further back, he wasn't gonna get even as close as I did. He was raised just like me so he knew about lightning. Frank didn't say anything and I said, "Well, we'll hear if it did."

Over on Sapelo at that very moment, Miss Catherine, Frank's mother, was out hoeing her garden. She had been bedding up some rows, getting ready to plant some sweet potatoes, before the rain came. She had stopped then and gone to the house, and when it began to let up, she said to Sug, Frank's sister, "Well, let me go outside and finish bedding my rows, and if it rain' again, the rain will water my sweet potatoes and I won't have to." Because it was work for her to fill a bucket at the hand pump, tote that bucket of water down to the field and pour a can or two of water on each newly planted potato set.

So she was back hoeing again, and all of a sudden, this *long* bolt of lightning split the heavens, and reached straight down and struck Miss Catherine. It knocked her down flat onto the ground, right into her potato bed. She never even saw it coming. But that jagged streak of lightning struck her down, the very same yellowish, reddish streak of lightning I saw from my window on St. Simons, that looked like it was striking something on Sapelo.

Sug was on the porch and she saw the lightning hit her mama, and she started screaming. She screamed like the world was coming to an end, and people came running from all directions to see what was wrong. Aunt Ruth Wilson and Miss Mildred Grovner and Miss

Rosa Mills got there first. Then someone rang the bell over at St. Luke's Church, which is just down from Miss Catherine's house. They rang the hurry-hurry-hurry-come-quick, ring of the bell, the disaster ring of the bell, and Uncle Allen and Aunt Annie Mae, that's Miss Catherine's sister, and Mr. Freddie Wilson and Mr. Jimmy Hillery and Mr. Caesar Grovner got there quick as they could.

Uncle Allen threw a sheet over Miss Catherine, loose like, so it wouldn't stick any more than it had too, because she had burns over most of her body. He and the other men managed to get Miss Catherine into his truck then, and he and Aunt Annie Mae raced down to the dock. Bennie Johnson was waiting, he was the captain of the *Janet* then, and he cranked up the motor on that boat and they went speeding off to the other side. They knew the only thing that could save her now was a doctor. They were *amazed* she was alive at all.

But Miss Catherine had not lost consciousness, she was still in her right mind and she could talk, however bad that pain was, and what Miss Catherine was worried about was her children. "Be sure and look after the children for me," she kept saying to Aunt Annie Mae and Aunt Annie Mae solemnly promised that she would.

It wasn't more than about thirty minutes after I saw that lightning flash that my sister Ada got a phone call. We were living next door to her and she had a telephone, so the family called Ada and she came over and told us Miss Catherine had been struck by lightning and that she was being rushed over to the hospital.

We went straight there, and I had never seen anybody with so many burns. Her back and her stomach and her sides and one arm and one leg were burned. Miss Catherine's skin was fiery red and blistered in some areas and darker in others, and there was gauze over the areas where the skin had come off.

The doctors had rigged up a tent-like thing out of plastic sheeting over most of her body, except for her head, because her face wasn't touched, and one arm and leg that weren't burned, and there was an oxygen tank nearby. But Miss Catherine was alive, she could talk, and she was hanging in there. Miss Catherine was definitely hanging in there and Frank and I took heart from that.

Back on Sapelo, heads were shaking and tongues were wagging, now, especially among the women. Any time disaster happens, people are gonna talk about it, and that's just what they were doing. Some people said the family never should have taken Miss Catherine to the hospital before they bathed her in milk, in milk and water.

See, the old people always said that the hottest fire that you can have is a lightning fire, and that the only thing that will pull the heat out from it is milk. If there was a lightning fire in the woods and there wasn't enough milk to put it out with, they said you were fighting a losing battle. "You'd have to wait till God sent rain," they said, "'cause that fire was too hot to out it with ordinary water." But in the rush to get Miss Catherine to the doctor, no one stopped to bathe Miss Catherine in milk and water.

Next, the women, some of the women anyway, got around to what was on their minds, really. That lightning strike was God's way of talking, they said. It was a sign from God that he was angry at Miss Catherine for some of the things she was doing and for all those outside kids she had.

Mama said so, Aunt Mary said so, Miss Clara said so, Aunt Beulah said so even, and she was a sister to Miss Catherine, now. So they condemned her. They been condemning her for years, anyway, because Miss Catherine actually did have outside kids.

She had lost her husband, Mr. Julius, in 1950. He died of kidney failure, the medical records said, but it was questionable kidney failure to some people, to the ones who looked to root and said he had been poisoned. But whatsoever way you believed, there was no question that Mr. Julius was gone.

He had died and left Miss Catherine with four children, four young children to raise. Frank was the oldest and he was not quite six years old. She had a heavy burden on her, and she just got a little eight-dollar-a-month pension after Mr. Julius died. Mr. Julius had been a butler to Richard Reynolds, he had traveled with Mr. Reynolds to his homes in Florida and North Carolina, but Miss Catherine only got eight dollars. What will eight dollars do for you when you got four kids to raise?

One of the deacons came to Miss Catherine's house to console her, and another guy did too. They started coming like they were gonna offer sympathy and help, and the deacons and the elders of the church *do* have a moral responsibility to help a sister of the church, now, but not the way this deacon did. Because Miss Catherine started having more kids then. She had four more kids after Mr. Julius died.

The other guy, the one that wasn't a deacon, ducked out after awhile but the deacon just took over. He took over and he scared off any suitors Miss Catherine might have had, and he got known as being the father of her outside kids.

The deacon was married. He was married to someone else, and his wife suffered in silence. He would tell people he wasn't blessed, because he didn't have any kids by her, and everybody knew that he was blessed by somebody else. After so many years, he came and went to Miss Catherine's house as he pleased and he didn't hide it.

Each time Miss Catherine had another child, her church would call her in. She had to go before the board of elders at her church and apologize for the mistake she made. They would take her back in as a member then, and she could be served communion. She went every time they called, because it was important to her to be a church member, she loved going to church.

But the deacon, he went to the other church over here, and his church never said a thing to him. He was not chastised at all. He got away scot-free, and that was unfair. It was unfair for sure, but it was the way things were done on Sapelo. Miss Catherine didn't go looking for that deacon, he came and sought her out at her house, but it was always the woman that people blamed, not the man.

Grandma didn't, she'd had her own share of outside kids and she wasn't gonna condemn anybody. Aunt Annie Mae didn't, because she has a much forgiving soul, but a lot of the other women blamed her. They befriended Miss Catherine to her face and behind her back they said mean, nasty things.

Miss Catherine was no dummy, she knew what they were saying, but she had the squarest shoulders you ever saw outside of somebody in the military. She held her head up, she looked you straight in the face, and she didn't let them drag her down with their bunch of talking.

She kept the gayer part of herself on top and the serious side on the bottom and she had a likable character, so she was hard to ignore. She worked at the Big House, doing laundry. She came home and starched the kids' clothes, she made quilts for them, she kept a garden, she fixed homemade ice cream and the best bread pudding you could find, and she actually felt blessed. To her it was like, "If God didn't want me to have these children, he wouldn't let me have them."

She made sure her children knew they were a blessing, she always told them so, and those children loved her. None of them ever said anything bad about their mama. They never did.

But with Miss Catherine lying in that hospital bed, tongues were working overtime. "*God frown* upon such a thing," they said, and that was enough to explain that lightning bolt to them.

It was an anxious time. Frank ignored the talk but he was worried about whether his mama was gonna make it, very worried, and I was expecting at that time, and he was a little jittery about that too. It was almost time for our baby to be born, our first child together, and in that summer heat, I was sure ready.

It was the mid-sixties, like I said, and some things were modern on this coast and some things weren't. Frank was working for the Sea Island Company and he had benefits, so I decided to have my child in the hospital. That was definitely modern, it was something that Mama, Grandma, and nobody else in my family had ever done. But the hospital was segregated, there was a separate wing for white patients and a separate wing for black patients, so things were not that modern, really. There hadn't been that much change here.

My baby decided to come on a Sunday evening and Frank took me straight to the birthing room, in the colored section, as the saying went, in the same hospital as Miss Catherine. So we had two members of the family in the hospital at the same time, a burn patient and a maternity patient, and I was giving birth and Miss Catherine was fighting for life.

I was in an off-white-color room with beige curtains and a hospital bed and glistening white sheets and a lamp glaring at me, and everything was all strange to me. It wasn't like being at home at all, not like being in my own bed, with Mama and Aunt Mary and all the women gathered around me, like when I had my first child. None of your family was allowed in, there were just nurses that you didn't know, and they were moving around like they were on automatic. They gave me a shot, without asking if I wanted one or not, and that shot was supposed to knock me out, but it didn't work. I knew everything that was going on the whole time.

The nurses were telling me to push, push, push. Then they were telling me, "You gotta hold it, you gotta hold it," and I said, "Y'all better make up your mind. This baby is ready to come."

"But the doctor ain't here yet. You can't have the baby till the doctor's here to catch it," the nurses were saying, and I was going, "Is that all the doctor gonna do? Catch the baby?" Then all of a sudden, my baby was coming through her door and the doctor was rushing through his door, and both were entering at the same time, and they met each other, and he grabbed my baby. An eight-pound baby girl.

They placed my baby on my stomach for a minute, then they whisked her away to be cleaned up and I didn't get to see her again till eight o'clock in the morning. On Sapelo, the women would have given her right back to me after they cleaned her up, and all the time they were cleaning, up, the midwife and the ladies would have been talking over every inch of that baby. They would have been saying what good lungs she has, and going, "Oh, my goodness, look at these little toes," and, "See how pink the fingernails are? This is gonna be a smart one here, look at those eyes. She's already lookin' at the world."

The sun was up and shining when they brought out a cart with all the babies to their mothers, wrapped up like little Christmas packages, and I had to unwrap that blanket and look at my baby and search her all over and see if everything was alright, because nobody told me nothing that night.

She was absolutely gorgeous, a small bundle with a full head of hair, black, silky hair, and big, bright eyes like Miss Catherine's. I took one look at her, and went, "Oh, my goodness, she looks just like Miss Catherine. She's gonna look just like Miss Catherine."

I nursed my baby and then I laid her down close to me so we could rest together. We were getting to know each other, enjoying our first visit with each other, when a nurse came in, a kinda heavyset lady with her white, starched uniform on.

She came into the room and she stood there. She didn't say anything. That nurse didn't move or anything. She just stood at the foot of my bed and looked at me and my baby. I looked up at the nurse and she turned and went back out of the room. And that was strange. Why did the nurse just come in and stand there? She didn't say nothing, she didn't do nothing.

Just like that, another nurse came in and I said to her, "Why y'all coming in my room so often? One nurse was just here not more than a minute and a half ago."

"Miss Bailey, nobody been in your room."

"Yes there was. One of y'all was in my room no longer than a minute ago. This heavyset nurse come to my door, come to the foot of my bed. She was in my room."

"Nobody been in your room," she said. "I woulda seen 'em if they was."

The nurse's station was just two doors down, she could see everything happening in the hall and she said nobody came this way. Not a single person. They didn't even have a nurse on the floor that looked like the woman that came into my room.

A little chill ran through me instantly and I got a lightheaded feeling, and I was thinking, "Okay, leave it alone. Let sleeping dogs lie." Because I knew right then and there that it was not a flesh-and-blood person that I could touch that had been in my room. It was the spirit of Miss Catherine come to see her grandchild. Her spirit left her body, left her sickbed and came to my bed because she wanted to see that grandchild. It was her very first grandbaby and she was gonna see it.

I wasn't too surprised, spirit-wise. I had always heard the old people talk about how a person can send their spirit, if they're sick or in trouble. So the spirit of a living person can walk; the body doesn't have to depart this earth first. I just had never seen that before, not at all.

The woman in the nurse's uniform that came into my room was the same size, build and height as Miss Catherine. Her skin was dark, just like Miss Catherine's. Only the shape of her face was a little different, it was a little rounder, so it was like part of her I knew, and the other part I didn't know.

I took a deep breath and said, "Okay, that was Miss Catherine. Her spirit came forward. That's all." When Frank came in, I told him, "I believe your mama came and visited me. I know she's in the bed down the hallway, but she came to see Terri," which is what we had named our daughter. Frank just looked at me, like "Naw," and said, "You think so?" And he let it go. He knew that things like that can happen.

We didn't get to take Terri in to see Miss Catherine. The hospital wouldn't let you take a baby into another patient's room, especially not into see someone as sick as Miss Catherine was, and I regret that. I've always regretted that, because Miss Catherine didn't make it. The hospital called Ada late one night, weeks after Terri and I had gotten home from the hospital, and said she had just passed. We had thought she was gonna make it, that there was no turning back if she had lasted that long. But pneumonia set in all of a sudden and she died of complications from it, just three days short of being in that hospital for two months.

But we had a new baby to remind Frank of his mama, and Terri was the spitting image of Miss Catherine. We have a saying on Sapelo, "One come, one go," and it has always been that way over here.

The old people will say, at the deathbed of a family member, "Yep, one goes, one comes." They'll look around to see what family member may be pregnant and say, "Aah, but there's another one on the way." And that takes away some of the sadness for losing that one. Because you get almost an immediate replacement.

Sometimes the child is born even before the person dies and that's the way it was this time. Miss Catherine must have known she wasn't gonna last when she came to see Terri, when her spirit came into my room. She knew she was going, but she lived to see her line continue, and she must have been peaceful at the end. She must have known that God couldn't be too angry at her if the one he sent to replace her looked just like her. One goes, one comes, as we say, and Terri came into the world and Miss Catherine went.

Chapter Twenty-Six

Coming Home

FRANK AND I CAME BACK TO SAPELO FROM ST. Simons in 1966 because I wanted to. He got a job with a new project the Marine Institute on Sapelo was starting to try to revive oystering along the coast, but he would have stayed in St. Simons if it hadn't been for me.

Life in St. Simons wasn't too bad but it wasn't home, and the black community there was beginning to be squeezed a little by development. All of St. Simons was. The whole island was on its way to being turned into fancy shops and high-priced homes for people moving into the Sea Islands. I could see what was happening and knew it was time to leave.

"Your mother's house is sitting there empty on Sapelo and it's an okay home," I told Frank. "We're gonna move in that house and stay there." And we did. But I was older now; I was twenty-one years old, and the civil rights movement had changed the way I saw things.

St. Simons, even though it wasn't a very big town, had helped me see the bigger picture. To be honest with you, I had never really focused on race as an issue before. Sapelo was a little different than most places because everybody who lived on the island permanently was black. I grew up not knowing there were restaurants we couldn't go into because we were black and that there were separate water fountains and separate schools for us. There were a few white kids on Sapelo, children of Cap'n Frank's and children of the post-mistress, and they went to the mainland to school, but they were older. I thought that was why, not that they were white.

I knew that Papa would get upset about the way the men on Sapelo were treated but he never fully explained. I knew that Grandma hated buckra, the kind of white man that got in your busi-ness. She said he was mean and conniving and that she'd rather pick shit with the chickens than work for that buckra man, which meant she'd rather scratch dirt and nearly starve than work for buckra. But in a way I had been kinda content because I didn't really understand what was going on. Always before, money had confused the issue to me. I figured that Richard Reynolds was rich so he deserved to be sitting in the front of the boat and that the white people who worked for him got better pay, so sure, they had more status. I never con-nected any of it with the color of our skin.

In St. Simons, I followed the civil rights movement on television, which is something I wouldn't have been able to do too well on Sapelo, because a lot of people, including Mama and Papa, didn't have electricity yet, so naturally, they didn't have television. I sat glued to my black-and-white screen and I saw protestors singing "We Shall Overcome" and it was inspiring. But I also saw how mean people could be. I saw the dogs and the whips and the jails, the cross burnings and the bombings and the slayings. I suddenly understood a little better a story Grandma told me about revenge in slavery days.

She said her grandmother had a slave master who was very mean and he had done something horrible. She was the cook, so as she cooked, she ground glass very, very fine and she put it in the master's food.

"Baby," Grandma said. "She grind that glass up and every other day she'd give him some of it and then he'd say his stomach hurt, and she'd give him a little bit, just a little bit of herbal medicine that she'd prepare herself and that made his stomach feel good. Then, a couple of days later, she'd go back and she'd put a little more of that ground glass in his food and he'd complain about his stomach aching again. She'd give him a little more herbal medicine to ease the pain and she'd wait a little and she'd put a little more ground glass in his food. She gradually kept at it till that glass did its job and he died."

She could have been whipped near to death by him or she could have been raped by him, or she could have had a daughter that he raped or a family member that he killed. Those were the things that usually prompted revenge. But whatever it was, it was such a hideous crime that she got even. She slowly killed him and his death probably was just put down to a continual stomach ache that irritated the heck out of him but no one could ever find the reason for.

Grandma didn't say who the master was. She didn't say whether this happened on her mama's side of the family, the Hall side that was descended directly from the Bilali side, or her father's side, the Grovners. She just let me know her grandmother, my great-great-grandmother, had told her the story herself, and she was serious about it. As serious as she could be.

In St. Simons, I served barbecue in a restaurant for a little while but mostly I worked as a maid and a babysitter. There weren't many jobs for black people then, it was a way to make a living and it was okay. I was a pretty independent maid and the families I worked for were neat people. The women would tell me what time they were coming back and I'd do whatever cleaning I thought needed to be done; my specialty was cleaning ovens and that always impressed them; and I also watched their kids. I didn't run into any problems, except for one time.

A few months earlier, President Kennedy had introduced the Civil Rights Act. One of the things he said when he did was that a Negro baby born in America had about one-half as much chance of completing high school as a white baby. That struck a chord with me.

On August 28, 1963, more than two hundred thousand people gathered for the March on Washington, which helped give some moral push to passing the act. A sea of black faces, and white faces too, had joined together in support of civil rights for black people. It was an historic moment and it was being broadcast live on national television. I was in a woman's home, ironing and watching the march at the same time, trying to see what rights my people were going to gain so that we could have a better life. She came in and saw me watching and clicked off the television.

It was her house, so she had the right to do that but I had the right to leave. I unplugged the iron and kept going and I didn't go back, even to get my pay, because she wanted me to remain ignorant. She wanted to act as if that march didn't have anything to do with black people on St. Simons.

I was watching television in my own apartment when Dr. King gave his famous "I have a dream" speech on the steps of the Lincoln Memorial, when he said that he dreamed of a day in our nation when people of all colors and religions can join together and sing in the words of the old Negro spiritual, "Free at last! Free at last! Thank God Almighty, we are free at last."

By the time I moved back to Sapelo, the Civil Rights Act had become law and so had the Voting Rights Act, but the Reynolds people had the same mentality as the woman who clicked off the television during the March on Washington. They were pretending that nothing had changed. That's when I took a good look around and started really disliking Richard Reynolds and his henchmen. The whole island was run like it was his private paradise. It was totally controlled. The jobs, the company boat to the mainland, *everything*.

People were afraid to voice their opinion about anything for fear they'd get fired, for fear they wouldn't be allowed to ride the boat between Sapelo and the mainland anymore, and for fear that repercussions would be taken out on their family. No one had forgotten what happened to Mr. Eddie Hall and his wife, Miss Mary.

A daughter of theirs had lived in New York for a long time but she had moved back and was living with her mom and dad at Raccoon Bluff. One Sunday afternoon she and Cousin Dorothy and Mr. Minus were all drinking together and they got into the company truck that Mr. Minus drove and came to Hog Hammock to visit someone. The Hall daughter got out and opened the gate so that Mr. Minus could drive through, and she got back in. But the truck door wasn't quite shut, and when Mr. Minus swung through, she fell out onto a very sharp live oak stump and was seriously wounded. She was rushed to a hospital on the mainland but she died of internal injuries.

The Halls had family members in New York, and unlike people

on Sapelo, black people there were used to suing people. They came and talked to Cap'n Frank and said that Mr. Minus may have been going too fast and he shouldn't have been driving the truck on a Sunday because it was a company truck and it belonged to Mr. Reynolds. They were trying to hold Reynolds responsible, and they threatened suit. The Reynolds people got mad and Cap'n Frank told the family they couldn't ride the company boat anymore. He said he was acting on orders and he probably was, but the company boat was used as a club to keep you in line. Almost no one had a boat of their own, you couldn't afford one, and if you couldn't ride the company boat to the mainland and back, you were marooned on the island.

Mr. Eddie Hall and Miss Mary were in their seventies and it showed how small hearted the Reynolds people were to tell an old couple they couldn't ride the boat anymore. Grandma and some of the other old people had a fit. "Buckra hasn't changed at all," Grandma said. "He's just like a lizard. He never changes his stripes." She had a field day with that buckra word.

Miss Mary's health was declining and eventually she got ill and Mr. Eddie knew he had to get her to a doctor. He still had his own wooden bateau and he snuck it over to the Duplin River, on the west side of the island. Then Allen Green, Uncle Allen, put Miss Mary and Mr. Eddie in his truck and drove them to Kenan Field, to the Duplin. He and Mr. Eddie loaded Miss Mary up in the bateau, covered her with quilts and Mr. Eddie, up in age as he was, started rowing to the mainland. The trip would take him two hours or more, depending on the tide and current.

Uncle Allen knew that when people found out Mr. Eddie and Miss Mary were gone, they would be saying, "How they got off the island? How they got off the island?" He expected he'd lose his job over it if his role was found out. So after he saw Mr. Eddie and Miss Mary off, he drove his truck up the road, then came back on foot with a brush and brushed out his tire tracks—so no one would know he was the one that helped them get off the island.

Miss Mary survived but she never got completely well. She stayed on the mainland with another daughter, so she could get to a doctor. She died not long after I got back to Sapelo, and the family hired a shrimp boat to bring her back to Sapelo so they could bury her. I don't know if they figured she still couldn't ride that boat or whether the family was angry and refused to bring her back on it. Either way, even in death, Miss Mary did not ride that boat.

The repercussions were such that you could be a landowner on Sapelo, with your people born and raised here for generations, but if you did something undesirable or that they didn't like, you could be ordered off the island. It happened to Asberry. Asberry was always high-strung and he shot a neighbor's dog after it tried to bite him. The neighbor complained and Cap'n Frank came down and demanded Asberry give him his pistol. He threw it in a creek and told Asberry, "God damn, you can't live here anymore. You gotta get your ass off the island."

Asberry was living with Mama and Papa, on private property. I told my brother, "Asberry he can't tell you to leave the island. He doesn't have the authority to do that." Asberry left anyhow. He did come back later but he never lived here again.

All this was going on even though Richard Reynolds was gone. He had died in 1964 but his death hadn't made any difference in our lives yet. The land was being run through the foundation he had set up, the Sapelo Island Research Foundation, and the men who had worked for Reynolds were still here, running the island exactly the same, as if they expected Reynolds to walk off the boat at any second.

Reynolds left the island in 1962, before I went to St. Simons, but there wasn't any fanfare about it. Everybody knew he was going to Europe with his new wife but nobody knew he wasn't ever coming back. He'd been here too long to think of that.

He had arrived on Sapelo in 1934. He was twenty-eight years old and he had just bought the island, or most of it anyway, at a bargain price from Howard Coffin. He had Coffin over a barrel because it was during the Depression and he was desperate for money. Coffin also owned Sea Island, an island over by St. Simons. He and his cousin, Alfred Jones, had started a resort on Sea Island for wealthy people, the Cloisters, and he needed money to keep it afloat.

Reynolds got Sapelo as a vacation home basically, since his home was in North Carolina, where his business was located, and he also had a house in Florida, at Palm Beach. In about 1959, he began spending most of his time on Sapelo though. His health was bad by then and his doctors thought an island life would be good for him.

There were people on the island that worshiped him but he called us "his people" in front of guests and that irritated me. I remember when he came to the new school once in the 1950s, and all the other kids went running up to him, "Mr. Reynolds, Mr. Reynolds," like he was something. I stood apart and watched and he looked straight at me, like, "Why is she not running up to me like all the others?"

He hired people who we thought were scoundrels and he didn't look too close at them. They did what they wanted to do, when they wanted to do it, in the name of Richard Reynolds. If someone actually got up the nerve to go to him and complain, he'd say he hadn't known we were being treated like that. He did dismiss a man once, an island manager before Cap'n Frank, who everyone absolutely hated. The guy was on the outs with another one of Reynolds's higher-ups and when someone on the island complained about him to Reynolds, Reynolds fired him.

Reynolds also stopped a summer camp he started for underprivileged boys after he happened to be at the dock at the end of camp one year and saw the boys being picked up in expensive automobiles. So he could have had a heart of gold for all I know. But to me, he was that lazy millionaire we did all the work for. He was always walking around with a cigarette in one hand and a drink in the other; he threw lavish parties for his guests and he had a whole string of wives

His first wife, "Blitz," Elizabeth Dillard, had been a family friend. She was fun loving and nice. She treated everyone in the Big House like they were people, not just someone working for her, so they loved her to death. The second wife, Marianne O'Brien, had been a movie starlet, and she was okay, though people didn't get to know her as well because she wasn't here as much. It was the third wife, Muriel Greenough, who he met at a society ball in New York, that nobody could stand. She was tall and stern and reminded me of Queen Elizabeth, the way Queen Elizabeth never looks happy.

The people working in the Big House had their own dining room and good meals, not filet mignon or anything like that, but very good meals. One day Muriel walked in and found them eating pork chops and she had a fit because she thought that was too good for them. She had a "let them eat fish and grits" attitude that didn't sit well with them. She acted like they were nobody and shouldn't be given special treatment.

She and Richard Reynolds didn't have too much of a honeymoon period before she started giving him holy hell and walking around with a six-inch dagger at her waist. Aunt Mary's job was doing laundry in the Big House then, and she said Muriel wore that dagger at all times. It would surprise me if Reynolds wasn't a little afraid of her even then, and things came to a head one day when Muriel was away from the island.

Reynolds had started having bad bouts of emphysema. He was a heavy smoker and he was suffering from all that smoke he put in his lungs. This particular day he had trouble breathing all of a sudden and he needed oxygen. Fred Johnson was there with him, he was one of the Johnsons from Hog Hammock, and he was a faithful retainer of Reynolds. Fred went to get Reynolds's oxygen bottle—it may have actually been the face mask you breathe through but he said oxygen bottle—and it was nowhere to be found.

Reynolds blacked out and Fred was frantically looking for that thing. Everybody rushed to help and they found it in time to save Richard Reynolds. It was buried in a closet under some dirty clothes—and what was it doing there?

Reynolds immediately wanted a divorce but Muriel didn't, and when he finally got her off of Sapelo, he posted guards. The guards were called night watchmen but they had guns and everybody knew what was going on.

The talk was that Muriel had threatened Reynolds and said that if she couldn't get him herself, she would get someone to, and he was scared to death. So, guards were stationed on the mainland, at Meridian Dock, and on Sapelo, at Marsh Landing Dock, to try to keep someone from slipping over. Richard Reynolds gave them orders to shoot first and ask questions later and Reynolds was rich, he might have been able to get away with that, but Papa was one of the guards. If Papa shot someone, I knew he was going to serve time. No hit man ever showed up though and Reynolds eventually got his divorce.

His fourth wife, Annemarie Schmidt of Germany, was with the medical team that was treating him. The housemaids said he was sweet on her and it turned out he was. She was nice but people didn't get to know her too well before Reynolds moved to Switzerland and died there, at age fifty-eight. When the news of Reynolds's death reached Sapelo, the old people said he died of his own product, because tobacco had killed the tobacco king.

"What are we gonna do without Reynolds?" one man said, and there were people who felt that way. I was sorry that Reynolds's life had been shortened, but I couldn't mourn him because of what he had done to people over here. By the time I came back in 1966, every black community on the island except for Hog Hammock had been closed. Everyone had been relocated into one location so that Richard Reynolds could have the rest of the land.

The relocation had taken place gradually. It was always just a few more families moving into Hog Hammock each year. You could see what was happening, though you didn't get the whole picture, and we were basically powerless to stop it anyway so you tried not to dwell on it.

First, Belle Marsh closed in 1950. Then Lumber Landing closed in 1956. Shell Hammock closed in 1960, when Reynolds wanted to build apartments there for the marine scientists. He offered to build new houses in the community for a few families in Shell Hammock and that sounded good but they turned out to be cheap, little pre-assembled-type wooden houses with a very inferior grade of wood that didn't hold up well at all. They were far from the quality of the concrete-block and terrazzo-floor apartments he built for the marine scientists.

After Shell Hammock closed, the Reynolds people turned the heat up on Raccoon Bluff until by 1964 everybody had left the Bluff.

Howard Coffin had started the thing of buying land from people at Raccoon Bluff, and he got quite a bit but people trusted him more. About the only thing people didn't like about him was that Coffin thought nothing about coming onto your property and snooping around to see if you had any moonshine and he got people arrested for it. He didn't like drinking and moonshine was illegal so he'd ride his horse around the island, looking to see if he could find any. Reynolds didn't do that. He liked his whiskey and he'd even send people out to tell you when the revenuers were coming so they never found anything. But other than that, people liked Coffin. He had a more personal touch and people thought he was more on the up-and-up in his dealings with them. They didn't feel forced to sell their land like they did under Reynolds.

There was more than one way to get people's land. The land you lived on over here was never owned by just one person. It was owned by all of the heirs of a family, even if there was just one person living there right then. The lawyers for Coffin and Reynolds must have known the law and we didn't, but they never told anyone that they needed to consult with other people in the family before they could sell the land. They just gave the person living on it some money and that was that.

In other cases, maybe someone in the family needed money for some emergency and so they borrowed a little bit of money from Coffin or Reynolds. Their people would ask, "What can we hold on to until you pay us back? You got a piece of land, don't you? We'll hold the deed on your ten acres."

Money was always short over here and as time went by and that person didn't repay it, no one ever reminded him that he owed it. He could end up dying without telling anyone in the family of the debt because he forgot it or was ashamed of it. Then, one of the higher-ups on the island would swoop in and say, "Well, your father borrowed fifty dollars on the land before he died and you don't own it any more." They'd say Coffin or Reynolds, whichever it was, had owned the land for years and you had only been living there through their generosity.

So, people lost their land and it didn't seem right to them but they didn't know they had any rights. There wasn't anything they could do about it. When some people learned more about the law later on, they'd say, "Well, they stole that land because my aunt signed it but no one else did." But it was a closed issue because who dared challenge the Coffins or the Reynoldses of the world at that time?

Many of the people left at the Bluff in the sixties were elderly people who lived in old houses and several were enticed into Hog Hammock with offers of land swaps and a new or remodeled house. So everything just combined and people were pushed into Hog Hammock whether they wanted to or not. There were each promised a house with electricity and a bathroom in Hog Hammock and when they moved, they got a bare bulb on a string and a room set aside for a bathroom that didn't have any fixtures in it or running water.

Uncle Allen had sworn that he wouldn't move out of the Bluff "until hell freezes over" but he did and hell isn't frozen over yet. We have a saying on Sapelo, "Money talks and bullshit walks," and that's the way it works most times. Uncle Allen was angry but in the end, he walked.

Mr. Eddie Hall was the last person to leave the Bluff. He held on as long as he could and when he moved into Hog Hammock in 1964, the Bluff was closed.

To me, the worst was what happened to Miss Frances and her husband, Mr. Reuben. They didn't get to move into Hog Hammock.

They were in their seventies, and they were told they didn't own any land. They thought they owned land at the Bluff but they couldn't prove it, and if they didn't have land to swap, they couldn't get a house in Hog Hammock. Miss Frances would have swallowed her pride to stay on Sapelo. When she had to leave the island, it broke her spirit.

In 1966, when I got back to Sapelo, everyone who was a member of the First African Baptist Church was still going up to Raccoon Bluff for church on the first Sunday of the month, just as people had been since 1900. I went too but it got harder and harder to go. We passed empty houses on the way, and then after awhile, the houses got torn down and we passed empty house sites and it hurt.

The church elders decided to build a new church in Hog Hammock since all the members lived there now and the Reynolds foundation donated money for it. The new church opened in 1968 and it was a happy occasion and a sad one too. A happy one because First A.B. was still alive on Sapelo and we had a nice, new cinder block building, but a sad one because that's when it really hit us that we had lost the Bluff. We wouldn't be going up there anymore, even for church.

The community formed by the three black men who had bought land there in 1871, almost as soon as they had been legally able to, had lasted ninety-three years. I said to Frank, "With a legacy like that, how did we mess around and let this happen? How did we lose that whole fighting spirit and determination?" We had lost the Bluff and nothing would ever be the same.

Grandma lived to see the Bluff close and her comment was, "Buckra always wanted it. He thought it was too good for colored people." To her mind and to most of us, it was a defeat. She died in December of 1968, just months after First A.B. moved. Grandpa had died in his sleep three years earlier. He lived into his eighties. His leg had gotten worse, he always used a cane, but he took care of Grandma until the day he died. His mind and his eyesight were good. He could lie in bed and shoot a squirrel off the limb outside his window with a single shot. After the Bluff closed and he died, there wasn't much left for Grandma. Her time and her world were gone.

◆

The Eye of the Storm

ONCE THE CHANGES STARTED, THEY WERE LIKE A force of nature that we couldn't stop. It was the late sixties, after all, and that was a time of tremendous change, and after the sixties came the seventies and they were change-filled years too. Change after change blew into Sapelo and some came in on a gentle breeze and others battered us with winds so fierce we thought we were gonna be blown right off the island. By the time the eighties rolled around, we felt like a special list of endangered peoples had been drawn up and that our names were on it.

In 1967, Georgia Power came to Sapelo, bringing electricity to everybody who didn't have it. I always tell everyone that Georgia Power made us all equal because all of a sudden, you could have electric lights in your house whether you were one of the favored ones on this island or not. And getting electricity didn't mean just that you could have lights around the clock if you wanted them, it was the whole nine yards. You could get an electric pump attached to your well and have running water and indoor plumbing and flush toilets and you wouldn't have to carry in the water from outside either. You could get a hot water heater installed and you wouldn't have to boil water in a kettle on the stove to do your dishes and take a bath anymore, and you could even get air-conditioning. Everybody could have these conveniences.

The Big House had been lit with lights the whole time I was growing up. Back in Howard Coffin's day, he had bought a big generator and when Reynolds came, he got a bigger generator and over time he wound up with three *huge* generators. He ran electric lines for the scientists when they came in the fifties, and over time electric lines were run to about half of the houses in Hog Hammock too. But it wasn't like one section of the community would get electricity and then another area would get it. A house in one area would have electricity and then you could skip maybe two more houses before the next house had it. If you were an outsider looking in, you would have probably thought there wasn't much rhyme or reason to who had electricity and who didn't, but if you were born and bred on Sapelo, you knew there was a certain type of reasoning behind it.

It worked like this: if I'd had my own house back then and they were running a line near me, Cap'n Frank would have asked one of the men in the community, the ones that always played up to him, "Well, do you think that Cornelia should get electricity?" "She don't need none," he would have said, and that would have been that. I was not from a family that worked in the Big House or had one of the higher-paying jobs, so we weren't considered to be part of the higher echelon and I wouldn't have gotten electricity. It was that simple. It was a private system and they didn't have to give you electricity. They gave it to who they wanted to give it to.

Some people would throw their pride aside and beg Cap'n Frank for electricity and kept on begging until they got it, but Papa was not like that. He was never one to beg for anything. He'd rather stick with his kerosene lamps than beg so he was among the half that didn't have any electricity while Reynolds was around.

So when the lights went on one Friday in October, 1967 in the first group of houses that Georgia Power got connected, it was definitely a day to remember. I was out in the front of my yard digging up the fall crop of sweet potatoes at the very moment a workman, on a pole right near me, flipped the switch. It was in the middle of the afternoon, so you didn't see a big difference right away, but when darkness fell over the island, I could see a bright light down the way in Miss Mildred Grovner's house where a kerosene lamp had always been lit.

Frank and I weren't in that first group to get electricity but that was okay because we weren't going to be oohing and aahing over the wonders of it. We had it when we were in St. Simons so it wasn't brand new to us. Within a couple of weeks everybody on Sapelo was hooked up to the new system, though, and then, for the first time in the history of the island, you could see lights shining all over the community.

Electricity had always been a shaky thing, even if you were lucky and had it, before Georgia Power came over. Whenever the weather was bad, Cap'n Frank or one of the other higher-ups would give the order to switch off the Reynolds's generators. There was a phone in the mechanic shop with a real loud ringer and the phone would ring and whoever was working in the area would go switch off the electricity.

Papa was the night watchman back then, so when the phone rang at night, he was the one to cut the power off. Some evenings I'd be visiting at someone's house who had electricity and it would start storming and the lights would go off and I'd know that Papa had thrown the switch. I don't think it bothered him one bit to throw that switch. He probably took great satisfaction in it. He didn't have as much as a bare lightbulb on a cord himself but he could turn off the lights on the island—and he'd just be doing what he was told to do.

But *now*, after the power company had come and gone, in the very last house in the community before the road went up toward the North End, there was a light on in Papa's house. Two years before man walked on the moon, Papa had finally gotten electricity.

That change came in on a mild breeze. It made people's lives a little easier. It was a good change mostly, though it pushed us into a world where it was hard to even imagine that the hag and the jack-o'-lantern had once ruled the dark of night here.

I told my kids about the hag and the jack-o'-lantern, I told them how nobody on this island was safe from the hag and how the hag could ride you like a horse, until you were too tired to practically move the next day. I told them how you could follow a jack-o'-lantern at night until you'd get so confused and turned around that you were hopelessly lost in the woods. But to my kids, the hag and the jack-o'-lanterns were legends from the past. To them, they weren't the real, living, mysterious beings they had been to me and everybody before me on Sapelo. My kids were living on the same island that I did as a child, yes, but they were growing up in a world where the power of magic and the old ways was fading away.

I had three children now. In addition to Stanley, Terri, and Julius, or "Lix" for short. In 1968, I was expecting a fourth child. I had planned to go to the mainland for the birth of my son Gregory, but I started having labor pains on a Friday night, long after the last boat had gone to the mainland.

Frank went and knocked on the door of Miss Katie Underwood's house, the midwife, just as menfolks here had done for gen-

erations, and Miss Katie, now in her nineties, came out of retirement
to deliver Greg. He was her last baby, because Miss Katie retired for
good after that and the reign of the midwives was over.

We no longer had a midwife to deliver our children, read the
knots in the afterbirth or see to it that the afterbirth was buried
properly so that every child, wherever he or she went in life, would
always be connected to Sapelo. Our midwives had always set the
rules for mothers-to-be and for the care of the new baby and the
mother, so that was about as basic a change as you could get. It had
been coming for a good while, but when Miss Katie delivered her
last child, it was like a wind that blew itself out all at once. We lost
something valuable.

The year 1968 also marked Papa's retirement. Cap'n Frank was
not one to mention the birthday of the men working under him
unless they were about to turn sixty-five. Then all of a sudden his
memory got good. "Ain't you got a birthday coming up?" he
reminded Papa shortly before the event. Papa turned sixty-five on
April 24, 1968, and his job was over that day.

So, it was like a cold wind being directed right at you. You were
turned out to pasture after years of being treated without too much
respect. Papa didn't get a Timex watch to while his time away with, a
pat on the back, a card or anything else that so much as said "thank you
for your many years of working." And he sure didn't get a pension.
You didn't get a pension working for Reynolds or his foundation.

You just got the little bit you put into Social Security and you
hoped that was right. The federal income tax system wasn't started
until after Papa began working, and for a long time Papa and the
other people over here didn't know a thing about it.

Papa knew what his weekly pay was that he got in a little enve-
lope and that's all. There was never anything on Papa's check that

said how much his total pay was or what was being taken out for taxes, and he didn't get a yearly statement either. He didn't know what he was paying in taxes until he started working at Blackbeard in 1957. Whatever taxes were filed for Papa and the other men before that, the Reynolds people filed without telling them about them. It's true that the tax forms would have been hard for a lot of the men to fill out on their own, but that isn't the point. You like to know what's being done in your name.

Papa put it all behind him like he did everything else. He was finished with it, it was "kitty-by-th'-door" to him. His shift and that of a whole generation of men and women he had worked with was over now. They were passing the responsibility of taking care of the island on to my generation and it wasn't any time at all until gale winds started blowing.

In 1969 we got the news that the North End of Sapelo was being sold to the state of Georgia to use as a hunting and wildlife reserve. It would be years before we found out that the state thought it owned the entire North End, including all of Raccoon Bluff, and while Reynolds had owned most of the land there, he hadn't owned all of it.

There were still a few black people from Sapelo that were hanging on to their family land at the Bluff. They weren't living on it, but it meant something to them, they owned it and they were paying taxes on it. But no one from the Reynolds foundation or the state ever notified black landowners of the sale, not before it happened, not when it happened, and not after it happened. The Georgia Department of Natural Resources, or DNR as we call it, just moved in. We discovered later the state was claiming the whole thing, because one man filed suit before the statute of limitations ran out.

Bill Brasher, who lives in Darien and is white, had bought some land from one of the old families at the Bluff, the Handys, and he said in court that the state was denying him access to it. The state argued that it owned the entire North End and the land couldn't be his but Brasher had a deed and he won. He did us a favor by coming over and personally telling us about his suit so that anyone who could show ownership could try to get their land back too. Some families did file claims, and they're still waiting for them to be resolved.

We didn't know anything about the terms of the sale of the North End back in 1969, but we were jittery about it because *wham!* Here came a big, new landowner over here. That hadn't happened since 1934. Everything was changing so fast we weren't sure of our footing anymore. We got very nervous about our future. It hit us for the first time that we could lose our island home if we weren't careful.

Geechee and Gullah people were being pushed off land they'd owned since Reconstruction all through the Sea Islands, so that fancy new developments could be built in places like Hilton Head and Daufauski Island in South Carolina. We had already been relocated into Hog Hammock, so what was there to protect us from being pushed all the way off the island? We felt battered, tossed about by storm winds ever since the early sixties, and now it looked like storm winds were starting to blow again.

Living on an island, storms are something we know about. We know that a hurricane can strike at almost any time the weather is hot. We hadn't had any bad hurricanes over here while I was growing up, we had been lucky for a long time, but every person on this island can tell when a storm is coming.

The rain starts in and keeps coming down harder and harder and it doesn't ever let up. The sky turns a dusty yellow, angry-looking banks of black clouds start rushing by overhead, stretching from horizon to horizon, and that's when the danger begins. The wind rises till all you can hear is its shrieking and howling, waves tear at the shoreline and the water comes crashing ashore.

There was a terrible storm on this part of the coast in 1824, during the days of slavery. Waves rushed in and covered all of Sapelo. All the crops in the fields were lost and the cattle were drowned. On a nearby island, every slave was washed out to sea, but on Sapelo, everybody was spared. Bilali was in charge here. The day before the storm he made sure that every black man, woman, and child was taken to the sturdy sugar and cotton houses, where they were safe behind thick, tabby walls.

There was a second terrible hurricane, in 1898. This one was way after Bilali's time. It was the storm that destroyed the hospital on Blackbeard Island and floated the lumber over to the Bluff that some of Bilali's grandchildren used to build the church.

At the height of the 1898 storm, waves as high as twelve feet broke over the west side of the island, and that's the side furthest away from the ocean. The winds smashed into the small, wooden houses everyone had and blew them into pieces and people climbed into trees, clinging to the branches to ride out the storm. Most people made it through but one family of black people drowned.

In every hurricane, there is an eye of the storm, a center of perfect calm and blue skies, and when it comes, if you don't know any better, you can think that the storm is over. But it's not. After the eye passes, the rain starts all over again, the wind shrieks again and the storm can lash out at you even worse than before.

That's what we feared in 1969, that we were in the eye of the storm, and the winds and rain were going to lash out at us again any minute. Our senses were yelling "storm, storm," but nothing too horrible happened right away, so, finally we took a deep breath and said, "Okay, they've got the North End, but we're still here." We relaxed awhile. Then the storm winds started blowing again.

In 1975, our worst fears were staring us in the face because the word was that we were on the chopping block, that the Reynolds foundation was entering talks with the state to sell the South End to the state—*all* of the South End, including Hog Hammock. And this time, unlike Raccoon Bluff where they owned most of the land, the Reynolds foundation just owned a small part of Hog Hammock. *We* owned most of it.

It would be easy to think, "We cleared the black people out of Belle Marsh. We cleared them out of Lumber Landing. We cleared them out of Shell Hammock and Raccoon Bluff. It wasn't too hard. We'll clear them out of Hog Hammock now and then we've got a whole package to sell the state." There were a little less than a hundred and fifty of us still on the island then, so they could have done it

Fred Johnson was the first to hear about the proposed sale. He was the one who had been a faithful retainer to Richard Reynolds and he was in tight with the brass at the Big House. He heard the news there and I wouldn't be at all surprised if someone hadn't let the cat out of the bag on purpose. Some of the brass over here were very opposed to letting the state get its hands on the South End. They liked running the island and didn't want to give that up.

The news spread through Hog Hammock quickly and when it did, we were angry. We had fight in our eyes. People were going around saying, "They done stole every place else, now they want to steal this place from us too. They even want to move us. Well, we're *not gonna* move again."

Fred Johnson called Ben Lewis in Savannah. Ben was born on Sapelo but had lived most of his life in Savannah. He was working at Savannah State College in public relations and he had contacts and knew the right people, so we ended up getting three lawyers on our side, including an African American lawyer who is now a judge in Brunswick. Under Ben's leadership, we formed the Hog Hammock Community Foundation. Our goal was to get the Reynolds foundation and the state to leave us out of the sale.

My name was one of the ones on the charter of incorporation but every person in Hog Hammock supported the new group. We had hot and heavy meetings, mass meetings, and everybody that could walk, crawl or creep came. The old folks like Mama and Papa, Aunt Mary, Uncle Glasco and Allen Green came. Everyone came and pitched in their ideas and reached into their pockets and gave money because a fire had been lit under us. We weren't used to organizing and speaking out but we were ready.

The attitude among people here toward Reynolds and his foundation had always been, "They got money, they're powerful, you can't fight them. You can't fight the white man." But the civil rights movement had made us realize that you *can* oppose someone powerful, and not only that, sometimes you can even win.

Ben got hold of a copy of the first set of papers on the proposed sale of the South End and he read it aloud at a meeting and Hog Hammock actually was included in the proposal. I was there when he read it. The Reynolds foundation backed off when they realized the stink it would cause to uproot us from the island. When the next set of papers was read aloud, we were no longer part of the sale. We had done enough to make them leave us alone.

When the Reynolds people pulled out, the state of Georgia strengthened its hold over all of the island, except for the community of Hog Hammock. I say the state but I really mean the Department of Natural Resources (DNR). Men in khaki shirts and green slacks soon were going all over Sapelo, bent on running things now that they considered it their island. They got into the ownership mentality pretty quick.

One of the rangers would drive up to the community yelling, "Cow on the ground, cow on the ground," whenever a wild cow was killed. They wouldn't touch the meat themselves, they weren't allowed to, but they expected us to come running to get it so we could eat the meat. I told Frank that we weren't going to do that. It reminded me of how slave masters used to expect people to come running for food and I didn't like it one bit.

We got used to DNR being here but we didn't get comfortable with them. The trust never developed between the state and us. How could it really? You could walk into a certain room in the DNR headquarters at Long Tabby, the site of the former tabby sugar house where people had ridden out the storm of 1824, and see a large map of Sapelo posted on a wall. The map had a big red circle around Hog Hammock with the words "to be acquired" written next to it. I saw the map myself and a lot of other people did too.

The tourists arrived soon. In 1977, DNR started half-day tours of the island for the public. We started getting a boatload of tourists almost every day. Our green marsh grass and white beaches had always been a barrier that kept the outside world out but not anymore. They drew people here by the thousands and that was a whole new thing to get used to.

We had other things on our mind that were more critical though. The number of jobs on the island was dwindling. DNR didn't need as many people working for them as Coffin or Reynolds had. Coffin had two hundred people working for him at one time and Reynolds had a sizable number too but DNR didn't plant crops or run a dairy. They didn't use the land in the same ways. They did keep everybody on till they retired, but as they retired, the jobs dried up.

The jobs didn't all disappear right away, but they did over time, until finally, there were just eighteen people in the community employed by DNR. People could tell what was happening and they started leaving the island in droves, so they could get jobs on the mainland. I looked around one day and said, "My God, my community is almost gone."

Our school closed too and that was a hard blow. It had gone to being an elementary school only, like it had been when I started there, and after the sixth grade, the kids transferred to the mainland. But we'd had our own school since Reconstruction and it was a source of pride to us, and all of a sudden, it was gone.

It closed in 1978. Some people who wanna puff and put wind in their jaw said, "Well, we closed the school for educational reasons, so the kids could get a better education on the other side," but that wasn't it at all. Those kids were getting the best education you can get, right here on Sapelo. The real reason it closed was that the state was closing a lot of small, rural schools during that time. Under the state's standards, you had to have 29.5 kids per teacher, and we didn't have 29 elementary school students left on the whole island. We couldn't meet what the state required in order to have even one teacher.

Maurice was in the third grade when the change came and after he went to school on the mainland, I started seeing a difference right away. He just wasn't being taught as much. We'd had teachers on Sapelo who really cared about the students and believed in homework and discipline. Once our kids went to the other side, I don't think they ever really caught up again.

Mostly, what they were learning from the first grade on, was to look to the other side for everything—for school and for jobs later on. When they got on the boat to go to the mainland for school and we waved good-bye, we knew we were losing them to the other side.

In 1980, at the beginning of a new decade, you could still go into the DNR headquarters here and still see the very same map of Sapelo with the red circle around Hog Hammock and the words "to be acquired" hanging on the wall there. It stayed on the wall until the mid-eighties when, during the uproar caused by Bill Brasher's land claim against the state, someone, I can't say for sure who, realized that maybe it wasn't too wise to leave that map up on the wall and quietly took it down.

I don't know what happened to that map. I never saw it again. It just disappeared. But we didn't for a minute believe that rolling the map up and taking it off the wall meant the state didn't want our land anymore, or that there wouldn't be other threats to our land as well. We couldn't rest easy at all. Our community was in trouble and it was as plain as the nose on your face that more storms would be coming our way.

She Who Has a Purpose

I HAD *LIVED* OUR CULTURE SO I KNEW A GOOD BIT about that part of my heritage, but I didn't know much about our history because so much of it had gotten lost. Slavery had been horrible and when it was over, people just closed the door on it and didn't want to talk about it anymore. There were also things that people had either forgotten or hadn't thought were important enough to pass down.

I didn't know, for instance, when the first Africans came to Sapelo and I still don't. I didn't know that they had been brought here because they had specific skills that the planters needed. I didn't even know, until it closed, that the community of Raccoon Bluff had been founded by three black men after the Civil War, just that black people had lived at the Bluff for a long time. And that should have been a *big* source of pride to us.

We didn't have a written history. We had what is called an oral tradition. It was a very rich oral tradition but there were huge holes in it, so many it was harmful to our view of who we were. You respect yourself more when you know you're someone with a history and we needed that over here.

What really got me started was hearing about the Ibos and Ibo's Landing, back when I was living in St. Simons. There is a spiritual that says, "Before I'll be a slave, I'll be buried in my grave, And go home to my Lord and be saved," and that tells the whole story right there.

A slave trader had a ship loaded with Africans from the Ibo tribe in southeastern Nigeria, sitting in a harbor in Africa, waiting for someone to buy its human cargo, when three Georgia planters agreed to the purchase. Most slaveholders would not buy Ibos if they had a choice because Ibos were considered a rebellious and unruly people and there were stories of Ibos' taking their own lives rather than submitting to slavery. But the Georgia slaveholders were in a hurry to get new slaves. They threw caution to the wind and said, "Okay, we'll take them."

Only a few slaveholders were wealthy enough to place an order with a broker for a shipload of slaves to be brought directly to them. Usually, Sea Island slaveholders traveled to Charleston or Savannah to buy slaves at slave auctions in those cities. But the Ibos were spoken for, so the ship sailed straight to the coast of Georgia, to Dunbar Creek on St. Simons.

From the crew's point of view, everything was fine until they offloaded the Africans. All hell broke loose then. The Ibos were angry, they were frightened and desperate to get away from their captors and through some miracle some of them managed to break free.

The crew members were screaming for help and fleeing for their lives and the Ibos who had broke free turned and walked into the water, *straight* into the water, like they were going to walk back to Africa. They had to have known they couldn't make it back to Africa. They knew how far away Africa was. They'd been in a ship for a month or more and all they could see the whole time was water,

water and more water. At dayclean, they saw water. When the sun beat down overhead, they saw water. At nighttime, by the light of the stars, they saw water. And in the end, they chose the water as their grave, rather than live out their lives as slaves.

Not all the Ibos walked into the water, just some of them. There were others that were still alive. Some of them came to Sapelo, because Thomas Spalding was one of three men who bought that shipload of slaves, along with John Couper, who owned the plantation Cannon's Point on St. Simons, and Pierce Butler of St. Simons and Butler's Island.

When I heard about the Ibos, I wondered, were those the same Africans that Ronnister Johnson told me about when I was growing up? The ones he told a story about who had run into the woods to hide and the master had said to let them stay there until they were ready to come out and behave? They could have been. If they were from that shipload, they would have been rebellious and frightened. It would make sense that they were the ones who ran into the woods in the area that later became known as Behavior. It was a slave community first, and Behavior Cemetery got located there after the community started.

The name of the ship the Ibos had been on was the *York* and we have a York's Landing on Sapelo, on the west side near Long Tabby on Barn Creek, where slaves were often unloaded. We had a guy over here named York Dixon when I was growing up. Could it be that the name "York" was passed down over here? Was his great-great-great-grandfather on that ship of Ibos? Just the very thought of it made me want to know more.

There were things even in my own family that I didn't know because the old people had taken so much history with them "to the grave and beyond," as we said over here. Grandma's skin, when she got older, lightened up to where she looked like a white person with a *light* tan. She hated that skin. She'd look in the mirror and say, "I look like a poor cracker, like buckra with that slappy skin," because her skin was getting loose, the way some white people's skin got as they aged. Now that I was older I asked Mama, "Mama, where did the white come from in our family?"

"Whatcha' mean?"

"Mama, you're fair, Grandma was fairer than you and Great-Grandma Harriet's was ever fairer, so where did the white come from?"

Mama got quiet. She didn't say a word. She wouldn't answer me for nothing in the world, but something happened somewhere back there. Bilali was dark and Hester was dark, but Hester's daughter, Sally, was fair. Within a generation after Bilali came to Sapelo, some white blood got in the family and it would have had to come from a plantation owner or overseer or a visitor to the island.

Most people over here who had some fairness in the family were not proud of it. They never made a point of saying, "I am better than you, my hair is straighter than yours," or anything like that. They'd blame that light skin on the Indians, even though there weren't any Indians here back when the fairness crept in. They would never say it came from a white man.

We did have a dish we called Mulatto Rice though, and it was rice with just enough tomatoes to change the color a little bit. It usually had onions and pieces of fried bacon in it too. Mama served it with fried fish. It was her favorite mixed rice dish, a change from the pure white rice we ate, and it was named after light-skinned people. That dish was as close as the old people usually came to acknowledging that there was some white blood in some of us.

Some of the old people I knew in my childhood were passing

now and I knew that soon it was going to be even harder for us to recapture some of our history. So when the state hired a professional genealogist, Mae Ruth Green, to do a genealogical study of black families who owned land on Sapelo at the time of the 1870 census, I was ready to help. Everyone in Hog Hammock knew that the Department of Natural Resources had brought Miss Green in with the hope that it would help resolve some land issues, but we figured something good would come out of the study. I was one of two people hired to help Miss Green track down and interview every descendant we could find. The old people were suspicious of outsiders, so I'd take her around to people's houses to help build trust and make sure the right questions were asked, and by the end of the study, each family had a written record of its members as far back as the Spalding era. That was something concrete that we hadn't had before.

One day I was riding the state boat to the mainland and a cousin of mine was reading a book, *Drums and Shadows*, published by the University of Georgia Press in 1940. It was written by the Savannah Unit of the Georgia Writers' Project under the Work Progress Administration, during the Depression, and the writers had interviewed black people on the Georgia coast in the 1930s, including people on Sapelo and all of the islands. They were looking for what they called "survivalisms," beliefs and practices that had been passed down from our African ancestors. I had never heard of the book, I didn't know anyone who did, but it had been around even before I was born and it was amazing. Simply amazing.

There were photographs of Katie Brown and Uncle Shed and mention of so many things that I had grown up with, from Brer

Rabbit stories to root and conjure. I found out from that book that harvesttime once was a big time over here. People would pray and sing the night through and when the sun rose, they would dance in a circle and beat drums and rattle dry gourds with seeds in them. I had heard the old people talk about there being drums here a long time ago but I had no idea they were used at harvest festivals, because we had quit having harvest festivals before my time.

I found out that Uncle Shed and other people over here remembered that a long time ago the entire funeral procession would stop at the graveyard gate and ask permission from the spirits to enter to bury their loved one in the "mother dust." I had grown up doing that, but now I knew the practice was a very old one that my ancestors probably brought with them from Africa.

I also learned the names of all seven of Bilali's daughters. I had known he had seven daughters, because of the Seven Sisters rose that we had over here, but now I knew them as Margaret, Bintu, Charlotte, Medina, Yaruba, Fatima, and of course, Hester, my great-great-great-grandmother.

After that, I redoubled my efforts to find out more about my ancestors but it was hard to find very much. History had recorded the life of Thomas Spalding because he was a plantation owner and he was prominent but no one had thought to record the lives of the Africans who were here two hundred years ago. There were a few mentions of Bilali, because he was the head driver, but there weren't many facts. He had gotten romanticized because he was different, he was a Muslim and he had so much power.

Spalding's friend John Couper, who owned a plantation on St. Simons, wrote Spalding that a man on his plantation knew Bilali and that they were from the same village in Africa. They recognized each other when Couper came to Sapelo to visit Spalding, and while the two plantation owners were having their visit, I imagine the two men from Africa were having theirs too.

The letter from John Couper is about the only document we've come across relating to Bilali. So, who was this man who had something so special that Thomas Spalding was willing to buy him and almost his whole family in order to get him?

We think Bilali was born in West Africa around 1760, possibly in what is now Gambia or Guinea. During that period, Muslim factions in West Africa were fighting each other and selling their prisoners of war into slavery. That may be how Bilali got enslaved.

Not everybody was captured in the woods by British slavers or tricked by a piece of red cloth. Some Africans were bartered and swapped and traded by other Africans. And while, if you're black, that could make you angry, to be honest with you, it made me feel better to know that. I never liked the story of people being tricked by a piece of red cloth. Although I know that did happen in some cases.

Bilali probably died not long after 1855. That would put him in his nineties when he died and that sounds right because three of his daughters lived to be in their nineties, a lot of his other descendants have too, and Grandma said that he lived to know all of his grandchildren and some of his great-grands. So, he lived a long and fruitful life.

He entered the picture on Sapelo sometime after 1802, the year Spalding started building what he thought was going to be a permanent empire for himself and his family. I suspect Spalding of being a picky shopper. He had a fifty-thousand pound loan from a British banker and he wanted the best seeds to plant on his newly acquired land and he wanted the best slaves to work it. He didn't just want people with muscle, he wanted people with know-how and he got what his grandson described as "hands skilled in the management of labor" from the British West Indies. He got Bilali and his family.

Bilali had been taken to the Bahamas as a slave. Spalding had lived in the Bahamas when he was a kid, because his father, who was a British loyalist during the American Revolution, had fled first to British Florida and later to the Bahamas. So, did Spalding remember Bilali from when he was a kid? Or did he ask family friends to find him someone who was an expert at growing the long-staple cotton that he wanted to grow? Did Spalding sail to the Bahamas himself to get Bilali? We don't know. But Bilali must have been running the plantation of his former owner to some extent, for Spalding to make Bilali the head driver on Sapelo.

By the time I came around, Richard Reynolds had gotten someone to write a fictional account of Sapelo's history. In the book *The Great Oaks*, by Ben Ames, a slaveholder who'd beaten his wife went riding out on horseback, Bilali followed him and the slaveholder's horse was found but he was never seen again. But that story is foolishness. If a slaveholder's disappearance had been linked to a slave, *no slave*, not even Bilali, would have escaped hanging back then. I've got a feeling that if black people of Bilali's time had been writing about him, they wouldn't have glorified him like a saint. Matter of fact, I suspect that a lot of people on Sapelo didn't particularly like Bilali.

Grandma always said, "As far back as my people can remember, they didn't particularly like our family that much." So that was an inkling right there that her family was not well liked, even after all those years, because of Bilali.

I think people respected The Old Man, but they were afraid of him. Afraid of his power. He was close to Spalding and he was put in the position of being their boss, and being the head driver, he would have been tough and strong willed, able to make men do what he said—*or else.*

There's a question mark on that "or else" too. The head driver, whether he was white or black, was usually the one who whipped the other slaves and there's nothing to say that Bilali did not do that. It was his job to make sure the crops were planted and harvested at the right time and he wouldn't have stood for any shenanigans. He may have treated everyone fair but when a heavy hand was due, he could have administered it to make sure it was done correctly.

There's a theory that Bilali was a student in Timbo, a center of learning and the capital of Futa Jallon, in modern-day Guinea, and that he was seized there and sold into slavery. But to me, there's a hole in that, because Uncle Shed said that Bilali's daughter Hester, my ancestor, remembered their village in Africa. She remembered parrots and snakes and that the lion was the most powerful of beasts. She said that the house she lived in was covered with palmettos and grass for the roof, and the walls were made of mud applied over a frame of sticks. And if Bilali had been a student, would he have had a family? Or could Uncle Shed have been confused and Hester, who we think was born in the Bahamas, had been telling Uncle Shed what her mother remembered from Africa? And would Bilali's family have been taken together from Africa to the Bahamas and then again to Sapelo? The odds against that seem very high.

We do know that Bilali could read and write. Whether he'd gone beyond the basics, I can't say, but it wasn't unusual for a Muslim to be able to read at that time. Where there were Muslim communities in that part of Africa, they made sure that their children learned sections of the Koran and were introduced to Arabic grammar. So even if Bilali hadn't gone on to advanced studies, he likely would have had some education.

White planters often credited Muslims like Bilali as being of superior intelligence. That probably had to do with the fact that a lot of them had some education, but it also had to do with their appearance. To the planters, the Muslims' Arabic-looking narrow features were indicative of a higher caste than the other Africans. The Europeans thought the Arabic features were closer to their own. Bilali might have thought he was superior too because he set himself above the others. His family held themselves aloof. So there were things about him that would have caused a divide right off the bat.

I think even if Bilali hadn't been the head driver he would have been different. I think his carriage and what he stood for would have set him above other people whether he was the head driver or not. He lived his life as much on his own terms as was possible for a black man in slavery times.

Knowing the little bit I did about Bilali made it all the more exciting when I saw a special exhibit in the lighthouse at St. Simons in the late 1980s. A photographer had put together photographs from *Drums and Shadows* of people like Uncle Shed and Katie Brown with photographs he had taken of people like Uncle Allen Green and even myself, who were still living on Sapelo, and you could see the similarities among us over the generations. That was neat but what really drew my interest was a rare book on loan from the University of Georgia Library in Athens: Bilali's journal.

It's a small brown book about the size of a Harlequin romance, with writing in a faded, reddish ink that could have been made from pokeweed berries or prickly pear cactus, both of which grow here.

The ink is smeared in spots, with blotches covering parts of words so it would have been hard to read even if I could read Arabic, but just to see it was something special—and it made my great-great-great-great-grandfather real to me.

Toward the end of his life, in about 1855, Bilali gave it to the Presbyterian minister in Darien, Francis R. Goulding. Goulding's son said that Bilali was "old and crippled and not able to work" at the time and lived on the mainland just opposite Sapelo Island.

Scholars have had difficulty transcribing it but the latest thinking is that it is a record of some of the religious teaching Bilali learned in his youth and practiced all his life. The wording isn't precise, it's more the way an old man would remember things from when he was young, but his love of his religion rings out from the pages.

According to a scholar of Arabic and Islam, the opening page starts off, "In the name of God the merciful, the compassionate, may the prayers of God be on our Lord Muhammad and his family and his companions."

One section includes instructions for washing of the feet before prayer and that brought back memories of how we were brought up to wash our feet before we said our prayers and went to bed and how in Papa's time, when people walked to church, they carried their shoes to keep them clean and when they got to the church the first thing they did was wash their feet and put their shoes on. They did not enter the church with dirty feet.

My first reaction was, so some of us were educated early on, far earlier than we had been given credit for. You see yourself according to what is told to you, and the myth was that none of the Africans had any education at all. From the view of us that slave masters passed down, you could almost believe that our lives started once we reached these shores. Then I felt proud. It was a good feeling to know that my ancestor could read and write and he had left a record of it. A good feeling to see *proof* that we came here with a history and culture of our own.

The name "Bilali" is African. The Mohammedan Mandingos, who lived in the upper Niger River Valley, which is in the area of West Africa we think Bilali came from, liked to give their children names that were Islamic or came from the Old Testament and New Testament and were found in the Koran. It's said that Bilali means "the first muezzin," the son of Ali, who was the son of Mohammed. "Muezzin" means "the crier who calls the faithful to prayer," and Bilali definitely was that. He was the one who called the faithful to prayer, a strong man who left a strong family behind him, whose influence was so lasting that when I was growing up, I was taught to always say my prayers kneeling to the East.

During the genealogy study we discovered a remarkable thing: all of us still living on Sapelo are related to Bilali. Whether through direct bloodline or through marriage, Bilali has become the father of us all. He is almost like the great live oak, not like the fictional oaks in the book Reynolds had written, but a living oak with vines and Spanish moss and resurrection ferns growing all over it. Live oaks have a root system that spreads far and wide, as Bilali has. His roots have spread all over this island and they're so deep that you can't tell where the tree stops and the soil begins anymore.

Somewhere along the way, I learned two things about my name. The first was that Cornelia, or Cornelius, for a man, was a name traditionally given to a child who was born on a Tuesday. I found a calendar for the year I was born and I checked and I was born on a Tuesday. Grandpa named me, he named most of Mama's kids, and I don't know whether he chose it deliberately or not, but in naming me that, an African tradition was bestowed on me. I also found out that "Nia," as I sometimes am called, means "she who has a purpose." So that was me—Cornelia and Nia—a woman born on Tuesday, who had a purpose, and I was beginning to discover my purpose at last.

When I first moved back to Sapelo, one of the old people started reminding me that I had been a special child, one who died and came back to life because I had a special purpose.

"The good Lord moved you back to Sapelo for a purpose," Sister Anna said. She was a Hillery who was called Sister Anna by everyone in the community. "God didn't bring you back here for nothin'. There's a reason why he brought you back here."

I'd heard talk like that all my life and it made me uncomfortable. I'd change the subject whenever it came up and duck the issue. Deep inside, I believed I had a purpose, but I always figured it would come about by itself if I just went about my business. And that's what I did. I took care of my family, I helped my community and I tried to further my education. I got a set of the Compton encyclopedia and I read a volume a week until I worked my way through the alphabet. I kept a dictionary by my side to look up the words I didn't know. When the opportunity arose, I got my G.E.D.

I never said, "Okay, I'm gonna be this or that." My purpose just grew out of who I was as a person—my curiosity about my people's history and roots, being a storyteller and learning to speak out. Before all the turmoil began over here, I didn't make a lot of noise. But when our community got threatened, I didn't have much choice. I had to speak out so that I wouldn't have regrets later. I learned to fight for what I thought was right, to be an activist in my own way. Those three things blended together and I became one who tells our stories for a purpose—to preserve our history and culture, remind us of who we are and help save our way of life on this island.

So, when the time was right, I discovered my purpose. It had been there waiting for me all along, just as the old people said.

I haven't told you about my becoming a storyteller, but it came about naturally. I grew up hearing stories every day of my life. Papa would entertain us with stories when he was in a good mood, Mama would tell us stories, Grandma would tell us stories and some of the old people I knew told stories. There was one man over here who was especially good at it, though, and he was known as *the* story-teller of the island. His name was Ronnister Johnson and Ronnister was it. He'd keep you cracking up.

He told stories around the clock, all day long. Whether you saw him at six-thirty in the morning or six-thirty in the afternoon, the next thing you knew, Ronnister would have you laughing yourself to death. He had a big laugh and you could hear him all over the community. "There goes Ronnister telling lies," someone would say. He was "Uncle Ronnister" to me and everyone else, even if you weren't related at all. As far as I know, I didn't have any close connection with him at all but I never tired of hearing Ronnister. Never. He lived next to Cousin Annie and whenever I'd go to see her, I'd stop and visit Ronnister. It would lift your spirit.

He was the one who told the story about the man and the rattlesnake. He said the guy went out hunting one day, he went out hunting by himself. And while he was hunting he got bit by a rattlesnake and he knew he was in trouble because he fell in a hole and there was nobody there but him. He decided, "I need help and I need help now," and he looked up toward the heavens and he said, "God, I need help. Come and come at once. Don't send your son because children have a habit of playing on the way."

I remember asking Ronnister, "Well, did the man get saved from the rattlesnake?" He said, "Yeah, he got saved. Somebody else saw him and he got saved." So he lived. But we had Ronnister to tell the story in such a way that you had to say, "Did he get saved? Did God come and save him in time?" Because he never made up things out of the blue. He'd just take bits and pieces of true things he'd heard and he'd put a light spin on them so he could get a good laugh out of them.

He wasn't around when the Africans who were rebellious were hiding in Behavior Woods. Even as a little kid, and little kids always think the old people have been around forever, I knew he wasn't that old—but he was the one that told that story. I would listen and remember everything he said and then I would see if anybody else might remember something else about the same thing and that way I could learn a little more.

I was at Ronnister's house once in the 1970s, and I was giving a tour to some students from a private school over in St. Simons. I was always giving private tours back then. Ronnister was singing "Down on Sapelo," a song he made up that had lines like, "No policeman you will meet, you can drive your Tin Lizzie nine miles on the beach," and he had everybody in stitches. Then one of the students said, "Now you tell us one, Miss Bailey," so I told one of the Brer Rabbit tales. I don't remember which one it was but the students laughed—not as hard as they laughed at Ronnister's tales because he was more seasoned, but they laughed, and I enjoyed it and I was on my way.

What really got me into it then, was that since I was already touring people anyway, the state made me a tour guide over here and I did that for a few years. I had to entertain people from seven-thirty in the morning until I put them back on the afternoon boat at four-thirty. There'd be up to twenty-eight people on the bus, or thirty if DNR overbooked, and I had to keep people entertained and occupied and not bored all day long by myself.

Believe me, that took some doing.

Everywhere we went, I would explain things and I would tell stories. The stories I told were true stories so I passed on history to them even in the stories. I didn't stay on one topic too long. I'd move back and forth, so they wouldn't get bored. So I'd drop one subject at a certain point and pick up another one and go with it awhile and then go back to the first one. I made sure to always drop one at a point where it was interesting enough that when I went back to it, people wanted to hear more. So really, the approach I used was a lot like Ronnister, when he told the story about the man and the rattlesnake. It was a natural way for me to tell stories, because Grandma and the other old people had told things that way. They told you just enough for what you needed to know right then.

It turned out that the more I told stories, the easier it got and the more I made them laugh, and pretty soon, people were asking for my tour. People were coming here from all over then and still do. They'd hear about Sapelo from some of the chambers of commerce and in other ways. One guy on one of my tours one time was from Canada. He and his family came and he said they'd seen me before, in Canada. I said, "You saw me where?" He said, "In Canada, on public television in Canada. I saw you." Some guy had been down here and had done a video that was on public television in Canada.

So that was it. It just went from there. I woke up one day some-

time after Ronnister had died, and the torch had been passed to me
and I was the storyteller. People gave me that title. I never gave it to
myself, but I enjoy telling stories that weave in our history and culture and keep them alive. Stories like that of a legendary animal I
saw when I was nine years old.

Even as a small kid I could walk anywhere on the island at night
and not be afraid, even if I was alone. My friends got so scared after
dark that some of them wouldn't even go to the other end of the
house unless someone was with them. Papa would brag about me,
"Yeah, that gal ain't scared of nuttin'. She's got the spirits walking
with her." And whether the spirits were there protecting me or not,
I always knew I was perfectly safe.

One winter day my friends and I stopped by the post office after
school so we could mail some letters for our parents. We had a little
time left before we had to be home and one of the girls suggested,
"Oh, let's go by the cemetery before it gets dark," so we walked to the
cemetery.

When we got to Behavior Cemetery, we perched up on the
wooden gate that looked out over the home of the spirits. Everything was so quiet and peaceful, with headstones here and there and
tall, green pine trees and live oaks with long, gray moss hanging
down. The late afternoon sun was streaming down on some graves
and shadows were forming on others and there was enough light to
see the flowers planted on people's graves.

"Oh, it's pretty. It's beautiful," one of the girls said.

We were sitting there staring at the scene and all of a sudden, the
sun went behind the trees—*whoosh!* One minute there was this red
glow in the sky and the next minute it was nightfall.

We jumped down off the gate to leave the cemetery and as we were walking down the road toward the community, giggling and talking, I looked back and *something* was coming after us. This huge animal that looked like a dog but not really like a dog was following us. Its tail was shaped like a dog's, its gait was like a dog's but it was the size of a young cow

"Hey, y'all. Look behind us. Do you see that?" I asked.

"What is it?"

"It looks like a cross between a dog and a cow."

There wasn't a dog on the island that big and I didn't think it was a cow. It was about four-and-a-half-feet tall and jet black, I mean *jet black*.

My friends were afraid of their own shadows so they took off screaming and running. I walked faster but I did not run. Something told me not to run.

I kept looking back and that dog or cow or whatsoever it was kept loping down the road behind us. It wasn't snarling, but it was definitely right behind us. When we got to Behavior bridge, which is about three-fourths of a mile from the cemetery, I looked back and it was gone. I didn't see it turn off into the woods. It just *vanished*.

I got home late and Mama and Papa wanted to know where I'd been. I told them about the dog that looked like a cow that chased us and they didn't say anything, not a word at all. They knew all the dogs on the island too and they knew it was no dog. It had to be a spirit of some kind.

A few years went by and then Doc, William Banks, Jr., told me his father, William Banks, Sr., has seen that animal too. Mr. William said he had been hunting one night near Behavior Cemetery and he looked up and here was this *big* dog coming toward him with flashing gold teeth and red eyes, the biggest dog he'd ever seen. The more he tried to run away from it, the more it chased him, and it kept after him until he got a good ways from the cemetery and then it stopped.

I didn't believe that story because I had seen the big black dog myself and it didn't have flashing gold teeth and red eyes. Doc said his father was serious though and Mr. William would tell jokes, but he wasn't one to make up stories so I never knew quite what to think until I read *Drums and Shadows* and found out that other people had seen the dog too.

Katie Brown said she had seen a shadow, and that's what she called a spirit that takes an animal form, and this one was one from the dark side of the afterlife. She saw a huge dog with a big tusk and long, thick hair like a Newfoundland one night and there "ain't ever been a dog like that on the island," she said. "He must be a shadow." She also said it was bad luck to talk about a shadow, that you must not talk about it if you see one and maybe that's why Mama and Papa didn't say a word about the one I saw.

Someone from the Johnson family saw the huge dog too. Grant Johnson had climbed over the fence of the cemetery to cut some wood without asking leave of the spirits to enter. He was cutting down wood as fast as he could, when all of a sudden, a big, black dog came after him, and Grant Johnson jumped back over that fence in a hurry.

So people had seen the dog that wasn't a dog for generations and I'd never even heard of it when I saw it. But it's like all of our stories over here. They have a lot of truth to them. And while the big black dog that roams the cemetery has looked different to people over time, the hounds of hell look different to everyone who sees them.

Chapter Twenty-Nine

I Flew Back

"YOU KNOW THOSE PLANES ARE FALLIN'?"

"Yes, ma'am."

"And you're still goin'?"

My phone was ringing off the hook with relatives and friends who thought I was crazy to fly so far away but I wasn't gonna let that stop me. I was *going* to Africa.

I wasn't planning to go off looking for my roots when I called my old friend Emory Campbell one day in 1989. I was just calling for help. I wanted Emory to come to Sapelo and talk with us about what we could do to prevent our land in Hog Hammock from slipping away. Some land in the community had just been sold to outsiders, the very first bit of land sold, and alarm bells were going off in my head because Hog Hammock's all we have left.

Emory's the director of the Penn Center in Helena, South Carolina, which is on the grounds of the first school for freedmen, and one of its concerns is helping those of us who are Gullah and Geechee hold onto our heritage and our land in the Sea Islands. It turned out that Emory couldn't come to Sapelo when I wanted him to because he was going to be busy packing his bags to go to Africa.

Joseph Momoh, who was the president of the Republic of Sierra Leone in 1989, had visited the Penn Center the year before and he was so struck with the similarities he saw between Gullah people in the Sea Islands and people in his country that he invited a delegation of Gullah people to visit Sierra Leone as guests of his government. The trip was being billed as a homecoming for Gullah people, since so many rice-growing Gullah and Geechee people originally came from Sierra Leone and neighboring countries in West Africa.

Emory told me who all was going and it sounded good but he didn't have any Geechee people from Georgia.

"Hold it a minute," I said. "There's nobody from Georgia. You can't leave the Geechee out. That's not right," I said. It does do to make a little noise sometimes. The delegation ended up being renamed the Gullah/Geechee delegation and we got the go-ahead for four Georgians to go. I lined up three people from the mainland—Lauretta Sams of Darien, who directs a project for African American youth called the Esther Project, and Frankie and Doug Quimby of the Georgia Sea Island Singers of St. Simons, who travel all over the United States teaching songs and games from slavery days. After I couldn't find a fourth person to represent Sapelo, I thought it over and said, "Okay, I'll go."

I had been on planes before but I had never flown such a long distance. Everyone from Frank on asked me, "You' goin' that far?" "Of course," I told them, and I knew just what I was going to do when the time came. I got on that plane, I fastened my seat belt, I said a silent prayer and then I didn't worry one bit about whether that plane was going to fall out of the sky or not.

As a matter of fact, I got on several planes. I went from Savannah to Durham, North Carolina, and from Durham to New York and from New York to Paris and from Paris to Africa. There were thirteen of us in the delegation and all of us were all so excited we stayed awake the entire trip to Africa. We didn't fall asleep at all. By the time the plane set down at Lungi Airport outside of Freetown, the capital of Sierra Leone, we were so tired, the only thing we wanted to do was go to the hotel and sleep.

It was dark, it was nine-thirty at night, Sierra Leone time, and we sat there quietly on a chartered bus that met us as we got off the plane. The bus traveled a little bit down the tarmac and then it stopped.

"Why'd we stop?" someone asked.

All at once, the press surrounded us, the British Broadcasting Corporation, The Freetown press, all kinds of press, and a public television camera crew from South Carolina that was making a documentary of our trip, "Families Across the Sea." There were bright lights everywhere and there were drums beating and *there were thousands* of people there to greet us, because announcements had been made about our trip. Sierra Leone is between Guinea and Liberia on the West Coast of Africa and is a little larger than the state of South Carolina. It has twelve different regions, and there were people from every one of those regions. Some of the people had come from hundreds of miles to see this delegation of Gullah/Geechee people from the United States.

All of a sudden, nobody in the delegation was tired anymore. I mean *nobody*. We all got our energy back quickly. The drums did it, the drums and the singing. I don't know quite how the drums did it but they did. It was like we had been here before, we had been to Africa, that this was our home and we were being invited back into our own home. The drums seemed to be saying, *"You're back! You're back!"* and celebrating our return.

We got off the bus and started mingling with the people and the paramount chief was pouring a libation to the north, east, south, and west. He looked at the delegation and for some reason he looked straight at me and handed me that first cup. I got a good whiff of it when I went to take a drink and there was not a drop of water in that cup, it was one hundred proof rum. "Okay, you're a guest. Keep a straight face," I told myself. I held myself with as much dignity as I could, looked straight back at the paramount chief, swallowed and passed the cup back. I was not gonna make a fool of myself since he had honored me by handing me the first libation.

After that first night we didn't feel like strangers; we knew inside that we were all kin.

Our luggage had been delayed so the next day President Momoh, as a gift of the government, sent us to a shop to get African-style clothes. I got a blue dress, a dress with rich reds, browns and golds, and an olive-green dress with a tie-dyed design that looked like a sand dollar. We wore our new clothes the whole trip. Even after we got our luggage back, we kept wearing our African clothes. We *preferred* them. The minute you slipped them on, those clothes changed you. Your head snapped back, you stood taller, your stride was different. You were more direct and you felt like you could have challenged the world and come out on top.

Everywhere I went in Sierra Leone, I saw similarities to Sapelo. *Everywhere.* In the faces of people, in the language, the food, the terrain and some of the old traditions.

Just looking at the people, I could see my grandmother, my mother, my father, my brothers and sisters, and some of the people there reacted the same way to me. One of the dignitaries said I was the spitting image of his sister and another said he had been watching me for two days and couldn't decide whether I was with the delegation or was one of the ladies from the Sierre Leone tourist department who were accompanying us. "No, I'm with the delegation," I said. "I'm from America," but to me, it was the highest compliment he could give me.

Africa has lots of countries and cultures so you can find all shapes and sizes and shades. But basically, people in Sierra Leone look like me. Most of them have my coloring, which is a rich brown. I saw very few people that were darker and I can count on my fingers the ones that were lighter. They are medium-sized people too, like I am. I'm five foot seven and hardly anyone was too much taller than me.

There were other things about the people in Sierra Leone that sang out "Sapelo" to me: the way the women carried bundles of everything from clothes to food or straw on their heads, like I learned to do as a child; how the older women tied an extra piece of cloth around their waists to support their backs; and how the men mashed down the back of old shoes, making them into modern day flip-flops, like we always did.

There are many different tribes in Sierra Leone and each has its own language. In order to communicate easily with each other, people speak a common tongue that's a good bit like the Geechee and Gullah spoken by the older people in the Sea Islands when I was growing up. They call it Krio, and it's the blend of English and African languages passed down by the descendants of freed black people who returned to Sierra Leone from the United States and Jamaica. When they'd slow down and speak slowly, it would go through your ear, it would go around in your head and you'd say, "Aah, I know what that is." That's how quick it was for you to get back into that. But you had to open your mind to it.

The food stirred up all kinds of memories in me. The weather was hot and they sold oranges on the street, peeled but with the frothy white membrane still on them so they wouldn't dry out, and that was how we did it at home. We bought some candy that was made of ground peanuts mixed with something sweet like molasses, and on Sapelo, we used to make a candy like that. If, as Papa said, your grinders were all gone, you could still chew it, so it was a hit with elderly people.

We ate so much rice when I was growing up that people called us "rice-eating Geechees" and in Sierra Leone, everyone eats rice. Rice and fish are the staple foods. In Freetown, you can even buy rice on the street, just like you would buy hot chestnuts or hot dogs in New York. You could either get a bowl of plain rice or rice with vegetables over it.

Out in the countryside, I noticed that they planted yams, which are like our sweet potatoes, in neat rows like we do and that they had lima beans growing on poles like we do and it reminded me so much of home. In King Jimmy's market in Freetown, a lady gave me some black-eyed peas and I was going. "These are the same identical peas we have at home." They had dried okra and smoked fish too because you don't have to refrigerate it and not everybody in Sierra Leone has refrigeration. Mama remembers when people on Sapelo would dry okra on the rooftops, before we had refrigeration, and the smoked fish in Freetown looked and smelled just like the fish we smoke on Sapelo. A lot of that fish was caught with cast nets, and everybody on Sapelo still uses a cast net. I can throw one too. I actually saw some guys in Sierra Leone fishing with cast nets and their nets were a lot like the ones Papa made.

Freetown is on the waterfront, and the Sierra Leone River is wide. It snakes around and has tufts of marsh grass, just as there are on the coasts of Georgia and South Carolina and North Florida. The terrain is similar, the seabirds are similar, the fish are similar—the similarities are just out of this world. I stood looking at the water one day, saying to myself, "Is this part of the reason, after slavery, why more people didn't leave the South and go up North? Could it be that there's something familiar about the land—that there's a link to our ancestral homeland that is remembered only by the soul?" I really believe that's what kept some of us in the South, no matter what the hardships were. Mama and Papa would never leave Sapelo and move to someplace like New York or Boston. There is something within them that says, "No, this look' more like our mother country. We can't leave."

What really knocked me out was finding traces of our traditions in Africa. The ring shout is fading away in Africa too but it is still done in a few of the smaller villages on special occasions. Some men and women from one of the outlying villages performed a ring shout dance for us one night. There were no young dancers with them, they were all in their sixties and seventies so that's a sure sign right there that the shout is disappearing. But the years they had on them didn't slow them down one bit. They were great, they had been doing it most of their lives and they had it down to a tee. I was watching an ancient part of Africa come alive before my eyes and it gave me a little chill to realize that I had grown up seeing Papa performing a dance that was centuries old.

The shout the people from the village were dancing was even about a bird. It wasn't the Buzzard Lope, that's a whole different shout, but it was about a bird and our feeling for birds was another thing we had in common. Birds were important both to people in West Africa and to Geechee and Gullah people in the New World because they are a symbol of freedom. They are free to go wherever their wings carry them. But I have a hunch that birds were even more important in the New World, because we definitely needed a symbol of freedom.

I watched every move the shouters made. They were moving in a circle to the beat of a stick and their arm movements were so graceful they looked just like birds flying. They moved their feet carefully too, not crossing them, just like people on Sapelo always were careful to do. The only thing different was that they used a drum for rhythm along with the stick and we always just used the stick. I don't know if we ever beat drums on Sapelo or if they were only used on special occasions like harvest festivals. They may have just beat them on special occasions, I don't know. What I do know is that people were forbidden to use drums on a lot of plantations. The slaveholders were afraid of the power of drums to stir people up, just like the drums beating, "You're back! You're back!" had moved us so much our first night here. The early Africans had such an ability to send messages back and forth between villages on their drums that the slave masters were afraid the Africans would use them to incite a revolt against them. They were probably right too. Some slaves had to have been thinking that way. Who wouldn't have? So that's probably why nobody in the Sea Islands used a drum, in addition to the stick, on the ring shout.

I was all wrapped up in the dance, enjoying it when the thought came to me, "These older people up there dancing should know something about the nubie." You remember Grandma's nubie? The object she used to answer her questions when she was sitting there humming to herself? I was sure the nubie must have come from Africa. Grandma had said it went all the way back, but I hadn't been able to find out a thing about it since being in Sierra Leone. I had asked some younger Africans about it and they had never heard of the nubie.

I waited until the shouters were through and then I started a conversation with a couple of the older ladies and one of them actually remembered the nubie. She described it to me as an object hanging on a string that you hold with one hand over the palm of the other and if it goes back and forth, the answer to your question is no, and if it goes around in a circle, the answer is yes—and I said, *"Aha!"* I had found the nubie in Africa.

I still didn't find out about its history or why it was called a nubie, but it was enough to hear her say, "Yes, we too have the nubie," and to know it was used for the same purpose. What could have been better except for her pulling one out of her pocket?

I was the nosy one in our delegation. The women from the tourist department would be going, "Miss Bailey? Miss Bailey? Has anyone seen Miss Bailey?" I was always wandering a little bit off from the rest of the group to talk to this lady or that because there was so much I wanted to know. I talked to one woman who told me that in the rural areas of Sierra Leone you can still find a few midwives and I asked if the midwives count the knots in the afterbirth to predict how many children a woman will have.

"Yes, they still do that."

"You're *kidding!*" I was a totally surprised. Not only that, a lot of people in Sierra Leone have grown up with the tradition of introducing the newborn child to the world within a week, just like we did.

I told several people about Ophelia and Uncle Nero's belief in the healing powers of the earth, and how he had wanted to bury her in the earth to draw the affliction out of Ophelia's limbs, and they believe in the same practice. It was just amazing how many connections there were, *amazing* how the old people on Sapelo had kept so many beliefs alive. We had more ties in common than I had ever dreamed.

Rice is by far the most important and the largest crop grown in Sierra Leone. We went to a rice farm in the lush, green countryside and that was fascinating to me since I had never gotten to see rice grown on Sapelo. Since I'd already seen so many similarities, I wasn't surprised at all to find that the rice is grown and harvested in the same exact way people on Sapelo did it until the 1940s, when it became cheaper to buy rice grown in Louisiana and Arkansas. The women at the rice farm even had a big wooden mortar and pestle to beat the husks off like the one Grandma used to have, and the African women even winnowed the rice in the old-fashioned way in huge, circular, shallow baskets made of coiled grasses bound with strips of fiber. I touched one and held it and those baskets were very close to the ones Mama used when she was young. In the Sea Islands, we call these baskets "fanners" and in Sierra Leone, they call them "fantas" so even the name is close.

Geechee/Gullah people in the Sea Islands are known for making and selling sweet grass baskets, especially around Charleston. On Sapelo, Uncle Allen was our most famous basket maker though we always had a number of people who knew how to make fanner baskets. When Papa was a boy, he learned how to make baskets from his Uncle Nero, and he and some other people used to sell them to Howard Coffin for fifty cents apiece, and Coffin would sell the baskets up North—for a big profit, of course. Papa even made a special rice fanner for Mama as his wedding present to her. About ten years ago, Papa finally passed his basket-making smarts on to me and now I know how too.

I was excited to see little boys in the rice field on the lookout for pesky "rice birds"—birds that swoop down and feed on the rice, because that was Papa's job when he was a kid. I couldn't wait to get back to tell him that even in this modern day, little kids in Sierra Leone still use the exact same kind of slingshot he used to chase the birds away. The African boys were whirling their slingshots around and letting loose a stone that got rid of the birds quick, at least for a little while.

Papa and Mama called the ricebirds that came to Sapelo the "May birds," because they would start arriving in May when the rice was planted. There were so many that you couldn't chase them all away so Papa and the other boys would set up homemade traps for them and then the women made a ricebird stew that was served over rice. It took a lot of birds to make a stew because those birds were tiny, but they were rich with fat from all that rice they had eaten and they made a delicious stew. So, nothing went to waste. The birds that ate the rice were eaten too.

When we first arrived at the village of Taiama, where the rice farm was, the paramount chief was calling the people together to greet us with huge horns that were the tribe's sacred horns, and to me they looked like they were ram's horns, and the children and the old people and everyone were coming from all different directions and lining up on both sides of this red, dusty road to meet us, while we were being led down the middle of the road between them. As we passed them, they began to close in behind us and they followed us into the village and that's when I *really* felt like I was at home. It was almost like when Grandma and Mama and the old people would call out, "C'mon, c'mon, it's time for sump'n to eat."

All we could hear were the voices of the people coming together and children singing and the horns blowing and the mixture of sounds went down to our very souls. I mean, it just penetrated, and it put us on a joyful level we'd never even known was possible before. Nothing beat it. *Absolutely nothing.*

They seated us on a raised platform under a roof so that the people in the village could see us, because we were honored guests, and we were served palm wine in bamboo cups. The palm wine looked and tasted exactly like the mash we used to use for making moonshine and I whispered to Lauretta Sams, "Don't drink too much of that stuff. It tastes smooth and cool and I know you're thirsty but it will get to you," and I sipped slowly because I knew just what it could do to you.

As leader of our delegation, Emory was the spokesman and he stood and told everyone how happy we were to be there with them. Then the village leaders dressed him in a ceremonial hat and a robe of coarse cloth that is a traditional garment worn by most paramount chiefs and they made Emory an honorary paramount chief. The cloth in the robe was what is called mud cloth, a heavy, close-woven cloth of natural fibers that is almost a tan color, and it is so strong it could easily last for a hundred years. It's plain but you can imagine the hands that made it and it's just as regal as any robe a king or queen ever wore.

I was sitting there watching as a woman came out with a woman's outfit draped over her arm, and all of a sudden my name was called. A woman from the village wrapped a skirt of gold fabric with a little bit of black and purple on me and then slipped a matching tunic over me and wrapped my hair in a piece of the same fabric and tied it over my left ear and they made me an honorary woman paramount chief. Once there were only men paramount chiefs but now there are women paramount chiefs too and they are just as powerful.

I didn't say much, just "Thank you," but I felt blessed, really blessed, because this was an honor I never expected in a million years. It made the whole trip. All of it was good but this gave me the deepest glow I've ever had in my life. The experience was absolutely out of this world. We were just in the countryside for one day but I still carry that feeling with me, in my whole being. *Always.* It changed me, it made me feel stronger, and I knew then I could do anything, go anywhere, and say what needed to be said from then on. I had this new power within me and I would never again be the same.

We learned a lot in Africa about ourselves. They gave us lectures at the Presidential Palace and the U.S. Embassy and we hung onto every word. We had to remember everything so we could tell people at home.

It was in Africa that I learned that our ancestors had the tradition of growing rice, not the slaveholders, and that they were brought to the New World because they could cultivate rice. That our ancestors built the canals and dikes and reshaped the coast into thousands of acres of rice fields. That the ports in Charleston, South Carolina, and Savannah, Georgia, specialized in importing people with rice-growing skills. That the slaveholders were willing to pay more for people with these skills. That they particularly liked to buy people from Sierra Leone and surrounding areas but that they would search the handbills advertising new shipments from the slave ships of Africans from anywhere along the coast of West Africa, from Senegal down to Angola, as long as they knew how to grow rice. That the wealthiest plantation owners placed orders with brokers for Africans from certain areas and that slave traders would then go find exactly what they were looking for.

It was in Africa that I learned why the connection between

Geechee and Gullah people and the people of Sierra Leone is an especially close one. That everywhere else in the Americas, except in South Carolina and Georgia, Sierra Leoneans were outnumbered by captives from other parts of Africa. That it was only in South Carolina and Georgia that Africans from Sierra Leone came together in large enough numbers to shape the culture and language. That because of the freedmen who returned to Sierra Leone, we had ties both going across the Atlantic and coming back. That as Geechee/Gullah people, we held onto more of our cultural heritage than other African Americans were able to, because living in the Sea Islands, we were more isolated than other black people in the United States were.

It was in Africa that I learned that instead of using the Underground Railroad and going north, a lot of Geechee/Gullah people who escaped from slavery went down to Florida and joined the Native Americans there, the Seminoles. That some of them intermarried with the Seminoles and over time came to see themselves as part of the Seminole tribe. That after the Second Seminole War, when most of the Seminoles were forcibly removed to Indian Territory, to Oklahoma, that people of Geechee/Gullah ancestry went too and that some of their descendants still live in Oklahoma. As a matter of fact, there were two people from Oklahoma in our delegation.

It was in Africa that I learned that the term "Geechee" most likely didn't come from the Ogeechee River in Georgia as many people said it did when I was growing up. That never had made sense to me, but *bam*! They put that label on us like there were no more ifs ands or buts about it. I think that people tried to figure out where that word "Geechee" came from that they heard black people call each other, and, not knowing anything about Africa, that's all that they could think of. The Ogeechee River runs near Savannah and it

was assumed that the Geechees had been associated with the plantations near that river. But Ogeechee is an Indian name, it's one of
three major rivers in Georgia with Native American names, and
when we did a genealogy check on Sapelo, none of our ancestors had
ever lived near there.

It was in Africa that I also learned that the terms "Geechee" and
"Gullah" were more likely to have come from there. That an
African American professor by the name of Lorenzo Dow Turner
was the first to point out that Geeche probably came from Kissi, pronounced "Geezee," a tribe that lives in the area where modern Sierra
Leone, Liberia and Guinea come together, and that it could be that
Gullah came from Gola, a small tribe on the Sierra Leone–Liberian
border. They were neighboring tribes so if that is true, they would
have had a lot in common before the enslaved Africans even came to
the New World. It's not for certain, history is rarely certain, and I
don't know how they will ever know, but that could very well be the
origin of the terms.

Dr. Turner got to know Gullah and Geechee people in the Sea
Islands during the 1930s and he spent years studying the way we
talked. He recorded some of our tales and our songs and he found
expressions people used and thousands of words still in use that he
could trace back to Africa. Most of the words he found had become
"private names" or nicknames, because in Africa people picked
names for their children based on such things as the day of the week
or the month they were born, how they looked physically, some
quality in their character or something they were particularly good
at. Geechee/Gullah people had continued that practice, even when
we didn't know that is what we were doing. On Sapelo, we named
our children mostly after someone in the family, so their given name
was an English name. Then, as they got older, they acquired nick-

names, and those were the ones that often followed the African pattern of naming children. There is a headstone for a Sunday in the cemetery, we had a July in my time and we still have a June walking around.

My husband, Frank, has a nickname, "Tata," which we were always told was English for "thank you." "Tata" was how we taught a baby to say thank you. But it turns out that in some parts of Africa, "tata" means "father" and is used as a term of respect for addressing an elder or chief. So I don't know how we really got the word "tata." English and African words were mixed together so thoroughly in Geechee culture that it can be very hard to say. But oddly enough, it was the kids in Frank's family that called him Tata. Frank practically raised his brothers and sisters. He was the substitute father after his father died.

At Harris Neck, Georgia, just across the marsh from me on Sapelo, Dr. Turner recorded an African song sung by a woman named Amelia Dawley. Her family had sung the song for generations and had passed it down even though they didn't know what the words meant anymore. Turner found out it was a Mende funeral song still known in Africa. The Freetown Players sang it for us and the way they sang it, it went like this:

Come quickly, let us all work hard
the grave is not yet finished
The heart of the dead
is not yet perfectly cool.

By "cool" they meant that the heart was not at rest—the member of their tribe had not been properly buried yet, so his heart was not at rest. It was a work song they sang while they were getting ready for the funeral. I did not know that song but the words didn't surprise me, because when I was growing up, people on Sapelo would rush to the church on hearing the death bell ring and ask, "How long ago did he die?" And someone would answer, "Not long, because the heart is still warm," and that meant that person had just died.

I had heard of Dr. Turner before, but not in any depth. I hadn't known, and this part I found out later, that he came to Sapelo and that he got some of his information from Katie Brown, Uncle Shed, Charles Hall, Frank's grandfather Balaam Walker, Tom Lemon of the Lemon family, and Sonny Dunham, the minister who married Mama and Papa. I had no idea of that at all.

When Dr. Turner's book *Africanisms in the Gullah Dialect* was published by the University of Chicago Press in 1949, people said he was crazy, because what he had to say was so different from what the researchers before him had said. They had been white and they had said that the way we spoke was taken straight from English—from how indentured servants spoke in the 1700s and early 1800s, mixed in with a form of baby-talk English that slaveholders used to get us to understand what they wanted. But those earlier researchers didn't know anything about African languages.

It was like they thought the sun rose and set on the English language only, that we had dropped all of our African words and all of our African selves when we came from what they called "the Dark Continent." The Europeans bought into the old idea that we were like a clean slate when we got to the New World and that slavery was a school that taught us everything we knew. Europeans had a very limited view of us. A very limited view.

Dr. Turner consulted with scholars in England who studied African languages and with some scholars in Africa and he knew several African languages himself, and he said that what we spoke was based on English, yes, but that it also owed much to African languages—and that the blend of the two can be called a language of its own. So he introduced a whole new way of looking at it. Even today, researchers use his work as a beginning point.

We sat there, very quiet, listening to every word, thinking these professors know more about us than we do about ourselves because so much of what they were saying was totally new to us. When we left the panel discussion, everybody was saying, "Good Lord, how come we had to come so far to learn all this stuff about ourselves?" We were grateful but felt so let down that we had to come thousands of miles to finally learn who we were. I was angry that I didn't learn these things in my own country. This knowledge should have been in our heads when we *went* to Africa.

We learned about Bunce Island too. Bunce Island is twenty miles from Freetown on the Sierra Leone River, at the furthest point inland the slaves ships could go without grounding. The British ran a very large slave trading operation there from about 1750 to 1800. A *huge* slave operation. Thousands of Africans were shipped off the island and sent to South Carolina and Georgia. We saw photographs of Bunce Island, so we knew basically what it was like, but later, when we actually went there, we weren't prepared just the same.

We rode a ferry to the island, just like the one you ride from the mainland to Sapelo, and it took about an hour to get there. When the island comes into sight, what you see are the ruins of the old slave trading fort and the walls around it that were mounted with giant cannons. The enslaved Africans were a valuable commodity so the British had those large guns to protect the place from traders on the river who might try to steal the Africans for themselves.

Everything is in ruins but there was enough standing that you could see what it had once been like. The British lived in this big two-story brick Georgian manor-style house with columns built with slave labor. The enslaved Africans were put to work well before they came to American shores. But that pretentious house didn't interest me. The people in that house lived in luxury while they kept their captives cooped up in tight quarters.

There was an enclosed courtyard behind the house that served as the slave yard. It wasn't very big, just about a quarter of an acre, and they would keep between two hundred to three hundred people there chained and parceled out in circles, with a trough of rice placed in the center of each circle.

There were three small rooms off the courtyard, one for the men, one for the women and one for the children, and the largest one, the men's, was only about twelve feet by twelve feet, so you know they couldn't have all slept in those rooms. Most of them probably just lived, ate and slept in the courtyard.

Walking around Bunce Island, I had the most horrible feelings. I was walking on the ground where many of my people had come from and everywhere I turned, I could feel their presence. I was walking right among them and it was almost like I had to walk carefully so I wouldn't step on them. It was like a part of them had stayed on that island always, like some part of them got stuck there behind and they were unhappy spirits. They were restless spirits. It was the most eerie feeling I'd ever had. You don't ever want to have that feeling.

Their spirits weren't like some wisp of fog or something. They were so real that I could have actually touched them and to me they looked like Papa and Mama and Grandma and all the people on Sapelo. The faces on them were just like the faces I see every day and I think some of my people definitely passed through this island. I was going, "I can see you my cousin, I can feel you," and I had this emotion of sorrow and of anger.

They didn't have any clothes on, they were chained and they were just sad. Sad people that didn't know what was happening to them. Some had already given up and they were the ones who would die onboard the ships on the way to this country, because they were defeated before they started. And at the same time there were some who were very defiant. They were gonna see this through to the end, no matter what became of them. So there were sad and defiant people together in that same courtyard, heads bowed on some and others looking straight ahead and wondering what tomorrow will bring. But absolutely defiant, refusing to look down, refusing to be defeated. That's right.

The Africans were led off Bunce Island in chains through a rock jetty that they probably built themselves and that was their last sight of Africa. From there they went twenty-five hundred miles away to the New World and never saw their families, their loved ones and their homeland again. I was standing near the jetty, waiting my turn for a small boat that was picking us up and taking us back to where the ferry was anchored, and this BBC reporter came up to me and said, "Miss Bailey, what are you thinking at this moment?"

I looked at her and said, "Woman, you don't want to know what I'm thinking at this moment," and she beat a hasty retreat. My thoughts were ugly, very ugly. I was so angry I wanted to shake someone. It took me awhile to compose myself after Bunce Island.

When it was time to leave Africa, none of us wanted to leave our new African friends. They had touched our hearts and we had touched theirs. There was crying and hugging before we got on the plane and then we sat too tired to talk and almost too tired to think. I did notice how big our plane was. I was thinking, "Gee we're not sardines, we actually can get up and move around." Our ancestors couldn't move at all in those cramped boats they were in and when they got to the New World they wanted to go back to their home in Africa. They wanted to fly back to Africa.

You may not know this but the Africans who came to the Sea Islands believed in flying. They actually *believed* in it. There weren't any airplanes back then of course but they believed *people* could fly. We had song after song about flying, songs like "I'll Fly Away" and the one we sang at church that had the verse, "When I get to Heaven, gonna put on my wings, gonna fly all over God's Heaven."

Flying was the only way for people to get back to Africa, to escape the horrible situation they were in, in this foreign land. They couldn't take a boat back. Even if they could steal a boat, I don't think they wanted to cross that water again anyway. It was too dangerous. So it was easier to dream they were free as a bird, on their way back home, and nobody could stop them. I know nobody physically can fly and our ancestors didn't physically get off the ground. But I can believe a big part of them left and went back home. Their minds and their souls flew back. It made that row they had to hoe a little shorter, to think of freedom. For the space of the row, they'd look at a bird overhead and they'd become that bird and fly back on the wind. They flew in their own way.

There were stories all over the Sea Islands of Africans flying back to Africa, and Uncle Shed told one in the book *Drums and Shadows*. He said those folks could fly, that some of the Africans said, "Master, you ain't gonna lick us," and with that they ran down to the river. The overseer thought he could catch them there but before he could get to them, they rose up in the air and flew away.

Uncle Shed said that happened on Butler's Island, over by

Darien on the mainland, and that's the way those stories were. They didn't happen on the island that you lived on but they happened close by. Just close enough to keep your hopes alive.

So, I did something my African ancestors on Sapelo dreamed of doing but didn't get to. I *flew* to Africa. I didn't fly like a bird, on the wings of a bird, I flew on the wings of man, but I flew just the same. They would have understood that, because they never for a minute let go of their dream of flying back to Africa. But what would have seemed odd to them, *very* odd, was that I was on my way back to the New World. I had two homes now, Africa and Sapelo, and I was flying back to my family and my home on Sapelo with a deep sense of pride instilled in me and a new set of fire in my eyes.

I had stepped foot on the soil my ancestors came from. I knew more of my people's history. The words "African American" had more *oomph!* behind them now because I had the inner power to back them up. I was determined that nothing or no one would ever defeat me again and I would be totally my own person from then on. I knew how to carry myself. I knew how to portray myself. I knew exactly who I was for the first time.

◆

Chapter Thirty

Watch Night

ON NEW YEAR'S EVE WE HOLD A CEREMONY CALLED Watch Night, and that's an old, old church service that reminds me a lot like our Geechee saying, "One go, one come," except instead of referring to one of your loved ones dying and one being born, you're watching the passing of the old year and the birth of a new one. So it's a natural time to reflect on my people's past and future on Sapelo.

On Watch Night inside the First African Baptist Church there's a rosy glow that makes you want to be there. The pulpit is covered with a dark red cloth, the seat cushions in the ministers' high-backed chairs are a wine-red, the upholstery on the wooden pews we brought down from the old church at the Bluff is a wine-red vinyl, and the pale red glass windows along the walls shine in the electric lights. Everything is a holy red for the blood of Jesus.

Back when I was young, Watch Night was the one night of the year we would bring the broomstick into the church to sound out the rhythm of the shouts. I've told you about the ring shouts that Papa used to do, but we had religious shouts too. These were faster and more upbeat than the Buzzard Lope. They were joyful shouts,

shouts you were lifting up to God. Some of them were very old, even older than the spirituals.

Some years we still bring the broomstick into church, but even when we don't, if you listen carefully, you can hear where it would go. You can *feel* the beat of the stick in the rhythm of the music and the way the women clap their hands and the men stomp their feet, and all of a sudden, the church comes alive. We start giving thanks for everything that happened in the past year and look forward to the new one.

In my mind, I can see the Watch Nights of old. I can see the church packed with people. I can see one of the men beating the broomstick and the braver of the old folks jumping up and going up front and cutting loose in merriment. I can see Miss Frances, Aunt Rosa Jean, Grandma, Miss Sarah Bell, Mr. James Spaulding, Bermuda Grovner, Uncle Joe, Mr. Charles Hall and all the other old people. They didn't raise their feet off the floor or cross one foot over the other, so it wasn't dancing—you weren't supposed to dance in God's house—it was more a shuffling movement of their feet. They stood straight and proud and went around in a circle counterclockwise, shouting up a storm to an old song like "My Soul Rocks on Jubilee."

'N Jubilee—'N Jubilee
A-a-a-h my Lord!
'N Jubilee—'N Jubilee
My soul rock on Jubilee!

The old people's souls *rocked*, the whole church *rocked* in a joyful noise. They gave thanks wholeheartedly for being alive to see another year and being able to come out to God's house to start the new year.

These days, and tonight, no one is going to go up front and move around in a circle for fear of looking foolish. We're a bit more sedate; more "seddity," as the old people called it when you were careful to dot your i's and cross your t's, and there's not even enough of us to fill the church, without relatives and friends coming from the mainland. There's so few of us left in Hog Hammock.

We outlasted the slaveholders and the wealthy tycoons, but can we make it in this modern era under the state? Our numbers are sinking fast and it makes me very scared. Whole sets of family names have vanished from the island. In 1870, there were forty-seven black families who owned land on Sapelo, and others who lived here. In 1950, there were thirty-six family names here. Today, there are only *nine* family names on the island. Our old die and our young leave and if we keep on going like this, we could all very well disappear forever from Sapelo.

On Watch Night, we are invited to stand up, one by one, and say what we are thankful for, and I have much to be thankful for. Sapelo is still an island of quiet beauty. Hog Hammock remains a small, private community where you can hear a rooster crow or a cow low in early morning, see a dog or two sleeping in the midday sun and hear an old car or truck rumble by on a dirt road at any time of day. I am fifty-five years old, and both my family and I are doing well.

My husband, Frank, recently retired from the state and is doing fine. Two of my sons are living on Sapelo and my daughter and another son are working on the mainland and raising families there, and who knows, maybe they'll move back one day too. My youngest child died a few years ago and that was a tragedy, but I have a grandson to keep his name alive. I have fourteen grandchildren in all, plus a foster son in the army and an adopted daughter who has been a part of our family for a long time.

Of my brothers and sisters, all of them but Gibb are still living. Winnie is on Sapelo, along with some of her children and grandchildren. Ada's in Brunswick. Barbara and my niece Elise remain in New York. They come home to visit and that's it.

Asberry is on the mainland and whenever I see him, he says, "What you got for me, Sis?" He works hard when he works, but when pay day comes, he plays just as hard and his money's gone. It's a sadness that Asberry hasn't done more with his life because he's bright. "I'll straighten up one day, Sis," he says, but he's in his sixties now. He'd better hurry up.

Papa's ninety-seven. His leg never did heal, but he can get around with a cane and he still laughs a lot and tells jokes. Mama died recently, at age eighty-nine, in a nursing home in Brunswick. She and Papa had been married seventy years and she had sixteen grandchildren, forty great-grandchildren, ten great-great-grandchildren and two adopted grands, so she was a rich woman. A very rich woman indeed.

Mama was brought home to Sapelo for her funeral on a chilly March day. She came back on the ferry, because even in death we still ride the ferry, and the rear deck of the ferry was completely filled with her casket, with beautiful floral arrangements of yellow, pink, red, purple and white flowers, and the luggage of people coming over. The inside cabin was jammed with relatives, friends, three preachers and choir members, all coming over to pay their last respects. The top deck was packed with members of a youth group on a tour, standing around the outside raling, shivering in the cold wind. So that was one crowded ferry for Mama's last ride across the water to Sapelo.

Up until the time Mama died she would look at me, if I had one of my younger grandchildren with me, and say, "Just look at you now, just as big and healthy. We thought we had lost you." She never forgot that, incident when I was three, not for a minute. They were ready to bury me.

I don't know what we would think now about a child who died and came back to life, or one who was in a trance and came back— besides being grateful to have the child back. But when the old people said I had a purpose, I knew I'd *better* have a purpose. I'd disgrace them if I didn't and that was unthinkable.

So I try to be as much as I can like an African griot. The griot kept the oral history of the tribe, as it had been passed down for thousands of years. He was in charge of remembering everything. He was a storyteller. He kept alive the names of tribe members so they would not be forgotten, as well as the events in the tribe's life— the good and bad and the pretty and ugly of their history. The stories weren't just for entertainment. Like the ones I tell, they have a purpose.

I tell our stories to help the folks on Sapelo keep our history alive, to help us take pride in the past, and to help us gain strength for the future, because I know that if our ancestors could get through everything they did and keep on going, we can face *anything* that comes our way.

I speak out for our culture wherever I'm asked to, from universities to elementary schools; from the Georgia Sea Islands Festival at St. Simons to the National Black Arts Festival in Atlanta, and even to the Smithsonian Institute in Washington, D.C. I speak out through newspaper articles and TV interviews, like a recent Public Broadcasting System series, *Africans in America*, which told the history of African Americans from slavery through emancipation. And when family and relatives come home to visit, I go to work.

Frank and I feed everybody, and once we've satisfied their stomachs with the foods they grew up with, like collard greens, fried fish, and sweet potato pie, and baked raccoon along with turkey or ham if it's Christmas, I give them something just as tasty to remember. Our folklore.

We still throw cast nets to catch fish on Sapelo. Some of us still make coiled grass baskets like the ones my mother and grandmother used for fanning rice. We still tell animal stories and we still pray to the East. But many of our Geechee ways have faded away.

Bolito's gone, or almost gone anyway. The state signed the death warrant for Bolito by starting its own lottery. Now Bolito is disappearing from this coast so fast that my grandchildren probably won't ever know anyone who plays it and they sure won't see anyone feeding a dime to a frog and looking for a winning number on its tummy.

Dr. Buzzard is fading away too. I get calls from time to time with someone asking, "Miss Bailey, living on an island, do you know someone who could help me?" And what they're asking is whether we have a Dr. Buzzard over here. I say, "Naw, it's gone," and that's the simple answer, because all of those who practice root are gone from Sapelo. But not all of those who believe in it are gone. The older generation still believes in root and will until they die.

Even the younger ones, like my own children, while they don't really believe, they don't totally disbelieve either. If you mention root, they get quiet and reflective. None of them say, "Oh, who believes in that old stuff anymore? Because it's a mind thing. If you believe in root then it has power over you. It doesn't matter how educated you've become. It will work.

But what about the spirits? Do we still believe in spirits?

The spirits are safe for now, even if we don't talk about them as much as we used to. We have people who believe in them. The older women do, I do, and I think my daughter Terri has sensed their presence. Terri and I were sitting around talking at the kitchen table a few nights before Mama's funeral and the back door to the kitchen kept opening. We'd get up and close it and it would open again and we'd close it again and it just kept opening by itself.

"Alright, Grandma, you close that door back," Terri said. Then she looked at me and said, "Ain't nobody but Grandma opening that door. She's comin' in to see what we're doin'."

Terri's three daughters were at the table with us and heard their mama talking about the spirit of their great-grandma, so more than likely they're gonna pick up the belief in spirits and how they can play tricks on you. That belief's not going to be lost any time soon.

When I first got back from Africa, I saw Africa in everything here, from our food to our folklore. I thought I'd get off that kick in maybe six months, but it's been eleven years now and I'm still seeing Africa in everything and finding new examples to boot.

A government official I met in Sierra Leone visited Sapelo and met Papa and said he was the spitting image of a former president of Sierra Leone. He took a photograph of him to show people when he got home. An African college professor told me that he too had grown up with the spirits being part of everyday life and with the hag. A man from Nigeria who visited here, saw some Life Everlasting and said to his son, "Look. We have this at home too." So Life Everlasting grows in West Africa. The only difference is that people there call the plant "never die."

Our stamp is all over this island, but you have to know how to see it. We put up a sign to let visitors know when they are entering Hog Hammock and we put one at Behavior Cemetery. Those signs are in our community, but the rest of the island is administered by the state, and on state land you will not see any historical markers commemorating our history and contributions to Sapelo.

There is no sign to tell you that the old slave community of Shell Hammock, where people were still living in my childhood, was located on the South End. The sign near the former community of Lumber Landing says "Timber Dock." The sign going to Belle Marsh says "Hunt Camp." The sign going toward the old community of Raccoon Bluff, founded during Reconstruction, says "Church Road." The old First African Baptist Church sits empty there and that's the only clue a visitor would have that some of us once lived at Raccoon Bluff. You can see ruins of tabby slave cabins at Chocolate, an old site on the North End, but they are from the 1800s. The markers for the era I grew up in are in our heads.

Culturally, historically and in every way but legally, this island is ours. But we feel threatened every day. All we have left is Hog Hammock and we've lost about twenty acres of it to people from outside the community. We can't let our guard down for a minute because so many people want our land. Some people study the tax rolls to see if they can find any of us slipping up on our taxes, so they can buy land at a tax sale. Other people have actually mailed letters to everyone in the community, enticing us to sell our family land. Then there is the state.

Officials with the Department of Natural Resources, or DNR,

deny they're after our land, they say they're doing everything they can to help our community, but it doesn't seem that way to us. For instance, DNR recently renovated the old lighthouse with tax dollars and public contributions and we're pleased to see them fix it up. But when it comes to renovating the old church at the Bluff, the story is different. They're willing to give us grants to help renovate the old church at Raccoon Bluff for cultural and church events, but they say that although the church is ours, the land it sits on belongs to the state. We say it can't be. Show us proof. No family from Sapelo would ever feel it had the right to sell the land under God's church.

It's a lot like the time the DNR tried to claim our land in Behavior Cemetery but couldn't prove it because that land had always been ours. But we're at a total standstill on the issue of the church land. Meanwhile, the claims filed years ago by Sapelo families on parcels of land included in the sale of the North End to the state haven't ever been resolved.

So it's hard to believe the state's too interested in our survival. The energy isn't going in that direction. It's more like they're playing a waiting game, waiting on us to leave or die so they can have the island to themselves. It reminds me of a story Papa told me. One day I went down to his house to take him some Sunday dinner and Papa said, "Hot dog. Good things come to those who wait."

I said, "Whatcha talkin' about?"

"Well, you came and brought me sump'n and the church send me over some food and I didn't have to cook today. Good things come to those who wait." Then he laughed and said, "That's what Buzzard told Hawk. But Hawk wouldn't believe him."

Papa said: "Hawk look at Buzzard and ol' Buzzard was jus'

sittin' there. And once in a while, he'd fly back and fo'th. Hawk said, 'What's wrong wit'choo?'"

Buzzard said, "Jus' waitin' on the letter of th' Lawd."

Hawk said, "You doin' what?"

"Jus' waitin' on th' letter of th' Lawd."

Buzzard, he was hungry but he was jus' waitin', havin' patience 'n' sittin' up there. Once in a while, he get off that limb and he fly round and he search for food and come back and sit.

And Hawk said, "Well, you jus' sit there and wait on the letter of th' Lawd if y' wanna. I'm gonna look for me sump'n to eat."

Hawk got up with *such speed* off that limb, *zzzzoom*! and he run right into a tree and break his neck. And Buzzard said, "Told you I was waitin' on the letter of th' Lawd."

I've got a pine tree in my yard with a big limb on it and it's not hard at all to imagine a buzzard sitting up there grinning at me. Lately, I've seen a bunch of buzzards high up in the sky over the community. Why are they circling the community? "Well, they hungry," people say. But I don't want us to be their prey. That's for sure. So we have to work together to prevent that.

One of my favorites of the songs we sing on Watch Night is "Amazing Grace." Everybody loves that song. We sang it all the time when I was growing up. The words cut to the depths of your very soul, especially the part that says, "Amazing Grace, how sweet the sound, that saved a wretch like me. I once was lost and now am found, was blind but now I see." My heart lifts as we sing it.

All the time I was growing up I thought "Amazing Grace" was a traditional spiritual, written by a man who was black. I thought he was describing how he was treated, because who would have been more a wretch than a black man who was a slave? But when I was in Africa I learned something that turned my thinking upside down. That song was written by a white man by the name of John Wooten.

He was an English clergyman by the time he wrote "Amazing Grace" in 1748, but before that he had spent part of his life trafficking in slaves. He was the captain of a slave ship that was a part of the Charleston slave trade. Some of the descendants of the people he helped sell as slaves may still be in the Sea Islands. A few could even be on Sapelo.

When I first heard that a slave ship captain had written "Amazing Grace," it was almost unbelievable to me. I couldn't help thinking, "Could that song actually come from the heart of a man who dealt in human souls and flesh?" God, he would have had to have done a lot of changing to be able to write that. He more than likely was describing himself and the deeds he had done.

Black people sing that song with so much feeling that if he's in Heaven looking down, he's probably saying, "Good Lord, that song has been immortalized by the very same people that I bought and sold." So that song gives me hope that maybe someday we will all come to understand each other better. It also makes me feel good to know the origin of that song.

I want to know everything I can about our history and our culture. It's when your heritage is denied and robbed that you hurt inside and you feel like there is something missing. I honestly think that if the slaveholders had kept better records, it would have promoted a lot of healing. If those of us who are African American knew what ship our ancestors had come on, what country they were from, and what tribe they were in, we would have had a better sense of who we are.

Watch Night

I was never ashamed of the fact that my ancestors lived in slavery times. I don't think of them as "slaves." I don't like that word, I don't dwell on that word. I don't use that word often, only occasionally, when it seems artificial not to. I don't use the term "slave owner" either. I say "slaveholder."

The period of history my African ancestors lived in was a time of slavery. There were more black people living in slavery, yes, but there were also some Native Americans who were slaves and there were white indentured servants who were practically slaves. Slavery was a terrible thing to live through, but I don't think the early Africans on Sapelo were that brainwashed. They believed in freedom. They were free to a certain extent. They made sure to retain their inner freedom at least some of the time and they held to their beliefs and ways. They couldn't have survived if they didn't. And after the time of slavery was over, it was a time to put that behind them, to turn things around and go on to something better.

We need to be proud of our ancestors from slavery days and of our old people who went through modern hardships and to learn from them that if you believe in something, strength comes from that. Your belief is your strength. Be proud of yourself and your culture. I love mine.

I want to build a praise house on our property. It will be a small, wooden praise house with little narrow benches like the ones of old, so that my grandchildren will see what a praise house is like and visitors will learn about them.

I will add one additional touch to the praise house I build. A small piece of stained glass that would never have been in one of those plain, undecorated tiny churches but definitely fits the mood. A pretty blue and green and yellow piece of glass with a small bird sitting on a branch, waiting to rise and fly. A symbol of freedom, a sea gull probably, because I was talking to a man who was visiting from Africa one day and he took a second look at some seabirds he saw and he said, "See that sea gull? The one with the black legs? It's from Africa." It must have gotten blown off course a bit, but that sea gull was here on Sapelo. It was waiting to fly with the wind back to Africa. To make that connecting voyage the early people here wanted to make and that we're still making.

I plan to set the bird in front of a window where it will catch the morning sun and let everybody know we are free, a part of us always has been free, and we will continue to be free as long as our minds and souls have the courage to take wing and fly.

The Watch Night service on Sapelo lasts until midnight, and by this time, after all the reflecting I have done, it's time to start looking forward to the new year. We're being thrust into the future and it's not going to be yesterday's Hog Hammock anymore. We're going to have to think about all kinds of things our forebears never had to think about.

We need to continue to educate people on the importance of holding on to their land for the next generation. We need to help older people who say, "After I'm gone, I don't care what you do with the land," because they don't know which of their children or grandchildren would best take care of it. And we need to reach Sapelo descendants who've inherited land here but have never set foot on the island, who may not have quite the same incentive to hold on to the land that those of us who live here do.

We also need a decent land trust, so that land can be held for people's descendants, or if they really need to sell it, for the community. We already have a community organization, SICARS, the Sapelo

Island Cultural and Restoration Society, exploring this and other issues. (SICARS has received funding from the Sapelo Foundation, a foundation of the Reynolds family, and we're pleased that some of this generation of Reynoldses are trying harder to extend a hand on Sapelo.)

We need more people living in Hog Hammock again. We need to campaign to bring some of our Sapelo-born and -bred descendants home. If we can't get enough of them, we may need to find some new people from a similar background who will recognize and respect our culture. Grandma got Grandpa off the boat, and she used to talk about the lady in slavery days who was waiting for a "fresh batch" of Africans so she could find a husband. So a little bit of hybrid vigor is good every once in a while.

We need new jobs to draw people back, ones that won't pollute the environment and will pay decently, so people can afford to live on Sapelo. We'd need new housing for them too, and this will take a lot of work. It's a tall order, a very tall one. Can we pull it off? I don't know, but we have to try to turn things around and reverse our luck.

I want us always to have a community on this island. A community of people who enjoy quiet living, value the land, and want to raise children in a place that's still a paradise for kids. I want the state and people everywhere to be proud of us and to realize the distinct historic and cultural value we have as a people who've lived here ever since the time of slavery. We're the *last* majority black population on a Georgia island that is reachable only by boat. Matter of fact, we're about the last majority Geechee/Gullah population living on a major island unconnected to the mainland in the *entire string* of Sea Islands, from South Carolina to Florida.

. . .

At five minutes to midnight on Watch Night, the church bell rings, with a quick pull of the cord, a bright ring you can hear throughout the community. It rings and rings as the old year goes out and the new one comes in.

We all leave the church and stand outside hugging and laughing and yelling, "Happy New Year!" The men go off a safe distance, aim straight up in the air and shoot their pistols and rifles off, and the fireworks from their guns fly up to the heavens. There's not a cloud in the sky, just the moon and millions of brilliant white stars shining.

Down at the last house in the community, a short distance from the church, Papa used to wake Mama saying, "Old lady, wake up. Almost twelve." Mama would say her prayers and Papa would go outside and shoot his gun off too. Mama's not there now, but she's probably watching just the same. Because over in the cemetery, the spirits are watching.

Bilali is watching, he has to be watching. He has become the father of us all. My ancestors Hester, Sally and Harriet are watching. Grandma Winnie and Grandpa John Bryant, Aunt Mary and Uncle Joe, Michael and Ophelia and all the others are watching.

The spirits will watch over us and over the island through the dark night as we search for the first rays of light in the sky at day-clean. They will keep on watching in all the days to come, they will watch until Gabriel blows his horn and everyone rises facing the East. This I believe, because it's what the old people believed.